LITERACY
A REDEFINITION

LITERACY
A REDEFINITION

Edited by
Nancy J. Ellsworth
Carolyn N. Hedley
Anthony N. Baratta
Fordham University

IEA LAWRENCE ERLBAUM ASSOCIATES, PUBLISHERS
1994   Hillsdale, New Jersey   Hove, UK

Lawrence Erlbaum Associates, Inc., Publishers
365 Broadway
Hillsdale, New Jersey 07642

Library of Congress Cataloging-in-Publication Data
Literacy : a redefinition / edited by Nancy J. Ellsworth, Carolyn N.
Hedley, Anthony N. Baratta.
    p. cm.
    Includes bibliographical references and index.
    ISBN 0-8058-1454-X. — ISBN 0-8058-1455-8 (pbk.)
    1. Language arts. 2. Reading. 3. English language—Composition
and exercises—Study and teaching. 4. Literacy. I. Ellsworth,
Nancy J. II. Hedley, Carolyn N. III. Baratta, Anthony N.
LB1576.L552   1994
302.2′24—dc20   93-24099
                                                          CIP

Books published by Lawrence Erlbaum Associates are printed on acid-free paper, and their
bindings are chosen for strength and durability.

Printed in the United States of America
10 9 8 7 6 5 4 3 2 1

*To Our Children
and Their Children*

Contents

PART II: LITERACY AND COGNITION

PART III: CONTEXTS FOR LITERACY

Preface

Periodically, the state of affairs in any area should be reconsidered. *Public education* has received little systematic analysis in its history, and *literacy* has received less. This volume attempts to fill some of this void. Throughout a child's schooling, questions will remain about the essential competencies of being a literate person. These questions, concerning public policy and educational practice at root, are the focal point of this volume. *Literacy: A Redefinition* presents discussions of major conceptual and practical issues that confront professionals in the field. A more integrated approach to thinking about the dimensions of literacy commensurate with society's needs requires that we focus on the future, transcending traditional definitions of literacy.

Advancing a professional knowledge base requires integrating new conceptualizations of literacy and current practices for its dissemination. This is rarely achieved as a single contribution: Hence, the power of presenting a range of viewpoints within one text. The advancement of hypotheses, theory, and application occurs as researchers and practitioners learn from each other to define the problems of schooling and seek solutions for improved delivery systems. The syntheses presented in *Literacy: A Redefinition* examine the issues on which educators must focus. The influence of researchers' conceptual models on practice arises as much from the questions they generate as from the solutions they propose; these chapters make explicit the questions that underlie a redefinition of literacy, as well as offer specific suggestions for implementation. They center our attention, offer direction, and identify critical features to be considered in the design and delivery of instruction.

Providing educational services is profoundly influenced by accelerating social and economic changes and by altered expectations of the responsibilities and roles of schools. Therefore, we focus on the trends and practical issues that educators will face in the next decade. Our concern is with all students: preschoolers through adolescents and adults, and those with learning, language, and cultural differences. This orientation seems to overcome practices that have been found to be educationally limiting or shortsighted. The volume is organized into three parts: "Reconception of Literacy," "Literacy and Cognition," and "Contexts for Literacy." Each of these sections examines an issue that needs to be debated by professionals concerned with literacy and the applications for its development.

Part I, "Reconception of Literacy," begins with a chapter by Zigler and Gilman, who propose a program to achieve better utilization and coordination of existing resources to ensure that all young children come to school ready to learn. Next, Calfee describes a program for curricular reform in literacy instruction starting with schools as they are and utilizing new techniques and ideas applied to daily activities to achieve fundamental change in the elementary grades. The next two chapters discuss trends in literacy. Venezky concludes that both printed books and hypertexts have important roles to play in an information society and notes that literate readership proficient in both communication and information processing will benefit greatly. Rose, Meyer, and Pisha then propose restructuring schools around new technologies that are flexible enough to include children in active exploration of a world whose knowledge base is no longer fixed in permanent ink. The final chapters in this section deal with changing populations for literacy. Baca, Escamilla, and Carjuzaa question language minority students' inclusion in the proposal reform, *America 2000*, documenting that such reforms continue to ignore the fact that our nation is an increasingly pluralistic society. In the concluding chapter of Part I, Garcia reports effective schooling practices and related policy issues for Hispanic children.

The second part of this volume, "Literacy and Cognition," opens with two chapters on thinking and literacy. Ellsworth describes an instructional program that employs a critical thinking schema to teach adolescents with learning disabilities to solve personal problems more effectively. Next, C. N. Hedley, W. E. Hedley, and Baratta present ways of increasing visual literacy through visual thinking and imagery; the case for the interface of visual thinking with verbal thinking as a curricular goal is made. In the following chapter, Stevens reports a study that supports the effectiveness of a multifaceted, cooperative learning approach to literacy instruction that may facilitate the mainstreaming of students with learning disabilities. Then London discusses the multicultural curriculum and develops a compendium of a literature of many peoples and places. This part of the book concludes with Silver's chapter, which reviews recent data on the biological origins of specific learning disabilities and the implications for the education of these children.

Part III examines new "Contexts for Literacy." Antonacci and Colasacco critique the current context for literacy instruction that fails so many of our students. They suggest a new context in which children are active participants in a multidimensional language arts experience. Next, Chiarelli proposes expanding the schools' partnership with families by involving them in family storybook reading during children's preschool years, thus building the skills that underlie literacy. Following this, Benson presents a vision of a new, rigorous vocational education program intended to serve as a major element of reform of inner-city secondary education. Milbrath discusses the philosophical underpinnings and specifics of a program to create environmental literacy. In a postscript, Didsbury looks to the needs of society in the future, quoting John Platt: "To survive, we must suddenly find out how to solve our problems in advance." Surely, one of the best ways to accomplish this objective is to educate literate citizens who can respond to the changing conditions they will encounter.

In conclusion, research on the training of literacy skills is a high priority in education—one supported by both public interest and professionals in the field. These chapters are intended to advance the way professionals think about approaches to literacy, the design of interventions, and the effectiveness of current and emerging practices.

The editors and authors would like to thank Fordham University for its support of the institute that brought together the contributors to this volume. Educators from across the country have made a good start for charting the educational future of a literate society.

Nancy J. Ellsworth
Carolyn N. Hedley
Anthony N. Baratta

I

RECONCEPTION
OF LITERACY

1

Literacy and the School of the 21st Century

Edward Zigler
Elizabeth Gilman
Yale University

U.S. schools are generally agreed to have reached a crisis point, leading educators, parents, and the national administration alike to express concern regarding the declining quality of schools and the concomitant decline in literacy. At the state and national levels, this concern has manifested itself in the proliferation of goals and reforms, notably the Bush administration's release of *America 2000: An Education Strategy* (U.S. Department of Education, 1991). The six goals contained in the America 2000 plan begin with "by the year 2000, all children in America will start school ready to learn." The other stated goals include graduation from high school, competency in basic subject matter, greater achievement in math and science, literacy for all adults, and ridding the schools of drugs and violence (U.S. Department of Education, 1991). These goals, however admirable, will not be realized without a deeper social understanding of what factors underlie the poor achievement of public school students, and especially what young children require to attain school readiness and to emerge from childhood as productive, literate adults.

To more fully understand what impairs children's ability to learn, it must be recognized that schools are not the only system to impact on the growth and development of the child. Experts generally agree that three systems, in addition to the school, largely determine a child's growth and development. These other systems are family, health, and child care (Belsky, 1981; Bronfenbrenner, 1979). A failure in any of the three systems clearly affects a child's capacity to benefit fully from a learning environment. As Bronfenbrenner (1990, p. 27) pointed out, the more we know about the conditions that "foster the development of human competence and character, the more we see these same conditions being eroded" in the social environment.

This chapter addresses the ways in which present social conditions have contributed to the impairment of learning and social development for many U.S. children, and describes a child-care and family support model, delivered through the school, that can ameliorate the destructive effects of these conditions. This model, the School of the 21st Century, provides a comprehensive program that expands the role of the public school to embrace the four systems that affect development and provides a means for teachers, parents, and communities to work together to give children a better chance to achieve their potential.

THE SCOPE OF THE PROBLEM

Teachers have become increasingly aware that a multiplicity of problems affect the performance of their young students. A recent survey of over a thousand public school teachers revealed that nearly 9 out of 10 beginning teachers believe that many of their pupils are too overwhelmed by family and other outside problems to succeed in class. Moreover, although some 98% of the teachers surveyed noted the importance of working together with parents, 70% observed that many parents consider schools and teachers as "adversaries" (Metropolitan Life Insurance Company, 1991). A recent report sponsored by the Carnegie Foundation for the Advancement of Teaching stated that today's children are suffering from the consequences of poor health care, inattentive or overworked parents, scarce child care and preschool opportunities, unsafe neighborhoods, mindless television programming, and isolation from adults. The report surveyed 7,000 kindergarten teachers, who revealed that 35% of their students entered school unprepared to learn. When asked what specific problem had the greatest impact on school readiness, most of the teachers cited "deficiency in language": Their students lacked the basic vocabulary and sentence structure skills needed for success in school (Boyer, 1991).

Some of the "outside problems," such as inadequate child care and inattentive parenting, afflicting many of today's young students derive in part from the major demographic changes the United States has undergone over the last three or four decades. Paramount among these are the dramatic increase in the number of mothers in the out-of-home work force and the number of single parent families, usually headed by women. Today, 25% of all children in the United States are being raised in single parent homes; for Black families, that number is over 50% (Children's Defense Fund, 1990). The number of school-age children whose mothers were in the labor force rose to 65% in 1990; for mothers of preschool children, the number is around 50% (Children's Defense Fund, 1990). Even more astonishing is the fact that nearly 54% of mothers of children under age 1 are now working outside the home (U.S. Bureau of Labor Statistics, 1990). It has been projected that by 1995, 75% of all mothers will be in the labor force (Hofferth & Phillips, 1987).

Economic strain also plagues young U.S. families. Most mothers who work outside the home do so out of financial necessity. Between 1973 and 1990, the median annual income for households headed by persons under age 30 fell by 32%; the child poverty rate for these families doubled during the same period, rising to 40% from 20% (Children's Defense Fund, 1992). Marc S. Tucker, president of the National Center on Education and Economy, noted recently that the level of poverty among children in this country is more than twice that of industrial nations with which the United States competes economically. Tucker observed that "it's not reasonable to expect those who grew up in poverty to achieve world-class levels in school and in the workplace" (Greenhouse, 1992, p. F14).

For single mothers, the economic situation is especially dire: In 1988, about one half of all single mothers had incomes below half of the adjusted poverty line (Child Care Action Campaign, 1988). Clearly, parents of young children, especially single parents, must work to support their families and they can do so only if they have child care.

Unfortunately child care is barely affordable for many young families and, when available, it is of extremely uneven quality. Many children are in care so poor that it seriously jeopardizes their growth and development. Whitebook, Howes, and Phillips (1989) conducted a study of 227 child-care centers in the United States and discovered that two thirds of the sites studied were "barely adequate" to meet children's needs. The issue of quality is likely to be even more critical in the case of family day care, in which a mother cares for five or six children in her home. Many of these arrangements are entirely unregulated; it is estimated that there are as many as 550,000 to 1.1 million unregulated family day-care homes in the nation (Hofferth, Brayfield, Deich, & Holcomb, 1991). Clearly, inadequate child-care settings are not characterized by the kind of individual attention and literacy activities children need to develop language skills and to become school ready. It has been found that children who do not develop adequate speech and language skills in the first years of life are up to six times more likely to experience reading problems in school than those who receive adequate stimulation (Clapp, 1988).

Parents are understandably concerned about the quality of care their children are receiving, yet they are forced to utilize the patchwork of services that exist in their communities. Surprisingly, it is the children of the working and lower middle class, the mainstream of the United States, who are least likely to enjoy high quality child care. The affluent can afford to pay for the best care and the poor often can benefit from subsidized, well-run day-care programs (Whitebook, Howes, & Phillips, 1989). Children today, even very young children, are also spending a startling amount of time away from their parents. In a survey of some 4,400 parents, it was found that 76% of infants and toddlers in center care and 69% of these children in family day care spent at least 35 hours each week in day-care settings (Willer et al., 1991). Under these circumstances, it is not surprising that parents lack the time to read to their children or to engage in the kind of enriching, leisurely conversation that forges family bonds and builds language skills. Despite this burgeoning use of supplementary care, the nation still lacks an affordable, comprehensive child-care network and has also failed to enact national regulations for child-care facilities.

Current social conditions, including the lack of a child-care system, place great emotional and financial strain on parents, who must juggle work and family responsibilities without adequate support from the social infrastructure. In 1987, a survey found that over 40% of employed parents experience stress, conflict, and guilt in attempting to function well as both parents and employees (Friedman, 1987). According to another survey, parents talk to their children, on average, just a few minutes each day (Boyer, 1991). It is ironic that at a time when the United States professes concern and even alarm about school readiness, as a nation we have failed to address the plight of children who are expected to enter school ready to learn after experiencing several years of inadequate or even destructive child care and minimal enriching interaction with their parents. Not surprisingly, increasing numbers of children have begun to show the ill effects of our deteriorating social fabric through inability to cope with the demands of school, family, and peer relationships (Zigler & Finn-Stevenson, 1991).

Older children are also the victims of these demographic changes. Often unsupervised after school, "latchkey" children may be predisposed to delinquency and other destructive behaviors. Poor supervision by parents and poor child-rearing techniques are among the most important precursors to delinquency (Farrington, 1987; Zigler, Taussig, & Black, 1992). Richardson et al. (1989) found that eighth-grade children who were unsupervised after school were twice as likely to engage in substance abuse as were children who had adult supervision. Clearly, educators alone cannot be expected to undo the potential destructive effects of social and demographic change once a child enters the formal school system. But today many educators have recognized that the lack of quality child care and other necessary social supports is harming many children and impairing their performance in school in both the cognitive and social spheres. As a result, schools in several states have redefined their mission in the community and adopted the School of the 21st Century model, conceptualized by Edward

Zigler in 1987 and presently being implemented nationally by the Yale Bush Center in Child Development and Social Policy.

UNDERLYING PRINCIPLES OF THE SCHOOL OF THE 21ST CENTURY

The 21st Century School model is the product of 25 years of thought and research in child development (Zigler, 1989). We know what the components of a successful family support and intervention program must be; it is only a matter of combining these into an affordable, comprehensive program that operates in conjunction and cooperation with the school system. To be successful, such a model must favorably impact on child health, family life, and child-care arrangements, as well as on formal schooling.

If a child is not healthy and does not have adequate nutrition, the other systems affecting development are almost moot. Poor prenatal care and poor maternal health predispose a child to low birthweight and congenital defects. The poor health trajectory thus established can plague a child throughout life. In fact the health care status of many U.S. children is inadequate, owing largely to the lack of a national health care system. Poor general health and nutrition in a child often impairs the ability to benefit adequately from even the best learning environment.

Support for the family unit is also essential. It is through the medium of the family that a child first encounters other important institutions like the school. Instability and inconsistency in care rendered by the family undermines the healthy effects of attachment bonds usually formed within the family environment. Variance in children's behavior and developmental outcomes is most dramatically affected by family factors. Thus it is essential to support and to educate parents about the importance of family bonds, which are strengthened by conversation, play, and reading to children to help prepare them for school.

Clearly the effect of inconsistency and instability in family care giving can be compounded by poor quality child-care settings, wherein extremely high turnover and inadequately trained workers are virtual norms (DeBare, 1991; Whitebook, Howes, & Phillips, 1989). Thus the 21st Century School model has the goal of establishing a stable, reliable system of child care that is also flexible enough to meet individual family requirements.

Finally, the school environment, another important developmental determinant, must be combined with the other three systems to form an integrated whole in which parents and educators become partners, not adversaries. The child spends thousands of hours in school, ideally building strong social, language, and other cognitive skills. The school should therefore be in a position to further the child's psychosocial development, based on and supported by the continuing, committed involvement of the family.

THE 21ST CENTURY SCHOOL MODEL

Predicated on the aforementioned imperatives, the U.S. school can be restructured to meet child-care and other needs now experienced by U.S. families. The 21st Century School model uses as its core the existing U.S. school facilities, buildings in which citizens have already made a close to $2 trillion investment. Traditionally school buildings have been in use for a limited portion of the year, open for a relatively short time during the day. The 21st Century School model sets out a plan for further use of these costly school buildings. There are ample reasons to make better use of existing facilities to provide early childhood services, such as parent education and support from birth to age 3, child-care programs from age 3 to 12, information and referral, and outreach and training support to family day-care providers. Such a comprehensive, centralized constellation of services not only makes access to services easier for parents, but also insures the kind of reliable, consistent care and support children need to make full use of the formal school environment.

Thus the School of the 21st Century would house two integrated systems. The first would be the traditional, formal school with which we are familiar, typically operating from 8 a.m. to 3 p.m., 9 months a year. The second would be a child-care and family support system operating from about 7 a.m. to 6 p.m., 12 months a year, to coordinate with the working day. The second system will be open to children from age 3 onward, for parents who need out-of-home care for their preschool children. The system is intended to be highly flexible: Mothers who do not work or who work part-time can use the facility for half-day nursery care, as needed. It is planned to function in a similar manner to the child-care systems in place in France and Italy today, where children attend preschool at age 3 (many at age 2) and receive early education and child-care services at the same time. In France, 90% of the children enter such programs at age 3. For French children under age 3, contractual government assistance for day nurseries has become a national priority and has spurred a major increase in the number of these facilities (David & Starzec, 1991).

This does not mean that formal schooling will begin at age 3; what will be made available is developmentally appropriate, high quality care for preschool children, the kind of play-oriented program that fosters language acquisition and overall optimal development. The second child-care component would serve school-age children, many of whom lack adult supervision before and after school. These latchkey children age 6 to 12 would be able to participate in supervised recreational programs before and after school and during school vacations.

In addition to this child care plan, the model incorporates three outreach programs, the first of which is a parent education and support plan for parents of children from birth to age 3. This component includes home visitation and supportive services for parents and children, such as health screening, parent education, and inoculations for the child. Such a program has proven entirely workable, and is modeled on the Parents as Teachers (PAT) program, which operates successfully in every school throughout Missouri and in locations in 35 other states (Missouri Department of Elementary and Secondary Education, 1986; Winter, 1985). The PAT program has been especially successful in enhancing parent–child communication and childrens' performance in achievement and language ability (Pfannenstiel, Lambson, & Yarnell, 1991).

The second outreach program is directed to family day care. Although the School of the 21st Century places child care for children age 3 to 12 within the school building, care for children 0 to 3 is still needed. A large number of these children are already placed in family day care. The 21st Century School child-care and family support system would organize all of these homes into a network, using the school as its center. This hub would have the task of training, monitoring, and supporting family day-care workers, thus creating a higher quality, more uniform system.

The third and final outreach program provides an information and referral service for families. There are some 200 or 300 programs offering services such as eye testing, food stamps, night care for children, and the like. An information and referral component, located within the school building, would help families make use of the baffling array of available services.

The guiding principles of this child-care and family support system are that parents are the primary raisers of their children and parents and schools should work together to insure that each child is given the best chance in life. The 21st Century School emphasizes constant communication between family and school and a high degree of parental involvement.

As noted earlier, the child-care and family support system for children 0 to 3 also includes home visitation, parental education, and health and developmental screening assistance. This support system is dedicated to the promotion of good relations between parents and the school staff, who are to be well trained in early childhood education and child development.

IMPLEMENTATION

Given the serious economic straits of many of our states and communities, the operational costs of implementing a 21st Century School are a major concern to communities considering such a plan. However, it is essential to evaluate the School of the 21st Century as an investment in human capital, or, as one school administrator put it, a way of "making better children." As such, we must take the long view, unfortunately not a typical vantage point for program evaluation in the United States. Benefits derived from successful childhood intervention programs are detailed in the Cornell consortium's analysis of a number of major intervention efforts (Consortium for Longitudinal Studies, 1983). The program benefits that emerged included improved grade retention rates, reduced placement in special education programs, fewer graduates on welfare, increased college attendance, and lower rates of delinquency (Berrueta-Clement, Schweinhart, Barnett, Epstein, & Weikert, 1984; Consortium for Longitudinal Studies, 1983).

Funding

Ideally, the public may one day assume the burden of supporting a child-care system, much as public education is now supported. For the moment, however, models such as the School of the 21st Century must be funded by parents, employers, and taxpayers, often in combination. In some districts, funding has come through local initiatives, with private foundation assistance at the start-up phase. Blocks of resources can also be made available to districts seeking to adopt a 21st Century School model. Frequently, funding for special education, high-risk children, drug-free schools, or other preventative programming can all be utilized to bring together a number of funding streams that can then underwrite the various parts of a 21st Century School and allow a commissioner of education or school administrator to fashion a comprehensive program. The program so funded might include a health component, child care, parent education, and staff training—all of which are arguably preventive in nature.

The school districts that have implemented the School of 21st Century model have found funding in a variety of ways. For example, districts in Missouri, Kansas, Wyoming, and Colorado have financed their programs largely through local initiatives and have received assistance from community and corporate foundations. In rural Wyoming, drug-free and at-risk program money is used, as well as parent education funding for the PAT portion of their 21st Century Schools. Local businesses also underwrite "scholarships" for parents who cannot afford fees for child care. In Missouri, the state-funded PAT program was created by statute and the state 21st Century School program was formed by supplementing PAT with child care and health components permissible under the statute. The Missouri program also receives direct Medicaid funds for child physicals, nursing staff, and the like. State legislatures can thus become directly involved in setting up 21st Century School programs. For example, enabling legislation in Connecticut has made that state's program a line item in the annual state budget. The Connecticut legislation that created three demonstration projects in 1989 was expanded the following year to authorize funding for five additional sites.

We have found that once these programs have been initiated, they can be operationally sustained through parental fees, structured on a sliding scale based on family income, for child-care services. To permit universal access, services are extended to low-income parents through a combination of state and federal subsidies.

Initial Planning and Program Administration

One important advantage of the 21st Century model is that it is flexible: School districts can adopt those pieces of the model that fit their local needs; the program may be varied so as to better utilize and coordinate, not replace, existing resources. Implementation consequently varies by site according to existing services and needs. Thus, in the state of Hawaii and in the city of Los Angeles, children receive before and after school care. In North Carolina, a network of school-based child-care centers has been proposed to serve only 3-, 4-, and 5-year-olds.

Typically, it is best to begin a program in three or four schools at first and to have that program satisfactorily operational before expanding to a districtwide or statewide program. Thus local concerns and strengths can be identified and incorporated into the local model before full expansion is undertaken. It is also important to inform and educate the state legislature, school administrators and personnel, the media, and the general public about the model to insure support for and commitment to the program once it is established. At the legislative and state government level, holding a conference on 21st Century Schools might be useful for information exchange before implementation is attempted.

At the point at which concrete planning begins, some of the services in the 21st Century School model may already be in place in some form in a given school district. For this reason, it may be wise to establish an advisory committee to review community resources and needs. Schools in many communities already sponsor preschool and school-age child-care programs, although typically in inadequate supply. All school districts therefore need not develop an entirely new system of services. In such cases, the program can be designed to supplement existing resources to better meet community needs, while acting as a hub to coordinate new services with preexisting ones. The goal for each site is to utilize resources to maximum benefit, coordinate these to insure program quality, and to provide families with a broad array of services to address individual requirements.

Site and program management is also a matter of concern. It is essential to establish clearly delineated lines of responsibility within the individual school and district, to insure cooperation between academic and other program personnel. Programs have dealt with management in somewhat different ways, but the appointment of a site coordinator has been found to be one satisfactory management solution. In Independence, Missouri, for example, each school runs its own program and the site coordinator reports to the school principal as to the operations of the nonacademic programs within the school. In Connecticut, a program administrator manages these programs, but reports directly to the superintendent of schools rather than to the principal. In each case, however, the administrator or coordinator is considered part of the school administrative hierarchy and attends all administrative meetings. This helps to foster teamwork and reinforces the view of the 21st Century School as an integrated program.

Although there are inevitable differences in the mode of implementation in each site, it is important to insure program quality and permit replication in future sites. Therefore, all Schools of the 21st Century must adhere to the guiding principles of the model and share the goal of providing high quality, developmentally appropriate care that is accessible to families. Because critical variables, such as staff training, program quality, and the level of commitment of school district personnel affect the performance of a 21st Century School, all participating sites are required to follow implementation guidelines developed by the Yale Bush Center. District personnel, from superintendents to child-care staff, are required to complete training on implementation and program operation. To further facilitate this educational process and to allow staff from existing or future programs to share their experiences and knowledge, a yearly Training Institute has been held at the Yale Bush Center.

Educational and Service Delivery Concerns

Despite the successful implementation of the School of the 21st Century in a growing number of sites, some criticisms have emerged. Some argue that schools, because of their academically oriented curriculum, are not appropriate settings for young children (Kahn & Kamerman, 1987). It should be acknowledged that the danger of an overly academic curriculum can exist in all child-care and early intervention settings, not only those based in schools. Moreover, 21st Century Schools address this issue by encouraging developmentally appropriate programs based on child-directed, cooperative play experiences. The hiring of staff trained in child development and early education is also stressed.

Other critics note that schools do not always have space available for additional services like child care and family support. However, in sites where space is a problem, modular buildings are being used by districts committed to implementing the program. Also, many participating school boards are taking family support and child-care service needs into account in developing their future space allocation plans.

Another concern has arisen regarding the issue of "turf" between existing child-care providers and the 21st Century Schools, and also between existing formal school personnel and child-care and family support staff. The first concern, that child-care providers in a community will be superseded by school-based child care, is an unlikely occurrence. The School of the 21st Century is a voluntary program and is operated on parental fees for service. Further, one stated goal of the program is to serve as the hub of other available services and to coordinate, not duplicate or replace, resources within the community. The program seeks to offer parents the broadest possible range of good quality services, including school-based care and other options like family and center child care. At present, there is such a dearth of accessible, quality child-care services that schools cannot possibly replace existing resources. School-based care will simply provide families with a much-needed additional option.

As to potential "turf battles" within the school itself, a number of administrators committed to program success have engendered an atmosphere of cooperation within their districts by clearly delineating the roles their staff members will play within the 21st Century School and by encouraging free discussion of the program during the planning and implementation stages. Typically, an environment develops in which teaching and child-care staff and parents are able to work cooperatively and effectively to the benefit of the children in the program and their community.

Union turf issues may also arise because custodial and other staff are needed to work hours other than those specified in their union contracts. If school employees are all in different unions, this can become a serious concern. Some states have resolved these problems by designating the 21st Century School components as "special projects," thus exempting the component from some of the rigid union guidelines. Another potential solution, proposed by the Connecticut program, has been to ask volunteer union workers to accept "flex time": to work the same number of hours but at different times. This method can save the program the expense of double and triple time wages required under some union contracts. Another possibility is to avoid having the program managed directly by the board of education. If the 21st Century services are subcontracted out by the school, union conflict and wage scale problems can be minimized. On the other hand, some union contracts present few difficulties to program administration; there is considerable variation from site to site. The key appears to be sensitive leadership that is able to create a spirit of cooperation among programs and staff members. Given this attitude, many union and pay scale issues can be creatively resolved.

EVALUATION

No plan for early intervention is complete without a means of evaluating its effects. To this end the Yale Bush Center has been evaluating how the School of the 21st Century program operates in several sites since 1989. Although the Bush Center is not an unbiased entity, it has designed an objective evaluation that has been reviewed by several prominent experts in child care and evaluation. Because the 21st Century model is a multicomponent program with multiple goals, the outcome evaluation includes not only individual level outcomes, but outcomes associated with the program, school-district, and community as well.

Results are still preliminary, yet these indicate that the program is working and meeting parental needs as to quality, location, and convenience. In one school district studied, 67% of the 221 parents surveyed who use the school-age services and 72% of the 141 surveyed who use preschool care report choosing the program for its convenience and quality. Of these, 19% of the school-age program parents and 41% of the preschool parents indicated that they enrolled their children because the program is operated by their school district.

Additional benefits have also emerged. One district, operating a program since 1988, has formed an advisory group composed of district officials, school principals, teachers, 21st Century School staff, and PTA members to oversee program operation. Such planning can ensure that the 21st Century services are not simply grafted onto the school but become an integral part of the overall school system. The preliminary evaluation indicates that successful integration of child-care and family support services within the formal school system is possible and has the support of parents.

Several ingredients for success have also been identified. As noted earlier, successful implementation of the five program services and coordinating these with the existing school system is dependent on the level of commitment demonstrated by the superintendent, principals, and teachers. Where such commitment has been lacking, the process of implementing the 21st Century model has been difficult. In some instances, turf disputes have emerged over such issues as selecting space within the schools for the child-care programs.

Staffing can also be problematic. As for many child-care programs, surveys of 21st Century School staff demonstrate that hiring personnel trained in child development or early childhood education can be a challenging task. However, to meet this challenge, school districts have offered training for their staff either within the school or through community colleges and have established "career ladders" to encourage staff to obtain additional training.

CONCLUSION

The nation as a whole lacks a comprehensive, affordable, and high quality child-care network and it has also failed to produce national guidelines for the regulation of child-care facilities. Families are floundering under the multiple stresses of parenthood and of the workplace, which remains for many workers "family hostile" rather than family friendly. Often, children are showing the effects of family stress when they enter school with inadequately developed social and language skills. All indicators suggest that the need for child care and other family support services in the United States will not lessen but will only increase in the future. Clearly, pervasive social and labor force trends in the United States have not been been reflected in national policies for workers and parents that support them as nurturers of the next generation.

After the many years of effort since the 1971 presidential veto of the Child Development Act, it appears that the child-care problem will not be resolved through the actions of the federal government. Seemingly, child care as a social policy initiative will one day resemble education: We will be able to expect federal government (as with education) to fund 6% or 7% of the cost, with these monies focused on poor and/or handicapped children; most of the funds needed for child care will be provided at the state or local level. A child-care federal tax credit has been instituted; however, an annual credit of $700 per child does little to assist parents who must spend $100 to over $200 per week for care. The recently enacted Child Care and Development Block Grant assists primarily the poor or near-poor, leaving working-class and lower-middle income families unassisted. Implementation of the School of the 21st Century model, with its early childhood and family support components, offers a comprehensive, economically feasible solution to our child-care and school readiness crisis. Only 4 years ago, the 21st Century School was an idea; today, examples of these schools can be found all over the United States. The first Schools of the 21st Century were established in Independence, Missouri. Subsequently, 21st Century Schools have been established in Colorado, Connecticut, Wyoming, Texas, Kansas, Iowa, and Arkansas. Beginning in 1992 in Kentucky, as part of that state's

School Reform Act, Schools of the 21st Century were to be set up in 131 school districts. Interest in this model is clearly growing, and we have every reason to expect that 21st Century schools, tailored to individual community requirements, will be springing up in many more school districts.

The 21st Century School program presents a workable means of creating a comprehensive system that incorporates family support and educational objectives. Most importantly, this model offers some assurance that our next generation will receive the kind of parenting and child care that will encourage, rather than threaten, optimal development, and provide children with a better opportunity to develop the language ability and other skills needed to succeed in school.

REFERENCES

Belsky, J. (1981). Early human experience: A family perspective. *Developmental Psychology, 17,* 3–23.

Berrueta-Clement, J. R., Schweinhart, L. J., Barnett, W. S., Epstein, A. S., & Weikert, D. P. (1984). *Changed lives: The effects of the Perry Preschool Program on youths through age 19.* Ypsilanti, MI: High/Scope Press.

Boyer, E. L. (1991). *Ready to learn: A mandate for the nation.* Princeton, NJ: Carnegie Foundation for the Advancement of Teaching.

Bronfenbrenner, U. (1979). *The ecology of human development: Experiments by nature and design.* Cambridge, MA: Harvard University Press.

Bronfenbrenner, U. (1990). Discovering what families do. In D. Blankenhorn, S. Bayme, & J. B. Elshtain (Eds.), *Rebuilding the nest: A new commitment to the American family* (pp. 27–38). Milwaukee: Family Service America.

Child Care Action Campaign. (1988). *Child care: The bottom line.* New York: Author.

Children's Defense Fund. (1990). *Children 1990: A report card, briefing book, and action primer.* Washington, DC: Author.

Children's Defense Fund. (1992). *Vanishing dreams: The economic plight of America's young families.* Washington, DC: Author.

Clapp, G. (1988). *Child study research: Current perspectives and applications.* Lexington, MA: Lexington Books.

Consortium for Longitudinal Studies (Ed.). (1983). *As the twig is bent: Lasting effects of preschool programs.* Hillsdale, NJ: Lawrence Erlbaum Associates.

David, M.-G., & Starzec, C. (1991). France: A diversity of policy options. In S. B. Kamerman & A. J. Kahn (Eds.), *Child care, parental leave, and the under 3s: Policy innovation in Europe* (pp. 81–113). New York: Auburn House.

DeBare, I. (1991, August 25). Tough to know whom to trust: Rules lax in big industry. *Sacramento Bee,* p. A1.

Farrington, D. P. (1987). Early precursors of frequent offending. In J. Q. Wilson & G. C. Loury (Eds.), *From children to citizens: Vol. 1. Families, schools, and delinquency prevention* (pp. 27–50). New York: Springer-Verlag.

Friedman, D. (1987). *Family supportive policies: The corporate decision-making process.* New York: Conference Board.

Greenhouse, S. (1992, June 7). The coming crisis of the American workforce. *New York Times,* p. F14.

Hofferth, S., Brayfield, A., Deich, S., & Holcomb, P. (1991). *The national child care survey 1990.* Washington, DC: Urban Institute.
Hofferth, S., & Phillips, D. (1987). Child care in the United States 1970-1995. *Journal of Marriage and the Family, 49.*
Kahn, A. J., & Kamerman, S. B. (1987). *Child care: Facing the hard choices.* Dover, MA: Auburn House.
Metropolitan Life Insurance Company. (1991). *The American teacher survey.* New York: Author.
Missouri Department of Elementary and Secondary Education. (1986). *Parents as Teachers Program planning and implementation guide.* Jefferson City, MO: Author.
Pfannenstiel, J., Lambson, T., & Yarnell, V. (1991). *Second wave study of the Parents as Teachers Program.* St. Louis, MO: Parents as Teachers National Center, Inc.
Richardson, J. L., Dwyer, K., McGuigan, K., Hansen, W. B., Dent, C., Johnson, C. A., Sussman, S. Y., Brannon, B., & Flay, B. (1989). Substance abuse among eighth-grade students who take care of themselves after school. *Pediatrics, 84,* 556-566.
U.S. Bureau of Labor Statistics. (1990). [Marital and family characteristics of the labor force from the March, 1990 Current Population Survey]. Unpublished raw data.
U.S. Department of Education (1991). *America 2000: An education strategy.* Washington, DC: Author.
Whitebook, M., Howes, C., & Phillips, D. (1989). *Who cares? Child care teachers and the quality of care in America* (Final report, National Child Care Staffing Study). Oakland, CA: Child Care Employee Project.
Willer, B., Hofferth, S. L., Kisker, E. E., Divine-Hawkins, P., Farquhar, E., & Glantz, F. (1991). *The demand and supply of child care in 1990: Joint findings from the National Child Care Survey 1990 and a profile of child care settings.* Washington, DC: National Association for the Education of Young Children.
Winter, M. (1985, May). Parents as first teachers. *Principal.*
Zigler, E. (1989). Addressing the nation's child care crisis: The school of the 21st century. *American Journal of Orthopsychiatry, 59,* 484-491.
Zigler, E., & Finn-Stevenson, M. (1991). National policies for children, adolescents, and families. In M. Lewis (Ed.), *Child and adolescent psychiatry: A comprehensive textbook* (pp. 1178-1189). Baltimore, MD: Williams & Wilkins.
Zigler, E., Taussig, C. & Black, K. (1992). Early childhood intervention: A promising preventative for juvenile delinquency. *American Psychologist, 47*(8), 997-1006.

2

Critical Literacy: Reading and Writing for a New Millennium

Robert Calfee
Stanford University

The times they are a'changing! An old millennium is fast ending and the new one approaches. Never mind that these timeposts are of mankind's own making, or that 1,000 years is an eye blink in the scheme of things. Calls for improved schooling seem to have accelerated, maybe for no other reason than our collective unease about the approach of the year 2000.

In this chapter I argue that, although U.S. schools are meeting our children's academic and social needs today as well as they have in the past, the education agenda has undergone a fundamental transformation. I describe a program for curricular reform in literacy instruction that, unlike other contemporary alarms, starts with schools as they are, and builds on the simplest of activities—the daily reading-writing lesson—to achieve fundamental change in schooling in the elementary grades. My argument rests on two propositions:

- *Critical literacy,* the literate use of language to problem solve and communicate, should be the primary aim of the elementary years of schooling.
- *The school as a community of inquiry,* a professional collective in which problem solving and communication are the norms, should be the aim of restructuring efforts.

My thesis is that these propositions are actually two sides of the same coin.

19

SCHOOLS IN THE UNITED STATES:
A GOOD JOB AND A NEW TASK

Readers accustomed to tabloid accounts on the state of U.S. schools may be puzzled by an earlier throw-away line. From *Nation at Risk* (NCEE, 1983) to the *New American Schools* (Mecklenburger, 1992), reports have bewailed the miserable state of public education, and have called for alternatives ranging from takeovers to privatization. In fact, a strong case can be made that our schools are doing as well today as at any time in recent history (Berliner, 1992; Bracey, 1991), and they are on a par with schools virtually anywhere else in the developed world (Jaeger, 1992). These assessments spring from standardized test performance, admittedly not the most adequate measure, but the one employed by detractors. Adjusting for changes in population demographics, the academic achievement of U.S. students has either remained constant or improved over the past several decades (Mullis, Owen, & Phillips, in press).

This accomplishment has come during a time when the proportion of students completing a high school education has increased from less than 1 in 8 to more than 7 in 8 (i.e., virtually every U.S. child attends school for 13 years), when children from ethnic minority and second-language backgrounds have become the majority in many schools, and when childhood poverty has reached epidemic levels in this country.

Moreover, these comparisons overlook the contribution of the schools to the social and emotional well-being of our children. Most developed countries subsidize their children through child-care facilities, medical attention, and other social services. In this country, the school is the primary caretaker for children at a time when families are experiencing turmoil unprecedented in the nation's history. Not even the Great Depression produced as many single-parent and no-parent families. In May 1992, when riots swept across Los Angeles, teachers and administrators in the Los Angeles schools served as unsung heroes and heroines, comforting children whose neighborhoods were shattered by violence and undermined by despair. During the week following the turmoil, attendance in the South Central elementary schools was higher than average — attendance by *teachers,* many of whom stayed with students even though they literally feared for their lives while driving to and from school.

Parents continue to view schools favorably, despite the onslaught of policy reports. The Kappan polls of public attitudes toward schools show that (a) while Americans give "schools in general" poor marks (C or lower), (b) parents think highly of their local schools (B or higher) (Elam, Rose, & Gallup, 1992). To be sure, some critics argue that our parents are simply complacent and self-satisfied, but these descriptions do not fit most parents I know.

The point of these remarks, however, is not to suggest that our schools are "fine"; to the contrary. But we should be cautious about undermining an institution that is crucial to the well being of our national democracy. Recommendations for transforming the current system, accordingly, need to respect the present accomplishments and services of the public schools. We are, after all, talking about tinkering with a system of 50 million student clients, 2.5 million teachers, another 2.5 million administrators and ancillary staff, expenditures of more than $5 billion in 1991–1992, and enormous capital invested in facilities and materials.

My reflections about educational change start from the assumption that elementary schools will remain pretty much as they are for some time to come in several important respects: relatively small sites open to all students in the local neighborhood, classroom teachers with 20–30 students, and so on. Within these constancies, however, certain innovations seem both desirable and feasible.

The justification for change springs from societal needs and pressures. As part of the economic summit convened by President-elect Clinton, John Sculley of Apple Computer has hit the front page with the statement that "in this new economy, the strategic resources are no longer just the ones that come out of the ground, like oil and wheat and coal, but they are the ideas and information that come out of our mind" ("Upbeat Clinton," 1992, p. 1).

Futurists discovered the "information age" several years ago, without exploring the implications for schooling in any depth. A quick response is to turn to technology; computers are the touchstone of the new era, so it seems proper to rely on them for schooling. Unfortunately, (a) it takes a good deal of education to become facile with a computer, and (b) computers are not especially warm and caring when it comes to children's emotional and social needs. Moreover, life in the information age is not simply a matter of interacting with smart machines; in fact, the hallmark of this new era will be effectiveness in teamwork and interpersonal communication.

Table 2.1 compares and contrasts two societies and two school systems — the "factory schools" characteristic of our industrial society since the Civil War, and the "inquiring schools" needed to prepare our citizens for the decades ahead. The matrix highlights the distinction between the inert, factual knowledge that has comprised the textbook-based curriculum of the past half century (and the preoccupation of developers searching for an ideal "packaged" curriculum in high-tech garb), and the open-ended, problem-oriented, interdisciplinary curriculum appropriate to future "real worlds." It contrasts instruction as frontal transfer of knowledge from teacher-expert to student-novice with instruction as management of collaborative efforts by student teams wrestling with genuine problems, instruction in which the teacher is facilitator, guide, and assessor.

The final entry in this matrix focuses on institutional conditions that will

TABLE 2.1
Contrasts Between the Factor and Information—Societal Views of Schooling

Industrial Society/ Factory Schools	Information/ Inquiring Schools
Curriculum	
Basic skills, functional literacy	Transferrable skills, critical literacy
Separate subjects: reading, writing, arithmetic, science, history	Integrated subjects: communication and problem solving applied to arts and sciences
Prespecified body of knowledge, information to be memorized, emphasis on content	Emerging knowledge, strategic approach to information analysis, emphasis on process
Print-based, standard textbooks and worksheets, "school" materials	A variety of technologies, including texts, electronic libraries, multimedia sources, "real" information from outside school
Instruction	
Teacher directed, student recitations	Teacher as facilitator of student learning and production
Individual work based on uniform processes and outcomes	Cooperative learning, group framing and solving authentic problems
Student is recipient of information; teacher is the source	Student as constructor of meaning; teacher as guide to resources
Uniform pacing for entire class or ability groups; micro-management of objectives	Pacing accommodated to student needs and interests; framed by long-term goals
Assessment	
Standardized tests; recognition and "fill in blank"	Performance-based assessments, emphasis on production of authentic projects
Predetermined outcomes for all students	Conceptually equivalent outcomes, variation in "surface" forms
Organization	
Hierarchical structure, principal as manager	Mutual decisions, principal as head teacher
Individual work by isolated teachers	Professional community of inquiry
Separate grade levels; pull-out programs and specialists to handle problem causes	Upgraded adaptations, schoolwide integrated services

support change in classroom conditions. Organizational and curricular-instructional reforms are not really independent. Sarason (1990) made this point with exceptional clarity when he noted that "teachers cannot establish and sustain conditions necessary for growth and development of children unless these conditions exist for teachers first" (p. 152).

How can the public schools achieve these aspirations within the realities of limited resources and needy clients? In the following sections, I describe two complementary programs, Project READ and the INQUIRING SCHOOL, which provide one answer to this challenge. According to my basic thesis, the primary target for change should be the classroom, and secondarily the school. I disagree with Sarason on the need to change working conditions for teachers first, if the implication is that institutional change must precede change in curriculum and instruction. To the contrary, I think it is possible to transform the essence of the teacher's "work" — the reading-writing lesson — in a way that makes effective institutional change easier and more effective. Moreover, unlike programs that begin with institutional restructuring, the strategy proposed in this chapter makes it less likely that a school faculty forgets why they decided to change.

CRITICAL LITERACY:
A WORKING PROGRAM IN PROJECT READ

During the last dozen years, in collaboration with colleagues in public schools around the nation, I have explored a model for fundamental reform of elementary education. The model comprises two components. *Project READ* is designed to provide teachers with the knowledge and practical skills to guide students in acquiring *critical literacy,* the capacity to use language as a tool for thinking and communication. THE *INQUIRING SCHOOL* employs *READ* strategies to coalesce an elementary school faculty into a professional community. The parts typically operate as a two-phase program. The first phase focuses on enhancement of classroom instruction, replacing rote learning of functional literacy with the challenge of critical literacy. The second phase emphasizes creation of a *community of inquiry,* the restructuring of the school around the goal of student success, using critical literacy as a tool for professional inquiry. In this section I first describe the curriculum and instruction frameworks that comprise *READ*, and then sketch the concept of THE *INQUIRING SCHOOL.*

Background and Context

In 1980 I began a collaboration with Graystone Elementary School in San Jose. Our modest goal was to improve elementary reading–writing instruction (Calfee, Henry, & Funderburg, 1988). Graystone epitomized a successful school: Teaching was efficient, test scores were high, and the school was well managed. To be sure, teachers and students expressed boredom, a lack of coherent purpose, and little sense of challenge. The faculty was quick to criticize the standardized basal reading curriculum, the piecemeal behavioral objectives, and countless worksheets. Their main concern was not higher performance (their test scores were adequate), but realization of a more engaging and challenging curriculum, of an education experience for students (and themselves) that was more coherent and authentic.

Working in concert, the teachers, the principal, and I constructed *READ* as a professional development program organized around two themes: (a) a shift from "basic skills" toward a more thoughtful and integrated definition of reading and writing, and (b) a shift from lockstep reliance on the textbook manual toward genuine decision making.

Although low key on the surface, the collaboration encompassed radical elements. We questioned the "stage" theory of reading that dominated basal instruction in the early 1980s. Learning to read progressed from letters to words to sentences to texts. The first-grader's job was to learn phonics under direct instruction by the teacher. Third-graders should be able to "read to learn," to get to the "good stuff." Writing was a peripheral consideration in any event. In contrast, we built READ around curriculum structures and instructional strategies that integrated comprehension and composition, that combined literary appreciation and skill acquisition, that embodied developmental integrity from kindergarten through the late elementary grades, that encouraged student projects lasting the better part of the morning and extending a week or more.

We questioned the teacher's role as "technician." The teacher's manual scripted virtually every action—questions to be asked, answers to be received. In the emerging READ model, the teacher's professional decisions were conceptually based, responsive to student interest and engagement.

Cognition and Curriculum

Starting from the mundane goal of integrating reading and writing, READ produced a paradigm shift by transforming curriculum and instruction from a behavioral to a cognitive enterprise. Curriculum based on behavioral principles rests on several assumptions and practices: A complex task is divided into a large set of specifiable behaviors, ordered by difficulty; students are taught each behavior by practice with feedback; differences in learning rate are handled by adjusting the students (faster students move more quickly and slower students are delayed, but the path is the same for all).

A cognitive approach to curriculum design rests on different assumptions: The mind depends on organization for effectiveness, and so purpose and coherence are essential in breaking down a complex task; metacognitive learning is more long lasting and transferrable, and so the learning context needs to be iterative and social; students' background knowledge and interests are different, and so the teacher's challenge is to point out alternate routes through a common curriculum.

At the outset, READ assumed that, in order to "teach cognitively," the teacher must understand cognitive principles. The challenge in early meetings with Graystone faculty was to portray cognitive theory engagingly and effectively. We approached this task by (a) constructing the simplest model of cognitive education we could imagine; (b) developing compelling examples, metaphors, and experiences; and (c) engaging teachers in refining the model and the techniques.

We developed the cognitive model summarized in Fig. 2.1. *Coherence* is a reminder of the limits of short-term attentional memory. The KISS

Fig. 2.1. Conceptualization of cognition, learning, and formal language; graphic framework employed in professional development sessions with teachers to portray foundations of *critical literacy*.

principle is from Peters and Waterman (1982) — "Keep it simple, sweetheart!" The message was straightforward: An organization that focuses on doing a few things well is more likely to succeed than one that is in constant chaos. Today's schools are certainly chaotic — how can we simplify complexity? In *READ*, we liken the KISS task to the task of carving a turkey;

unless you can find the joints (a task requiring a kind of x-ray vision), you will make hash. Today's curriculum of fractionated factoids has no staying power. What we need to do as educators is decide on a few important "chunks" of organized skill and knowledge that are worth teaching well, hence the emphasis on coherence of both curriculum and instruction. As will be seen in the following section, READ replaces thousands of basal objectives with four broad domains, an application of KISS.

The linkage between prior experience and new learning is the essence of *connectedness*. The incredible diversity of today's students is a challenge to connectedness. The key is to make contact with what students *do* know (rather than emphasizing what they *do not* know), and to build on that knowledge. The principle applies equally to teachers' learning. For example, suppose the workshop goal is to explain the lack of coherence in a basal curriculum (or a standardized test) organized around hundreds of behavioral objectives. For teachers experienced with the basal, little is gained by a frontal attack. The turkey metaphor connects quickly to this issue by concretizing the principle that neither teacher nor student can *comprehend* hash. To be comprehensible, a curriculum must comprise a few distinctive segments, each with its own language and concepts. The turkey metaphor links this complex but powerful cognitive principle to everyday experience.

The third *C* is *communication,* which begins with a concept of central importance for defining *critical literacy:* the distinction between natural and formal language registers. This idea, springing from psycholinguistics and cultural anthropology, assumes that all children enter school with a fully functioning linguistic system, but they vary in the natural language acquired during childhood and their familiarity with the formal language that is the standard for school and for society.

Formal language entails several contrasts in style with natural language (Figure 2.1). The differences have less to do with the *medium* and the *message* than the *manner.* For example, a teacher appears in traffic court; the plea may be completely oral, but the style is formal. Returning home, the teacher writes to a "significant other" about the day; the note is written, but the style is natural. Such downhome examples allow teachers to envision the power of instruction based on critical literacy. The kindergarten class discussing a favorite story is achieving literacy, even though the children are still learning their ABCs — if the discussion attends in explicit manner to critical features of the narrative. The "language experience" approach of the 1960s was based on similar practices (e.g., Ashton-Warner, 1963), but lacked a conceptual foundation. The natural–formal contrast does not deny the importance of print as a medium. To the contrary, its value arises because it supports explicitness and memorability. But the Greeks were literate long before they invented the alphabet.

The second category under communication, *metatalk,* is essential to the concept of critical literacy. Cognitive psychologists introduced metacognition three decades ago to describe the phenomenon of "talking about thinking." The human capacity to reflect is uniquely linked to possession of language, but is not an automatic consequence thereof. Vygotsky (1978) argued persuasively that reflectiveness emerges through a developmental sequence that begins with self-centered children's efforts to make themselves "understood" by others, leading eventually to the capacity to "understand" themselves.

The explicitness of formal language connects it to critical literacy; both are related to the notion of metacognition, and all three concepts are linked to the *social dimension* of language and literacy. In everyday usage, *criticism* refers to harsh judgments; for the Greeks, however, a critic was an individual capable of rendering explanation and judgment about the merits and shortcomings of a particular event or object – a connoisseur, if you will. *Functional literacy* is the capacity to use language to "do" something – to read a want ad or use a technical manual to fix a leaky sink. *Critical literacy* includes the capacity for action, but also incorporates a broader sense of understanding and insight, and the ability to communicate with others about "texts" whether these are written or spoken. It is the difference between understanding how to operate the lever in a voting booth versus comprehending the issues needed to decide for whom to vote and why (Freedman & Calfee, 1984).

Undergirding READ is the firm conviction that reading and writing instruction in the elementary years is the source of critical literacy for most children, and the equally strong belief that virtually every child is capable of this achievement. Present practice promotes functional literacy. The first-grader silently marking a worksheet has no opportunity for metacognition or any need to explain. What is required is a social curriculum that provokes and supports discourse and explication from the earliest grades onward.

Curriculum Structures for Critical Literacy

What must a student learn to become critically literate? What is the scope of the course, and what is the sequence for introducing various elements of the curriculum? Rather than relying on a prescripted basal textbook, the *READ* design emphasizes a few critical tools that allow students to engage with virtually any topic. These tools give the teacher freedom as a professional; they are simple for students. No longer is the teacher the possessor of all knowledge; instead, the aim of READ instruction is to pass on to students the "secrets" for analysis and synthesis of knowledge.

In the READ curriculum, reading and writing are integrated. Imagine a school day in which literate activities permeate every minute, supporting authentic engagement with literature, science, social studies, mathematics, the arts, and humanities—even the conduct of the class as a community— where reading and writing are not listed on the day's agenda. This image stands in sharp contrast with current practice, especially in classrooms serving children at risk for school failure, where large segments of the school day are devoted to direct reading instruction, where the focus is on skill acquisition, and where the content lacks interest and relevance.

Achieving these aims requires a strong design. In "carving" the curriculum of critical literacy, READ divides reading and writing into four "chunks": narrative, exposition, concept and vocabulary development, and decoding-spelling. These four components embrace virtually the entire literacy curriculum; grammar is incorporated within the discourse forms, and poetry is neglected.

Each component is in turn subdivided into a few distinctive elements, each with its own structures and technical terminology. For instance, narrative (Fig. 2.2) comprises four key elements: character, plot, setting, and theme. These building blocks apply to fairy tales as well as Shakespeare. The figure sketches how each element might be structured during a lesson. Plot, for instance, can be "drawn" as a story graph or divided into episodic units.

The "character weave," for example, is a convenient way to engage third-graders in discussion of "Little Red Riding Hood" and the "Big Bad Wolf." Imagine a class assignment where the task is to rewrite one or more classical fairy tales from the perspective of the "bad guy" (or gal); "Little Red Riding Hood" has already been done, but think about the possibilities for developing the character of the witch in "Hansel and Gretel."

When should the various elements be taught? The READ design provides a common curriculum for teachers from kindergarten through the middle school years, and so this question must be answered developmentally. The character matrix serves equally well to contrast Charlotte and Wilbur in *Charlotte's Web,* or Hamlet and Othello in the Shakespeare plays. The challenge for teachers is to believe that young children can appreciate and apply high-level concepts for analysis and synthesis, for comprehension and composition.

The experiences of READ teachers shows that kindergartners are fully capable of such achievements when the texts, tasks, and language are developmentally appropriate. Young children are capable of fairly sophisticated analysis of characters and plot, but it helps if the teacher reads the story and makes a record-picture of their discussion (they have trouble making notes). First-graders can appreciate *Charlotte's Web,* if taken in bite-size chunks. Fourth-graders will see this same story from a different perspective, but may not be ready for *Hamlet.* Young children can also compose rather compelling narratives (e.g., consider the opening line of a

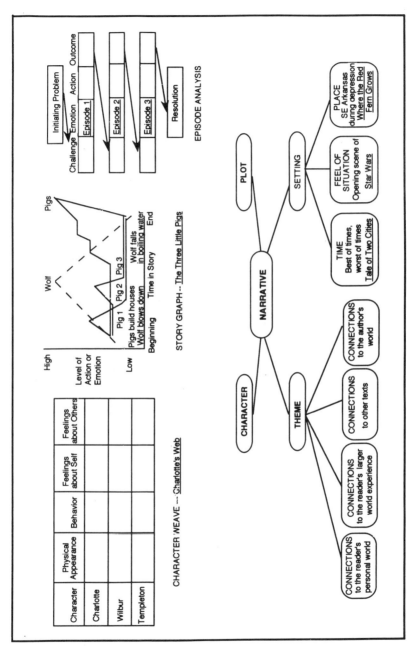

Fig. 2.2. Graphic portrayal of four major "chunks" of the READ curriculum for the reading–writing curriculum for the narrative genre.

29

kindergarten production in South Central Los Angeles — "My life is broke!").

The other three *READ* curriculum domains, sketched in Fig. 2.3, are described elsewhere (e.g., Calfee & Drum, 1986). The basic approach is the same as for narrative. Each domain is subdivided into a few distinctive

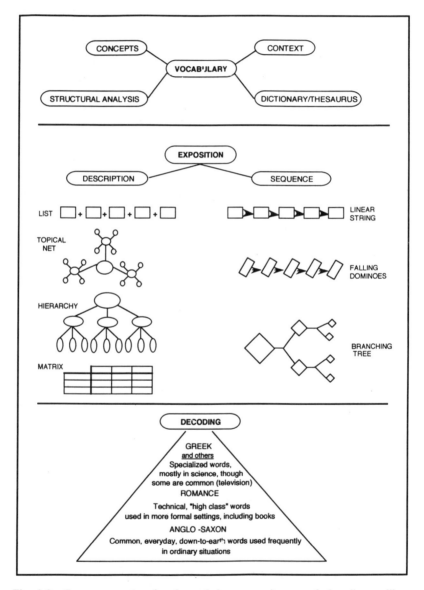

Fig. 2.3. Summary portrayals of vocabulary, expository, and decoding–spelling components of the READ curriculum.

categories, each encompassing structures for analysis of ideas and texts, for reading and writing.

Instructional Strategies for Critical Literacy

Decisions about what to teach may be independent of decisions about how to teach, but the student is more likely to achieve success when these decisions complement one another. Unfortunately, it is not uncommon for higher order thinking to be taught through recitation, and for a textbook exercise designed to promote creativity to provide the correct answers.

During the Graystone project, we developed the instructional design in Fig. 2.4. The left-hand column is a variation on Madeline Hunter's Five-Step Lesson Plan, which was popular at the time. We simplified the original to four steps, created an opening that was shorter and more explicit, emphasized student engagement and cooperative activities in the middle, and introduced the notion of a closing review. The right-hand column shows three themes for integrating a lesson: The *content* is the "stuff" of the exercise (e.g., "The Three Little Pigs"), *process* refers to the analytic focus ("We'll look at the characters and events in the story"), and *structure* is the graphic structure for pulling the pieces together. Content, the emphasis in most basal lessons, becomes the occasion for analysis and synthesis.

The READ lesson design differed from existing practice in several ways. First was the recommendation to focus on a few critical conceptual outcomes in a lesson. The typical basal lesson included objectives in vocabulary, comprehension, decoding, and so on, a combination altogether lacking in coherence. Second, the basal lesson was teacher directed, with the teacher relying on the teacher's manual for both questions and answers (Cazden, 1988, analyzes the *interrogate-recite-evaluate* syndrome in a classroom discourse). The READ lesson emphasized genuine discourse, with teacher questions designed to evoke a wide array of responses. Third, the precedence of process and structure over content was a major conceptual shift. Fourth, we encouraged productive activities at the end of the lesson in place of the typical worksheets.

During subsequent years, as we observed countless READ lessons, we realized that the preceding design was easily routinized by teachers and students — and for administrators, who in some instances developed checklists based on the lesson design in the upper panel of Figure 2.4. Teachers complained of stultification, and this feedback led to the development of the model in the lower panel: *C*onnect, *O*rganize, *R*eflect, and *E*xtend (the CORE model; Calfee, Chambliss, & Beretz, 1991). Unlike the stepwise design, this model is flexible and iterative. Any given lesson may call for emphasis on one or another of the four elements. The order is not critical;

LESSON DESIGN

Opening

Explicitly introduce lesson goal
  --content
  --process
  --structure

Middle

Lesson development
Active student involvement
Cooperative activities
Small-group problem-solving
    discussion

Closing

Review lesson
  --content
  --process
  --structure

Follow-up

Reinforce and extend lesson goal
Productive activities

Content

Substance of lesson

Process

Methods of analysis -- taking the
    problem apart

Structure

Methods of synthesis -- putting the
    pieces together

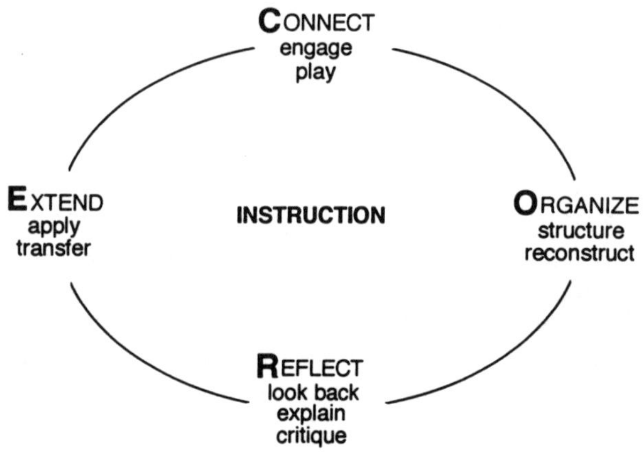

CONNECT
engage
play

EXTEND
apply
transfer

INSTRUCTION

ORGANIZE
structure
reconstruct

REFLECT
look back
explain
critique

The CORE Model of Instruction

Fig. 2.4. Alternative views of lesson design in the READ instructional plan.

reflection may come before organization. The model can be applied at many levels: a 20-minute lesson, a 3-week thematic project, or untangling the confusion one student faces with a spontaneous 30-s "connection."

Here is a brief application of the READ strategy. The lesson is from a second-grade class in inner-city Chicago. Of several stories the teacher had selected for "fun reading," the children's favorite was *The Napping House* (A. Wood & D. Wood, 1984), a "cumulative tale [like 'frog on a log'] in which a wakeful flea atop a number of sleeping creatures causes a commotion with just one bite." The children knew the story virtually by heart, from the opening picture of Granny asleep in her cozy bed in the napping house, through the subsequent episodes in which one creature after another piles up on Granny, to the climactic flea bite that unpacks the startled collection. The children were already "connected" to the story, and so, after rereading the story, the teacher's next step was to organize the narrative by sketching the sequence of characters and episodes (the house, granny, the child, the dozing dog and snoozing cat, and finally the wakeful flea).

The curriculum focus in this lesson was narration, highlighting the interplay between characters and episodes that are the crux of this story. The "work" of the lesson began with the question, "Suppose we write our own story, something like *Napping House,* but different. Where shall we put the story [establish the setting], what characters shall we put into the story, and how shall we start it?" These questions include both reflection and extension in the CORE model. The task goes beyond story comprehension to story composition, where the students are asked to imitate a rather complex model.

Not surprisingly, given that the youngsters were attempting this task for the first time, their first suggestion was to rewrite the original story — "You need a house, a bedroom, a granny," and so on. The teacher pushed them: "Let's make our own story. We can put it in a different place; what are some places in a house besides the bedroom for a story?" You will notice that the final question actually provides a scaffold for the students' thinking. After some discussion, including serious consideration of the bathroom, students decided on the "cooking kitchen," where they portrayed the mother making pizza, joined first by her child (considerable discussion about whether a boy or girl, resolved by choosing twins), then a dog, a cat, a rat (not the mouse of the original), and finally a flea. As the characters evolved, the teacher sketched the emerging story on a large piece of paper stretched across the chalkboard. The children struggled with the climactic event; what should be the consequence when the flea bit the rat, and so on? Finally a boy suggested that the pizza explode, filling the kitchen with pepperoni and sausage and cheese; this resolution was a big hit!

The lesson illustrates several features of the READ strategy. The teacher made extensive use of graphic structures (both semantic webs and story maps), almost incidentally in support of the tasks. The discussion covered both comprehension and composition; whereas the students' story was modeled on *Napping House,* the task of inventing a resolution was a genuine challenge. Finally, although the teacher guided and scaffolded the class discussion in this introductory lesson, she also revealed a deep appreciation of the social dimension of learning, which opened opportunities for interchanges promoting explicitness and reflective thought. If Vygotsky was correct, metacognition (the ability to think about thought) depends on social interactions; it is not an automatic consequence of practice. Metacognition is valuable in its own right, because it fosters strategic thinking and undergirds "high-road" transfer.

The social model also supports the development of formal communication skills that will serve students throughout their adult lives. Worksheets and routinized responses may suit a factory society; the information society requires talent in effective teamwork. To thrive in the future, students must be facile in group processes, whether in college, in their careers, in government business, or in the increasing complexities of personal life.

A SEGUE: FROM *READ* TO *THE INQUIRING SCHOOL*

As the previous example illustrates, READ is as much about writing as it is about reading. The research on authentic comprehension as reconstruction of text supports this strategy (Spivey, 1987), and the concept of literacy as social constructivism is also consistent with the techniques. READ contributes to these ideas through its detailed "engineering" of graphic structures and group problem-solving strategies to support these concepts, moving them from idealizations to practical realities.

For teachers accustomed to following the basal scripts in the teacher's manual, the power of these ideas can be frustratingly elusive on first encounter. We have viewed this "problem" as another challenge in program design: how to provide classroom teachers with an experience that provides an "aha" about the power of READ structures and strategies in a social situation that affects them as adults. The following example illustrates one approach that we have developed for professional development workshops.

The exercise begins by asking the group to spend a few minutes writing an essay on the prompt, *My life as a writer.* Reactions to this "assignment" are varied; some participants begin immediately to fill their paper with prose, whereas others frown and wince. After a couple of minutes, the group is interrupted and asked to discuss their text with a neighbor: "Talk about what you were writing, where you were going with the story, how you decided what to write." Participants always enjoy this part of the process!

The participants are then asked to start the task anew by jotting personal reflections under three headings: How I *learned* to write; when I *had* to write; when I *wanted* to write. The facilitator prods the participants' memories — "Who was your first writing teacher? The writing teacher you liked best? Your most recent writing test? A friend with whom you have corresponded?" After a few minutes of reflective note taking (actually a semantic web), participants discuss their notes with a neighbor, adding additionally to their list as they emerge from the exchange. In the final segment of the exercise, each participant designs a draft, beginning with a theme and selecting episodes from the previous notes to illustrate the theme. You will notice that, in organizing a narrative composition, the writer begins with the theme and then adds episodes to fit. An especially memorable theme from one teacher: "Whenever I try to write something, the paper bleeds," the teacher's way of expressing her dread of the red-penciled comments that had thwarted her efforts to become a writer. In another session, a teacher organized her essay around the value of writing in her life, from her imaginary childhood friend to a personal diary that sustained her through an unhappy marriage.

The point of this exercise is to demonstrate the power of READ structures and strategies for "grownups," even teachers! The preceding example Connects, Organizes, Reflects, and Extends, all in a matter of 15 min! One of the more distressing features of life as an elementary teacher is the isolation and "juvenilization" of everyday experience. The lack of opportunities for professional contact, and the continuing focus on low-level basic skills is stultifying. READ makes it possible for the teacher to introduce students at every age to the "good stuff," to genuine literature and authentic topics, while ensuring that students move toward high-level accomplishments in well-defined curriculum goals. READ provides a common technical language that cuts across grades and roles, opening the way for professional interactions.

This "story" has a happy ending. Several years ago, we observed a dramatic transformation in several READ schools: Teachers began to extend the strategies of critical literacy beyond the classroom to encompass other facets of their professional work (Calfee, 1992; Calfee & Wadleigh, 1992). Grade-level teams planned joint projects with semantic "webs"; teacher committees agendized school meetings around "weaves" or matrices; faculties integrated categorical programs using "time-weaves."

We finally realized that these schools had evolved into a remarkable new form, the INQUIRING SCHOOL. Schaefer's (1967) vision is of the *school as a center of inquiry;* it is an institution that routinely conducts practical research on practical problems, where teachers and principals work as a professional team, where leadership springs not from the "man on horse-back," but as a collective enterprise — not by external mandate, not by top-down dictate, not by imposed "research" methods, but by transferring techniques for effective language use from the classroom to encompass the entire business of the school. The path to power was neither bureaucratic nor managerial, but educational (Cuban, 1991).

The move from READ to THE INQUIRING SCHOOL has taken different shapes in different location (Calfee & Wadleigh, 1992), not as the result of a preplanned design, but through simple serendipity. Although each site is distinctive, they share certain themes in common:

• The school's central agenda is *improved classroom practice* for promoting critical literacy throughout all the grades.
• *Professional collaboration* is a hallmark, in pairs of teachers, grade-level teams, and over the entire community, regular classroom teachers, resource specialists, and administrative staff.
• *Shared decision making* is a daily reality, through collaborative lesson planning, "metalessons" (demonstrations in which one teacher conducts the activity while another gives running commentary), and a continuing review of the school's educational missions.

The INQUIRING SCHOOL design does not include any novel elements beyond those in READ. The driving idea is that professional knowledge is the source of professional power. The READ structures and strategies comprise a body of professional knowledge, but in some form they are also available to every educated person. The "click" comes when a READ cadre realizes the power of the techniques for *both* their students *and* for themselves as professionals.

CONCLUDING REMARKS

The READ/INQUIRING SCHOOL model is presently being implemented in more than 100 schools throughout the United States, mostly in large urban areas serving large numbers of students at risk for academic failure. The key ingredients in the model are quite simple: (a) the local elementary school has the power within itself to reform curriculum and instruction; (b) fundamental change builds on new ideas and techniques rather than extra money, innovative materials, or institutional restructuring; and (c) reading and writing is the foundation for the elementary school in moving from the factory age to the information society.

Skeptics have posed various questions and concerns about the feasibility of the model: Schools already have too much to do; what if "they" won't let us change the curriculum; what about test scores? Schools are certainly chaotic today; READ/INQUIRING SCHOOL actually simplifies the agenda by focusing on critical literacy, and connecting other programs to this central concept. Districts, states, and even the federal government certainly mandate curriculum goals; although I have not compiled the complete collection, my estimate is that elementary teachers in Los Angeles are responsible for curriculum mandates that, if stacked on top of one another, would be several feet tall — not including teachers' manuals and tests! Some mandates are quite prescriptive and others are amazingly vague. The bottom line is that they are largely unenforceable, partly because they are contradictory, but also because the authorities lack the personnel to visit local schools.

Administrators beyond the local school level are often attentive to test score performance. Although READ is not especially compatible with the worksheet-oriented instruction that supports standardized tests, students tend to do well on these measures when the program is fully implemented (Calfee et al., 1988). And visitors to READ classrooms are frequently impressed by the climate of motivated students engaged in productive work, especially writing and project activities.

Like almost any other site-based innovation, however, READ/INQUIRING SCHOOL does entail risk, because it brings responsibility. There is safety in "doing what you are told." But this response is not professional, nor is it effective in meeting the challenge that confronts elementary educators in today's world. One of my favorite children's stories is Lionni's (1985) Swimmy. The hero, a little fish, is the sole survivor when a giant tuna snaps up his cousins. After wandering through the wonders of the ocean floor, Swimmy happens upon another school of cousins hiding in the shelter of a large rock. The school is uneasy about Swimmy's entreaties to explore the sea around them. He thinks about the problem for a while, and then persuades his friends to join together with him, shaping a giant fish from their small bodies — "And so they swam in the cool morning water and in the midday sun and chased the big fish away!" That is the message of THE INQUIRING SCHOOL — to unite as colleagues, to experiment and inquire, all of this toward the goal of ensuring that all children achieve their full potential academically, personally, and socially.

REFERENCES

Ashton-Warner, S. (1963). *Teacher*. New York: Simon & Schuster.

Berliner, D. C. (1992, February). *Educational reform in an era of disinformation*. Paper presented at the meeting of the American Association of Colleges for Teacher Education, San Antonio, TX.

Bracey, G. W. (1991). Why can't they be like we were? *Phi Delta Kappan, 73,* 104–117.

Calfee, R. C. (1992). The Inquiring School: Literacy for the year 2000. In C. Collins & J. N. Mangieri (Eds.), *Teaching thinking: An agenda for the twenty-first century (pp. 147–166). Hillsdale, NJ: Lawrence Erlbaum Associates.*

Calfee, R. C., Chambliss, M. J., & Beretz, M. (1991). Organizing for comprehension and composition. In R. Bowler & W. Ellis, *All language and the creation of literacy* (pp. 79–93). Baltimore, MD: Orton Dyslexia Society.

Calfee, R. C., & Drum, P. A. (1986). Research on teaching reading. In M. Wittrock (Ed.), *Third handbook on research on teaching* (pp. 804–849). New York: Macmillan.

Calfee, R. C., Henry, M. K., & Funderburg, J. A. (1988). A model for school change. In S. J. Samuels & P. D. Pearson (Eds.), *Changing school reading programs.* Newark, DE: International Reading Association.

Calfee, R. C., & Wadleigh, C. (1992). Building a learning community through inquiry. *Educational Leadership, 50*(1), 28–32.

Cazden, C. B. (1988). *Classroom discourse: The language of teaching and learning.* Portsmouth, NH: Heinemann.

Cuban, L. (1990). Reforming again, again, and again. *Educational Researcher, 19*(1), 3–13.

Elam, S. M., Rose, L. C., & Gallup, A. M. (1992). The 24th annual Gallup/Phi Delta Kappa poll of the public's attitudes toward the public schools. *Phi Delta Kappan, 74,* 41–53.

Freedman, S. W., & Calfee, R. C. (1984). Understanding and comprehending. *Written Communication, 1,* 459–490.

Jaeger, R. M. (1992). World class standards, choice, and privatization: Weak measures serving presumptive policy. *Phi Delta Kappan, 74,* 118–128.

Lionni, L. (1985). *Frederick's Fables.* New York: Pantheon.

Mecklenburger, J. A. (1992). The braking of the "break-the-mold" express. *Phi Delta Kappan, 74,* 280–289.

Mullis, I. V. S., Owen, E. H., & Phillips, G. W. (in press). *America's challenge: Opportunities for higher standards.* Washington, DC: Office of Education/OERI/NCES.

National Commission on Excellence in Education (NCEE). (1983). *A nation at risk: The imperative for educational reform.* Washington, DC: U.S. Government Printing Office.

Peters, T. J., & Waterman, R. H, Jr. (1982). *In search of excellence.* New York: Harper & Row.

Sarason, S. B. (1990). *The predictable failure of educational reform.* San Francisco: Jossey-Bass.

Schaefer, R. J. (1967). *The school as a center of inquiry.* New York: Harper & Row.

Spivey, N. N. (1987). Constructing constructivism: Reading research in the U.S. *Poetics, 16,* 169–192.

Upbeat Clinton opens economic conference. (1992, December 15). *San Francisco Chronicle,* pp. 1, 8.

Vygotsky, L. S. (1978). *Mind in society: The development of higher psychological processes.* Cambridge, MA: Harvard University Press.

Wood, A., & Wood, D. (1984). *The napping house.* New York: Harcourt Brace Jovanovich.

3

Literacy and the Textbook
of the Future

Richard L. Venezky
University of Delaware

Since early in this century U.S. book reading habits have been found wanting. Gray and Munroe (1929), in summarizing 150 studies done prior to 1929 on reading habits of adults, concluded "that young people and adults engage more in reading short, unrelated types of material and less in reading longer selections and books, or materials which are closely related" (p. 260). Surveys of reading habits in the United States have shown that the amount of time spent reading books varies with education (e.g., Parsons, 1923, cited in Gray & Munroe, 1929, p. 35), as does the particular parts of the newspaper that are read, with the more highly educated tending to focus more on the informational parts and the less educated, on the entertainment parts (Kirsch & Jungeblut, 1986). Total amount of time spent reading books in 1977 was only about 5 minutes per day for employed men and about 4 minutes for employed women (Robinson, 1977).

Compounding this less than salubrious situation for the book is a recent report on literacy among U.S. young adults that found distressingly low levels of literacy among a large segment of the surveyed population (Kirsch & Jungeblut, 1986; Venezky, Kaestle, & Sum, 1987). Literacy and schooling are closely linked and therefore literacy and book reading are closely related, with the more literate tending to read more books. But even among certain segments of the more literate, book reading is not popular. For example, among the population over 56, only 29% claim to be book readers and this dichotomy cannot be explained by physical condition (Library of Congress, 1984).

Adding to the uncertain future of the book is electronic technology. With inexpensive, handheld computers, complete with high volume storage media and voice synthesis, who needs a book? Want to absorb yourself in *Anna Karenina?* A simple, spoken command to your satellite-linked, all-weather portable will bring the complete Tolstoy oeuvre in a flash from an electronic library, automatically charging your MasterCard a small reader's fee. Say "read *Anna Karenina*" and the voice synthesizer will kick into action, "Happy families are all alike; every unhappy family. . . ." And why should a medical student lug a fat, heavy copy of *Gray's Anatomy* onto an airplane if it and just about anything else in print can be accessed through a lightweight portable?

Satellite-beamed libraries may not be available just yet and handheld computers may not have the screen resolution and voice synthesis and recognition desired for comfortable listening and viewing, but these features are closer than a decade away. Already voice recognition systems are used in specialized contexts such as baggage handling and medical reporting. Voice synthesis has not reached the quality of digitized speech, but it is approaching that point. Wireless communication is available for laptops, and more powerful handheld computers are announced every month.

Against this backdrop of limited literacy, unsustainable attention, and expanding electronic technologies, what future is there for the book and especially the textbook, which for almost 2,000 years has been a central fixture of education? This chapter is a background briefing for those who wish to predict the future of books or to take steps to shape this future. Its focus is primarily textbooks and its concern is both with the future of these artifacts and of the abilities required to read and understand them. Lest the previous two paragraphs raise the specter of technohype, of a panegyric to bits, bytes, and pixels, let me reassure the discerning reader that the disposition of ink on paper plays more than a plaintive role in what follows.

A BRIEF HISTORY OF TEXTBOOKS

The earliest texts used for education were probably the various books of the Bible and the poetry of Homer (Cubberley, 1920). Books especially for instruction developed later, beginning with Aristotle's *Metaphysics, Physics, Psychology, and Ethics.* Other popular texts in the Middle Ages included Donatus' grammar, Ptolemy's *Mechanisms of the Heavens,* and Boethius' *Geometry.* Prior to the 12th century, however, most instruction was not given from the original texts but from abridged compendiums. These included such works as Boethius' summaries of Aristotle and Plato and various attempts to combine all classical learning into a single text (e.g., Isidore's *Origines*). Textbooks were circulated as manuscripts, generally equivalent in length to a modern text of 70–137 pages, and were sometimes in catechetical (question–answer) form (Cubberley, 1920, p. 164, fn 1). No attempt was made in these compendiums to teach or even to motivate learning. Their sole purpose was to summarize secular knowledge required for either the church service or for the study of theology.

With the awakening of intellectual life in Europe in the 13th century, translations of classical works were rediscovered, primarily through contact with Moslem learning in Spain. Within a century the works of Aristotle, Euclid, Ptolemy, Cicero, Galen, Hippocrates, and other classical writers were standard fare in the European universities, where they remained in most cases until the mid-18th century. Although most textbooks up to the 16th century were written in Latin, the Protestant Reformation brought a flood of vernacular materials. By 1529 Martin Luther published in German his translation of the New Testament, the *Greater* and *Smaller Catechisms,* and his own version of a primer. By the end of the 16th century, primers in vernacular languages contained the alphabet, syllable tables, and even some secular material, all oriented toward teaching children to read and to know the primary church rituals (Davies, 1974).

The earliest settlers to North America brought with them a variety of English textbooks and continued to import textbooks from England until well into the 19th century. But textbooks were also published in the Colonies, beginning with the first press established in Cambridge, Massachusetts, in the mid-17th century. When the first U.S. Copyright Law was established in 1790, John Barry's *Philadelphia Spelling Book,* Jedidiah Morse's *American Geography,* and Samuel Freeman's *Columbian Primer* were among the first materials to be protected.

For several centuries elementary-level textbooks were undifferentiated by age or grade level and gave little, if any, pedagogical advice to the teacher. Complex prose and an adult vocabulary were common until the 1820s and 1830s when the ideas of Rousseau and Pestalozzi began to influence U.S. educational thought and practice. Modern U.S. textbooks are a creation of the second half of the 19th century when the common school movement had created a sufficiently large market to make textbook publishing profitable and canals and roads allowed national distribution of materials at low costs. Large specialty printing houses like Truman & Smith in Cincinnati, Ohio, could do a multimillion dollar business in textbooks by marketing across the entire country. Ray's *Practical Arithmetic* and the *McGuffey Readers* were successful not just because of their intrinsic merits as pedagogical materials but also because of the marketing skills of their publishers.

The total value of book production in the United States increased through the second quarter of the 19th century at nearly twice the rate of increase in the total U.S. population, growing from $2.5 million in 1820 to $5.5 million in 1840 and $12.5 million in 1850, with textbook sales accounting for almost a third of these totals (Trubner, 1859, pp. 89–90). School materials were purchased not only by parents and individual schools but more and more by school districts. With the introduction of the age-graded school, textbooks for the elementary grades began to be issued in graded series, with a separate book designated for each grade level. Earlier graded series had been published, particularly for reading, but the widespread development of graded series for reading and mathematics did not occur until the second quarter of the 19th century (Venezky, 1992).

Sullivan (1927) noted that "when people could not read, who wrote the ballads of a nation may have been more important than who made the laws. After literacy and schools became general, the authorship of school text-books became important" (p. 9). Authorship of elementary textbooks has shifted since the 17th century from the single writer who truly wrote and edited the work to committees of authors, selected as much for their name, gender, or race appeal as for their abilities to write instructional materials. Modern elementary textbooks are most often not written by the people listed as authors, but by writing houses that specialize in the development of textbook series, or by in-house editors/writers.

Textbooks today are assembled more than they are written, leading to what Barzun (1945) described as the impersonal voice. "The truth drones on with the muffled sound of one who is indeed speaking from a well" (p. 66). With some texts, especially those created through the electronic contributions of large numbers of people, the notion of authorship may not apply. The National Library of Medicine, for example, has created a hepatitis data base through consensus of experts. Perhaps we have finally arrived at virtual authorship.

HOW TEXTBOOKS ARE USED

In idealized curricula, textbooks are often relegated to a minor role or eliminated altogether. Rousseau, for his imaginary pupil, Emile, allowed no textbooks until the age of 18, when well-chosen histories were recommended. Prior to this time, only *Robinson Crusoe* was advised. Similarly, Dewey opposed prepared curriculum materials, especially textbooks. His University of Chicago laboratory school curriculum was constructed around fundamental occupations, the socioindustrial arts of mankind, sequenced as they emerged in history. In contrast, other educators like Hoole, Comenius, and Pestalozzi used textbooks to introduce educational innovations.

Modern textbook usage varies by a number of factors, including grade level. At the elementary levels, teachers appear to be heavily dependent on textbooks, but contrary to popular opinion they do not follow them slavishly (Stodolsky, 1989). Studies of science textbook use indicate that almost 94% of all elementary science teachers teach from a textbook (Weiss, 1987). Elementary reading series (i.e., basal readers) appear to be written more for robots than for discerning human beings. Accompanying each student text is a parallel teacher's edition, with a reduced impression of each page of the student text and often a fully scripted guide to its instruction. The teachers/robots are told not only what to do step by step — as if they were preparing an elaborate sauce — but also what to say.

Secondary-level textbooks are also heavily used by teachers, but given the specialized training of secondary teachers, dependence on texts is less than what is found at the elementary level. At the college level, and to some degree at the upper secondary levels, textbook use varies by field. Kuhn (1970) divided textbook usage patterns into three classes. In the first, characterized by music, graphic arts, and literature, students are exposed directly to artists' works; textbooks (with the exception of handbooks and the like) play only a secondary role.

The second of Kuhn's classes, centering on philosophy, history, and the other social sciences, uses textbooks heavily, but also assigns parallel readings in original sources, the classics of the respective fields. Thus, experimental psychology courses might assign an original article by Thorndike or Skinner; U.S. history courses, the Declaration of Independence, the Bill of Rights, and speeches by Patrick Henry and Abraham Lincoln.

In contrast to these groups, the natural sciences (his third class) use textbooks exclusively until research begins on a PhD. "Why, after all, should the student of physics, for example, read the works of Newton, Faraday, Einstein, or Schrödinger, when everything he needs to know about these works is recapitulated in a far briefer, more precise, and systematic form in a number of up-to-date textbooks?" (p. 165). To this trichotomy, we should add a second dimension that contrasts textbooks with journal articles, technical reports, and conference presentations. Basic courses across all disciplines would tend to use textbooks more than this latter class of materials, whereas more advanced courses, which tend to investigate cutting-edge ideas, would depend more on recent statements as reflected in current journal publications and the like.

A further contrast might also be made between developed countries where teachers are generally well trained, particularly at the secondary and college levels, and developing countries where teacher training is still limited. In the latter case, according to Altbach and Kelly (1988), textbook dependency is significantly higher. Teachers at all levels in industrialized countries also have teaching aids (charts, films, etc.), copying machines, computers, and libraries to supplement and support their presentations, thus reducing their dependence on textbooks.

LITERACY AND TEXTBOOK COMPREHENSION

Comprehension of science, math, and social studies textbooks, what K–12 teachers call content-area reading, is a serious instructional problem.

Students who grasp the plot and author's purpose in narrative fiction do not always demonstrate the equivalent expertise with expository materials. The elementary reading and language arts curricula are constructed primarily on narrative fiction; little space in the readers and little classroom time is devoted to strategies for reading high information texts or everyday documents like TV schedules, advertisements, and instruction manuals. If the skills required for content-area reading were the same as those required for fiction, then what problems exist in content area reading might be attributed to the conceptual load of the texts involved.

However, critical differences separate comprehension of narrative fiction from comprehension of exposition. First, the reader's task with fiction is to follow and appreciate authors as they lead us through the plot, revealing events, thoughts, and feelings as they choose to present them. Few stories are written to be read in any other order than that presented by the author. The reader's task is invariant across time and texts: read, understand, enjoy. The text is a tightly constructed whole, to be consumed in its entirety.

With expository materials, the reader is usually pursuing a well-specified task that generally varies across texts and readings: determine how to reset margins, find which breakfast foods are low in sugar, decide which type of bank account is best for your children. These are problems to be solved with the aid of texts; the solutions might be found by skimming, reading marginal notes, studying a graph, repeated reading of selected selections, or other strategies that actively engage the text as if it were a loose collection of facts and ideas rather than a continual thread of episodes that build one on another.

Only in school-based reading are expository texts treated as if they were stories, to be engaged in a linear path. "Read the chapter and answer the questions at the end" exemplifies the artificial world of the content area classroom, but not the true use of expository texts and everyday documents. Strategies and materials exist for teaching content-area reading (e.g., Herber, 1978; Lapp, Flood, & Farnan, 1989), but they have made only modest inroads into the secondary curricula and minimal entry into the elementary reading program. As a consequence, teachers undervalue and underassign reading in the content-area classroom (Rieck, 1977) and students pass to adulthood with insufficient skills and experience for higher levels of expository and document reading (Kirsch & Jungeblut, 1986).

A second limitation on literacy acquisition is that even with the constructivist perspective that now pervades reading instruction, literacy is still viewed either as a collection of skills or as the deconstructionist's intellectual anarchy where any reading of the text is legitimized. This may be informative and ameliorative for reading Nabokov or Barth, but for warranties, bus schedules, and prescription labels it is a formula for disappointment and pain.

Literacy requires active, autonomous engagement with print; autonomy, however, requires knowing when and how to supplement and extend the text with knowledge one brings to the reading task. For expository texts and everyday documents, extraction of an unambiguous meaning is critical, regardless of what obstacles the author may have strewn in the reader's path. Hiatuses in the text must be filled to match what the author intended, not what readers find most agreeable, unlike fiction where the author often invites readers to interpret the text according to their own experiences and dispositions.

REPLACEMENTS FOR THE TRADITIONAL TEXTBOOK

Over the past 40 years a number of variations and replacements for textbooks have appeared. Some of these, like the programmed textbook, represent alternative approaches to instruction, realized in traditional textbook form. Others, like on-line texts, are alternative approaches to the delivery of textbook material. Although each of these creates some alteration in the traditional relationship of reader to text, none makes as radical change as hypertext and none challenges as directly the definition of *textbook* and *author* as the basic concept of hypertext. The potential of each of these alternatives to guide the future of textbooks varies, however, from minute (programmed textbooks) to substantial (hypertext).

PROGRAMMED TEXTBOOKS

Programmed textbooks were a dead end on the phylogenetic scale of pedagogy, spawned by Skinner's *programmed instruction.* The theoretical base for programmed instruction was *operant conditioning,* a behavioral approach to training that reduced complex tasks to small steps that minimized failure (Skinner, 1954, 1963). Success at each step was rewarded immediately, although alternative reinforcement schedules were also used. Through these training regimens, rats, pigeons, and other animals were led to do complex dances, peck at different patterns of colored dots, or navigate complicated mazes. Skinner extended these ideas to human instruction, primarily through teaching machines that had already been used experimentally for testing (Benjamin, 1988).

In 1958, the same year that General de Gaulle became French premier and Nabokov published *Lolita,* Skinner signed a contract with Harcourt Brace Publishing Company to develop a new teaching machine for high school and college-level use. This project failed and the two parties to it parted ways within a year; nevertheless, Harcourt Brace decided to transfer the

English grammar materials they had developed for the project to a textbook form. This was published in 1960 as *English 2600,* where the 2,600 represented the total number of steps in the program (Reid, 1969). Over the next decade Harcourt Brace issued a total of 16 programmed textbooks. Each was composed of a series of multiple-choice questions, with branching instructions attached to each answer alternative, thus allowing students to navigate a path through the material according to their responses. Correct answers were revealed along with the next page (i.e., question) to be read, thus giving the required feedback.

Programmed texts proved to be relatively expensive to write and edit; for the reader they were uniformly boring with little room for the author's style and little place for a teacher (Feldhusen, 1963). Because failure was to be avoided, each question was written to ensure a 90% to 95% correct response rate. At this level of simplicity, readers did not need feedback to tell them whether or not they were correct. After about a decade of effort, Harcourt Brace closed its programmed instruction division; no other major textbook publisher, before or since, has tried this approach to textbook organization.

In retrospect, a programmed text is simply a reduction of a textbook to a rigid, boring form. Authorship is still evident and a textbook exists with which the reader interacts, albeit in a nonlinear manner. Different readers might engage different portions of the text, but this might occur with a more traditional text, especially when the author suggests that the reader, for whatever reason, might skip over certain sections. W. Somerset Maugham (1944/1992) used this device in *The Razor's Edge,* where in the introduction to section VI he informs the reader, "I feel it right to warn the reader that he can very well skip this chapter without losing the thread of such story as I have to tell" (p. 242). The story is still Maugham's, however, and the reader takes what Maugham presents, plus or minus the marked chapter. Whether continually programmed or only occasionally programmed, this form of text has had an infinitesimal influence on textbook design in the past and shows no potential for influence in the future.

On-Line Texts

At a number of sites around the world, texts are stored on-line, for access by anyone who requests them. The National Science Foundation provides on-line access to its publications, including descriptions of grant programs and lists of grantees. The On-line Computer Library Center (OCLC), which provides on-line cataloguing for hundreds of university libraries in North America, is also experimenting with text delivery. Electronic Information Delivery On-line System (EIDOS) will deliver selected pages of on-line documents on demand. It is based on the finding that up to three quarters of all text use is analytical examination or consultation of relatively short sections.

With on-line text browsing, most relationships of author, text, and reader remain intact. However, readers no longer have a physical artifact to hold and to access as they choose. They might be charged for each page they access or each request they make for access, plus the number of words or characters transferred to their workstations. Depending on how access to the text is controlled, the reader may be able to access selected portions of the text nonlinearly, for example, all sections that refer to a designated topic or that contain specific words. The text remains intact; only the paths of retrieval are enriched.

On-line textbooks, that is, the electronic delivery of a traditional text-book, will probably have a limited but increasing acceptance over the coming decade. For the person who wants to consult one or more textbook treatments of a specific topic: a computer sorting technique, conjugation of the Latin verb *facere,* the Teapot Dome Scandal, immediate, 24-hour-per-day access to an on-line textbook library would, at the right price, be desirable. A library catalogue could be searched, one or more appropriate texts located, and the desired sections down loaded for viewing or printing. Would an entire class of psychology 101 students, however, want to have access to their textbook only by computer? Probably not, especially if the computer version were simply an electronic image of the printed text. The added convenience of on-line access would be outweighed by the reduction in graphic resolution and available viewing/skimming area.

Customized Publishing

A textbook today is assumed to be the coherent product of an author or group of authors/writers, whether a college-level physics text by a Nobel laureate or an elementary-level basal reader by an army of identified and unidentified writers. Whether on the East coast or the West coast, readers of Kernighan and Ritchie's *The C Programming Language* (1978) can expect to find a tutorial introduction starting on page 5. But with customized publishing, these conditions no longer hold. Through a device that not only allows adaptation of a text but also generates indexes, paginates, prints, and binds, textbooks can now be tailored for individual instructors (McDowell, 1989). The tutorial introduction in Kernighan and Ritchie, for example, might be tailored for a class of business majors, with programming examples constructed around compound interest, stock prices, and other economic relationships. Instructors might then add their own preface and even problems at the end of each chapter. Different instructors might tailor the text for humanities students, focusing on natural language programming.

Authors of future textbooks might generate base texts, with alternative chapters that individual instructors could then configure for their particular needs, much as one builds a necklace from a collection of beads of different types, colors, and shapes. Copyright presents an obvious limitation on what might be tailored; the first company to offer customized publishing restricted this service to a few titles that the company had copyrighted itself. Beyond this issue are the questions of what is the text and who is the author. Customizing extends from abridgement through selection of author-generated alternatives, to revision and inclusion of work not produced by the original author. Abridgement raises no major issues about text or author; selection raises a question about text that is no different from that raised by different selections of novels and short stories for a Hawthorne reader; but reworking opens up both questions for debate. At what point is *The C Programming Language* no longer *The C Programming Language*? At what point are Kernighan and Ritchie no longer its authors? These issues have both legal and practical implications and hypertexts confront them even more strongly than customized publishing. As a future direction for textbooks, customized publishing is an interesting concept, but one with limited application. Most instructors are probably not interested in revising existing textbooks and not all authors will agree to have their materials modified by others. Furthermore, if the result of customizing is strictly a print product, xeroxed notes and replacements for the original text may be a more convenient and economical route to the same end.

HYPERTEXT AND HYPERMEDIA

Imagine reading a Shakespearean play on a computer screen, for example, *Othello*. The text rolls forward in a normal manner from act to act and scene to scene. But special icons or buttons appear in the margins that allow you to skip from one place in the text to another, or from a text component to some alternative document, such as a dictionary. One button might be labeled "Next Scene," another "Next Act." Other buttons might be associated with particular characters—Iago, Desdemona, Roderigo, and so forth—and allow you to skip to the next or previous lines for any of them. A "Definition" button might allow you to call up a definition for any designated word or phrase, and an "Interpretation" button might bring to the screen one or more interpretations of a line, scene, or even the entire play. You can read as you choose, following characters or scenes, calling up definitions and interpretations, moving forward or backward in the play.

This is the basic idea of hypertext, a concept first proposed in 1945 by Vannevar Bush, director of Scientific Research and Development during World War II, but not developed until the 1960s (Conklin, 1987). The first practical demonstrations of hypertext systems were made by Doug Engelbart of Stanford Research Institute and Ted Nelson, director of the Xanadu Project, who is credited with coining the term *hypertext*. Until recently the idea was known primarily to computer scientists working on information organization. The term *hypertext* does not appear in the *Oxford English Dictionary Supplement* (Burchfield, 1976), nor *Webster's New Ninth Collegiate Dictionary* (Mish, 1983), nor the second edition of the *Random House Dictionary of the English Language* (Flexner, 1987), but it does occur in the recently published Random House *Word Menu* (Glazier, 1992).

If to the description just given we now add buttons labeled "Speak" or "Show," that allow a line, passage, or scene to be heard, perhaps with choice of actor or actress, or to be seen as it was filmed, we have *hypermedia*. But hypertext and hypermedia have important applications in the design of computer delivered textbooks and have already been applied in a variety of areas. Rather than *Othello* as our model, we might consider a high school meteorology text. A table of contents would be linked to the text segments so that selecting a particular entry in the table would lead immediately to that segment of the text. Similarly, the index would also be linked to the text so that selecting an index entry would take the reader to the referenced portion of the text.

Technical terms would be linked to glossary entries and perhaps, through labeled linkages, to opposites, members of the same class, superordinate nodes, and so on. From terms like "desert" one could retrieve a list of the world's major deserts (with pictures of each), maps of specified desert areas, and even animations of how a particular desert was formed over time. Links or buttons might also exist for literary references, bringing *The Rime of the Ancient Mariner* to a window on the screen in relation to "water" or "ice." Another button might link aphorisms, metaphors, and idioms to specific weather phenomena: raining cats and dogs, gulley-washer, and so forth.

Many buttons might serve pedagogical purposes, much like the original design of the Time-Shared Interactive Computer Controlled Information Television (TICCIT) system, where special keys would bring a simpler definition, an example, or an alternative summary (Bunderston & Faust, 1976). Problems could be linked to concepts, and solutions and explanations linked to each problem; alternative explanations, animated diagrams, and other visual representations might be linked to each concept that is introduced. Other links might bring material from chemistry, physics, or geology texts that is required for understanding particular concepts. Then, buttons could link comments made by the instructor or by other students to the particular parts of the text to which they pertain. With enough effort, the entire contents of a major library might be interlinked so that for the on-line reader the boundaries between texts were no longer visible.

Fiction developed especially for hypertext has been marketed since 1987 when Michael Joyce's *Afternoon, A Story* was released on floppy disk. A company in Massachusetts now offers a stable of both fiction and nonfiction in a hypertext system called Storyspace, which they advertise as "serious hypertext." Coover (1992), who directs the Brown University Hypertext Fiction Workshop, calls hypertext "interactive, polyvocal" technology, "freeing the reader from domination by the author" (p. 23).

Hypertext is possible through systems like Storyspace and Macintosh HyperCard/HyperTalk, which allows buttons or links to be made conveniently across text components (*lexias*). With HyperCard, pictures and speech can be attached to any point in a text. (With another Macintosh system, video clips can be added.) With these properties, hypertext and hypermedia could do everything that customized publishing promises but then much more. At the same time, hypertext and hypermedia create new perspectives on authorship, on text–reader relationships, and on literacy.

Authorship

If texts are richly interconnected, with links to dictionary and encyclopedia entries, atlases, novels, poems, and so forth, and personal comments from readers are also included, not only is authorship in question, but the whole notion of text, at least in the traditional sense, evaporates. What a reader sees is no longer a well-defined text, with specified beginning and end, but an open network where from any point a path can be specified to reach anything ever written! As new materials are generated, they also are richly linked into the network, section by section, paragraph by paragraph, so that their individual identities are disguised. A novel might still be read from beginning to end but it also can be read in selected parts, or interwoven with other works by the same author or with related works by other authors. Reviews, interpretations, and potentially even comments by the author might be linked to different parts so that the total available work is no longer simply the "novel," but some complex of information with the original novel serving as a local core.

For textbooks, the interconnections are potentially richer, with a greater number of supporting and explanatory segments linked to each idea, concept, and term. For a college textbook, every concept might have available explanations and background materials at each lower level, besides problems, solutions, definitions, literary links, biographical and historical essays, and so forth. Although an author for each potential segment might be identified, the total number that might contribute to what a typical reader encounters in accessing a "text" could be quite large.

Roles might be assigned for developing a richly interconnected textbook, with separate writers for explanatory material, problems along with their solutions and solution plans, historical and biographical material, definitions, and graphical representations. Then, highly creative editors/linkers would locate and link appropriate literature, art, and music references, lower and higher level treatments of the same topics, aphorisms, meta-phors, and other relevant language forms, and other materials that support, reinforce, or extend the original work. These supereditors would need to ensure that a reader/browser can navigate the network without getting unduly lost.

New Literacy Demands

Intelligent reading of a hypertext involves not only the ability to interpret text and graphics but substantial navigational ability. If one is not to be dominated by the author, then choices must be made. Turning from page to page is no longer the optimal approach to either understanding or enjoy-ment. The reader must apply metacognitive skills continually, deciding when to branch to a definition, an example, a historical sketch, an explanation at a different level of difficulty, a problem, or some other information. Self-monitoring is critical for using a hypertext well. (On the other hand, hypertext can be entertaining for those who have no purpose to their reading. Select buttons at random and see what turns up. Wander from node to node like a cow across a summer meadow, grazing here and grazing there with no greater purpose than satisfying an immediate appe-tite.)

Appropriate use of new information technologies like hypertext and hypermedia require information-processing skills, the forgotten component of the elementary and secondary language arts programs. The information age has yet to penetrate the schoolhouse door where narrative fiction still dominates the reading programs (Venezky, 1982). The typical basal reader, from which most K–8 reading programs are taught, contains 85% or more fiction, with expository materials limited mostly to biography. Author's purpose, plot, and character are the goals of reading comprehension and "good literature" the badge of valor for any basal series.

Informational texts require special skills for appropriate use. Skimming for general organization, note taking, rereading, and active analysis of charts, graphs, diagrams, and pictures are all required for understanding, but seldom mentioned in instruction for narrative fiction. The logics of "if . . . then," "while," and "until" are critical to understanding conditional properties, yet these are rarely given overt attention in the language arts class. Teachers assume that the skills required for narrative fiction are sufficient for informational reading. But there is no single main point to electricity and magnetism or to the settlement of North America. The author's purpose in describing the growth of cities is to describe the growth of cities and is rarely an issue in comprehending the text content. There is no plot to the description of the geography and culture of Central America, and the characters, if introduced, are important mainly for their historical roles and not for their personalities or emotions.

What is needed for the coming century is a totally new language arts curriculum for the elementary and secondary schools, constructed around communication and information processing. Observing, analyzing, interpreting, reorganizing, and creating should frame all instruction. Classroom tasks should be motivated by communication and information-processing needs; writing letters to obtain information, creating charts for allocation of classroom responsibilities, debating the pros and cons of particular school or city regulations, preparing an environmental protection plan for the county, and so on. Literature still has an important role in this curriculum, but does not dominate it. Literature, with art, music, and dance, form a collective of expressive arts. Students should experience them directly and also learn their histories, their technologies, and their unique properties. Surrealist painters and romantic composers should have no less a claim on the classroom than transcendental writers. Emerson and Thoreau should be no more celebrated than Magritte and Mendelssohn.

Hypertext and hypermedia have revolutionary potential for textbook design. This potential, however, cannot be realized fully through single texts rendered in hyperform. Instead, large collections of interconnected materials are needed with reference works (dictionaries, encyclopedias, etc.) and accumulations of supplementary notes included. Like finer wines, hypertext books should improve with age as richer and richer connections are created to supporting and extending materials. Who will control the linkages created for a rich set of materials and how readers will learn to navigate through such a universe remain to be determined, as are the economic arrangements that would ensure both authors and readers.

THE FUTURE OF THE BOOK

But where will books as we know them today fit into this future? Will the U.S. penchant for short excerpts and vapid prose eliminate all desire to read serious works? Will the printed textbook be relegated to museums and historical society dioramas? Will the prophecy of Ecclesiastes, "Of making many books there is no end," be proven false? Will the bathroom and the beach be the last locales where books are enjoyed? Almost a decade ago the U.S. Senate authorized a study of the changing role of the book in the future. This study, carried out by the Librarian of Congress under the auspices of the Center for the Book in the Library of Congress, resulted in one of what no doubt will be many studies on the future of the book (Library of Congress, 1984). Among its many predictions was that the videodisk would rapidly replace the how-to book. But technologies are rapidly evolving, with some bursting like spring flowers into everyday use and others seeping more gradually into niches in the consumer market. *Books in Our Future* contains no mention of either the fax machine or hypertext, technologies that existed in 1984 but were not considered major agents of change at the time. The fax machine has clearly altered the way we communicate documents and other messages. Hypertext is only now beginning to alter how we store information.

Book production will continue to be sustained both by the beauty and fascination of print on a clear, white page and the desire of the reader to have a visible specimen of the works of a favored writer, whether fiction, poetry, or exposition. I might prefer to have my encyclopedia, dictionary, and thesaurus on-line, but William Shakespeare, Amos Oz, Ann Tyler, and Stephen Gould I prefer in self-contained, printed volumes, to carry in a briefcase, to read on a train or plane, and to sit on my shelves as reminders of ideas and voices that speak to my intellect and imagination. Francis Bacon said, "Some books are to be tasted, others to be swallowed, and some few to be chewed and digested." Tasting and perhaps even swallowing I can do on-line; for chewing, however, I want the real McCoy.

Hypertext and hypermedia will be a continuing challenge to those who organize information and instruction, a challenge to create connections across ideas and domains of knowledge, to organize words and concepts so that new, more powerful relationships can be discovered. In a humane information society, both printed books and hypertexts have roles to play. What each requires, however, is a literate readership that can actively seek and utilize information but that at the same time treasures a well-constructed phrase, a crisp description, and a clear explanation.

REFERENCES

Altbach, P. G., & Kelly, G. P. (1988). *Textbooks in the third world: Policy, content and context.* New York: Garland.

Barzun, J. (1945). *Teacher in America.* Boston: Little, Brown.

Benjamin, L. T., Jr. (1988). A history of teaching machines. *American Psychologist, 43*(9), 703–712.

Bunderston, C. V., & Faust, G. W. (1976). Programmed and computer assisted instruction. In *75th yearbook of the National Society for the Study of Education* (pp. 44–90). Chicago: University of Chicago Press.

Burchfield, R. W. (Ed.). (1976). *A supplement to the Oxford English dictionary* (Vol. II). Oxford: Clarendon Press.

Conklin, J. (1987). Hypertext: An introduction and survey. *Computer, 20*(9), 17–41.

Coover, R. (1992, June 21). The end of books. *New York Times Book Review*, pp. 1, 23–25.

Cubberley, E. P. (1920). *The history of education.* Boston: Houghton Mifflin.

Davies, W.J.F. (1974). *Teaching reading in early England.* New York: Harper & Row.

Feldhusen, J. F. (1963). Taps for teaching machines. *Phi Delta Kappan, 44,* 265–267.

Flexner, S. J. (Ed.). (1987). *The Random House dictionary of the English language* (2nd ed., unabridged). New York: Random House.

Glazier, S. (1992). *Word menu.* New York: Random House.

Gray, W. S., & Munroe, R. (1929). *The reading interests and habits of adults: A preliminary report.* New York: Macmillan.

Herber, H. L. (1978). *Teaching reading in content areas* (2nd ed.). Englewood Cliffs, NJ: Prentice-Hall.

Kernighan, B. W., & Ritchie, D. M. (1978). *The C Programming Language.* Englewood Cliffs, NJ: Prentice-Hall.

Kirsch, I. S., & Jungeblut, A. (1986). *Literacy: Profiles of America's young adults.* Princeton, NJ: Educational Testing Service.

Kuhn, T. S. (1970). *The structure of scientific revolutions* (2nd ed.). Chicago: University of Chicago Press.

Lapp, D., Flood, J., & Farnan, N. (1989). *Content area reading and learning: Instructional strategies.* Englewood Cliffs, NJ: Prentice-Hall.

Library of Congress. (1984). *Books in our future.* Washington, DC: U.S. Government Printing Office.

Maugham, W. S. (1992). *The razor's edge.* New York: Penguin. (Original work published 1944)

McDowell, E. (1989, October 23). Facts to fit every fancy: Custom textbooks are here. *New York Times,* pp. D1, D11.

Mish, F. C. (Ed.). (1983). *Webster's ninth new collegiate dictionary.* Springfield, MA: Merriam-Webster.

Reid, J. M. (1969). *An adventure in textbooks, 1924–1960.* New York: Bowker.

Rieck, B. J. (1977). How content teachers telegraph messages against readers. *Journal of Reading, 20,* 646–648.

Robinson, J. P. (1977). *How Americans use time: A social-psychological analysis of everyday behavior.* New York: Praeger.

Skinner, B. F. (1954). The science of learning and the art of teaching. *Harvard Educational Review, 24*(2), 86–87.

Skinner, B. F. (1963). Reflections on a decade of teaching machines. *Teachers College Record, 3,* 168–177.

Stodolsky, S. (1989). Is teaching really by the book? In *88th yearbook of the National Society for the Study of Education* (Pt. 1, pp. 159–184). Chicago: National Society for the Study of Education.

Sullivan, M. (1927). *Our times: The United States 1900–1925: Vol. 2. America finding herself.* New York: Scribner's.

Trubner, N. (Comp. and Ed.). (1859). *Trubner's bibliographical guide to American literature.* London: Trubner.

Venezky, R. L. (1982). The origins of the present-day chasm between adult literacy needs and school literacy instruction. *Visible Language, 16,* 113–127.

Venezky, R. L. (1992). Textbooks in school and society. In P. W. Jackson (Ed.), *Handbook of research on curriculum* (pp. 436–461). New York: Macmillan.

Venezky, R. L., Kaestle, C. F., & Sum, A. M. (1987). *The subtle danger: Reflections on the literacy abilities of America's young adults.* Princeton, NJ: Educational Testing Service.

Weiss, I. R. (1987). *Report of the 1985–86 National Survey of Science and Mathematics Education.* Research Triangle Part, NC: National Science Foundation.

4

Out of Print: Literacy in the Electronic Age

David Rose
Anne Meyer
Bart Pisha
Center for Applied Special Technology, Peabody, MA

Classrooms are dominated by a technology that is inadequate to meet the challenges faced by teachers today, and antithetical to the challenges they will face tomorrow.

For over 500 years, print technology has provided access to knowledge in our classrooms. So dominant has this technology been that teaching the skills for using print technology—reading and writing—has become a central preoccupation of schooling. The very structure of our classrooms, the schedule of our school day, and the nature of our pedagogy have been built on the bedrock of print.

Now, our educational system is in crisis. Education professionals, the business community, and government leaders are calling for national education goals, school restructuring, new methods of assessment, and innovative models for effective learning. Among the most pressing challenges are the need for:

1. Inclusion (providing an education that includes, rather than excludes, children of differing abilities in mainstream settings).
2. Individualization (providing an education that is flexible enough to match the individual needs of its students).
3. Engagement (providing an education that engages students in active construction rather than passive reception).

We explicate each of these, and argue that print, a fixed medium, is inadequate to meet these challenges or to serve as the primary medium in educational reform. We propose that what is required is a flexible, malleable medium: electronic multimedia.

THE CHALLENGE OF INCLUSION

Today's classrooms must offer equal educational opportunities to an increasingly diverse student body. Students who would otherwise be in segregated placements are being educated in mainstream settings. Known by many labels—learning disabled, physically handicapped, attention deficit disordered, visually handicapped, culturally disadvantaged—these students have been isolated in special programs, tracks, or schools for decades. In addition, children with diverse racial, ethnic, and linguistic backgrounds have long been poorly served in our schools, and have been segregated in various ways.

Separate "pull-out" programs or completely separate programs have proven to be both ineffective and expensive. Throughout the country the move to "mainstream" all, or almost all, special needs and "at-risk" students is widespread. For pedagogical, economic, and ethical reasons, this movement has enormous appeal. Reasonable voices of concern have been raised, however. Mainstreaming, after all, has a history of failure, not of success. Decades ago, what are now called "special education" students were routinely maintained in the classroom. They were removed for good reason; regular education teachers were ill equipped to handle the diversity. The question on many people's minds is whether there have been any changes that will make teachers any better prepared than 30 years ago. Without changes, the reentry of students with special needs will look more like "warehousing" than education.

THE CHALLENGE OF INDIVIDUALIZATION

Teachers have long understood the need to adapt their approaches for students with different levels of preparation and ability. Adapting the pace of instruction, the time allotted to individual tasks, or trying out a different explanation are all methods of individualizing instruction. Such methods place great burdens on the teacher, who must be the fulcrum of any such adaptation. In crowded classrooms, the ability to provide a flexible interface between a single curriculum and many different students is a formidable task.

Moreover, two recent trends in education will make the task even more difficult for teachers. The first is the trend toward inclusion. With an even broader array of students, the task of individualizing instruction becomes even more difficult for the teacher. For many teachers, the task of successfully integrating children with moderate to severe disabilities stretches their capacity to individualize beyond the breaking point.

Secondly, spearheaded by Gardner's Theory of Multiple Intelligences, there is increasing recognition that children's learning styles and preferences range far more widely than is represented by current curricula, and far more widely than most educators have assumed. Based on verbal reasoning, traditional curricula value one kind of learning and one kind of learner. To adapt these curricula to match the range of "intelligences" that are now in vogue would be a gargantuan enterprise for any individual teacher.

To truly individualize the curriculum, we need to expand the means by which information is made available, the methods students may use to find and use information, and the avenues for self-expression that are considered acceptable. Music, art, and drama need to become legitimate means of expression rather than being regarded as adjunct activities. Sound, video, and images need to become legitimate tools for learning and presenting ideas.

THE CHALLENGE OF ENGAGEMENT

Innovative programs around the country are showing what Montessori, Piaget, and others said long ago: Children learn most effectively when they actively construct their own knowledge. The best learning occurs when children can manipulate elements in their world, discovering rules and properties by active experimentation and play. Researchers, including Pogrow (1990) and others, showed that even, or maybe especially, children who are achieving marginally if at all with rote, out-of-context skills instruction, can flourish when given the opportunity to explore complex concepts actively.

THE LIMITS OF PRINT

Successful inclusion, individualization, and engagement are key components in critical educational reform. In our view, print is inadequate to meet these challenges, primarily because of its fixed nature.

By its very inertness, print actually creates barriers to inclusion for many students. For example, students with dyslexia, cognitively capable of functioning in the mainstream, have difficulty processing printed linguistic symbols, both in reading and in writing. Their inefficiencies with print technology, not their inherent disabilities, lead them to be excluded from history, science, literature, geography, and social studies.

Similarly, print's fixed nature precludes the ability of teachers or publishers to build the capacity for individualization into the curriculum itself. Print presents information in one way for everyone. Where students' varied styles call for alternative formats and presentations of information, they find a single medium. *Individualization rests entirely with the teacher, a formula for failure.*

Finally, print does not invite experimentation and active learning. In fact, print's permanence almost dictates the opposite approach, suggesting that students should absorb material as is, rather than learn about it by altering or experimenting with it.

THE PROMISE OF MULTIMEDIA

We need a new medium of exchange between teacher and student, a malleable medium that allows for inclusion, individualization, and engagement. In our view, that medium is electronic multimedia. With this computer technology, we can design new tools for teaching and learning, tools that will be a key to solving the current educational crisis.

How can electronic multimedia answer the challenges we currently face? Our view has evolved during the course of the Center for Applied Special Technology (CAST's) Equal Access Research. In this grant-funded project, we have collaborated with four school districts to redesign their classrooms, using multimedia as a core technology for including all children in active, collaborative learning. In the course of mainstreaming severely disabled students, we have gained insights into the opportunities that electronic media offer for all students, with and without identified disabilities. An example will illustrate:

Matthew is an 8-year-old boy with cerebral palsy. A very bright youngster, Matthew can control only the muscles of his eyes and his chin. He cannot sit up, walk, move his hands, or talk. For Matthew, print technology is a barrier — he cannot hold a book, turn its pages, write on paper, or erase mistakes. The inclusion of Matthew as an active learner in the classroom requires a more accessible technology.

A key step in making the curriculum accessible for Matthew was to bring the material into the computer. By using digitizing technology to capture pictures, text, and spoken words, we created electronic versions of the print materials he needed. Once the material was in electronic form, we created alternative on-screen formats, including varied supports for Matthew's learning. Using a switch controlled by his chin, Matthew can activate buttons to turn pages, have text read aloud, or select and place letters into a written document. With the same system, he can browse books of interest to him, work with his mathematics curriculum, select and place graphics and sounds in his own compositions, and present his work to teachers and peers. Matthew can also use the computer to practice specific words he is having difficulty reading or spelling. Because multimedia can present information in varied formats, Matthew is included with his peers in challenging, intellectually appropriate curriculum.

Studying Matthew's dilemmas and developing solutions have led us to understand that the enhancements and flexibility afforded by multimedia can expand opportunities for all students. In fact, inclusion, individualization, and engagement are all served by the flexibility of multimedia. Supports for individuals with widely varying needs can be built into a single piece of curriculum, and then activated selectively by students or teachers. For example, format options can include enlargeable text for beginning readers or students with visual impairments; choices for highlighting words and sentences on the screen to support focused attention; digital or synthetic speech to help with word decoding, instantly translatable into numerous languages; numeric, graphic, or animated display of mathematical relationships; and many others. These options can be customized for individual students or for the varied learning goals of different tasks. Alternative forms of presentation—available to publishers, teachers, and students—include digital sounds, speech, and music; still and animated graphics; synthetic speech; and live video. These options legitimize the communicative strengths of children with varied intelligences, styles, and preferences. And because representations can be transformed, recombined, and changed, electronic multimedia provide an ideal environment for experimentation. Electronic media provide nearly infinite alternatives for active learning, exploring, and self-expression.

CONCLUSION

American education is structured around a technology that is 500 years old. We have reached the limits of that technology and it would be a fatal mistake to restructure our schools around those limitations. Instead, we should restructure schools and design new teaching and learning approaches around new technologies; technologies that are flexible enough to respond to the diversity among children and malleable enough to include all children in the active exploration of a world whose knowledge is no longer fixed in permanent ink.

REFERENCES

Gardner, H. (1983). *Frames of mind: The theory of multiple intelligences*. New York: Basic Books.
Pogrow, S. (1990, January). Challenging at-risk students: Findings from the HOTS program. *Phi Delta Kappan*, pp. 389–397.

5

Language Minority Students: Literacy and Educational Reform

Leonard Baca
Kathy Escamilla
Jioanna Carjuzaa
University of Colorado, Boulder

AN HISTORICAL PERSPECTIVE OF EDUCATION REFORM

Concern about school reform and restructuring efforts have been raised by many researchers (Goodlad, 1984; McCaslin & Good, 1992; McCollum & Walker, 1992; Sarason, 1990). McCaslin and Good (1992) did an extensive review of current school reform efforts with a focus on the interrelated areas of school and classroom management and instruction. They concluded that in order to reform schools significantly, we must consider the various constructions of students in the popular culture and the larger educational community. Without understanding schools and communities, efforts at school reform are destined to fail. They also found that too many reforms are undertaken for political rather than educational reasons; hence, many reforms are irrelevant or self-defeating because they are symbolic and expedient.

To illustrate this concern, McCaslin and Good (1992) offered the following example: It has long been said that schools do not need more money; they need to be more efficient with the money they have. For U.S. schools to be successful, they need to be run more like U.S. businesses. In short, corporate models will improve public schools. Ironically, business is increasingly concerned with productivity. It is difficult to pick up a newspaper or popular magazine without reading about U.S. business lagging behind the Japanese, the South Koreans, and/or the Germans. Further, there is a feeling that U.S. business has lost its competitive edge, and now ranks only sixth in the world. The question then becomes, if such is the state of U.S. businesses, why do we want to use them as models for school reform? The assumption that corporate models in education will improve the schools may be an erroneous one.

In order to gain a perspective on trends in education reform, a look at major reform documents during the past decade is in order. Although the demographic composition of the United States has continued to dramatically change, the proposed reforms have consistently ignored the soon-to-be-majority, minority population. According to Reyes and McCollum (1992), the educational needs of nonmainstream students, especially language minority students (LMS), were not addressed by the core reform programs of the 1980s, nor are these students mentioned in the six national education goals outlined in *America 2000: An Education Strategy* (1991). Reyes and McCollum proceeded to argue that these recent reform policies emphasized educational excellence and often overlooked the needs of the growing population of language minority students. They accuse America 2000 of not only ignoring LMS students, but also of advocating the implementation of instructional practices that the research has proven to be detrimental to students whose first language is not English.

"During the last 10 years, according to recently released 1990 U.S. Census data, the number of Americans of Asian or Pacific Island background more than doubled, the population of American Hispanics grew by more than one third, whereas U.S. White and Black populations grew only by approximately 6% and 13%, respectively" (Hornberger, 1992, p. 197). Despite this demographic reality, the latest reform effort still assumes that the student population has remained the same, that is, consists of a majority of students who are from White, middle-class families.

EQUITY AND EXCELLENCE

After 14 months of intense activity by the 18-member National Commission on Excellence in Education, *A Nation at Risk* (1983), a 36-page reform text appeared. With its three essential messages, it became apparent that the trend in education reform was switching from a pursuit of educational access to a pursuit of educational excellence. These three messages were as follows: (a) "Education is the one factor that undergirds our prosperity, our security and our stability"; (b) U.S. schools are tilting toward mediocrity and not toward excellence; and (c) we can expect the best and we ought to work to get it (Goldberg, 1984, p. 15). The conflict between equity and excellence was summed up by Strike (1985): "Shall we spend our education dollars on the education of the poor or on our future scientists and engineers?" (p. 405). Although Strike gave examples of norm-referenced and criterion-referenced scenarios for excellence, he stated that any notion of excellence defined within the context of human capital theory is going to be norm-referenced.

During the early 1980s, the Reagan administration was concerned with limiting the federal government's involvement in educational policy. Reagan wanted to reduce federal spending on education. According to Bell (1986), then secretary of education, "President Reagan's basic policy of allowing the marketplace and free enterprise to work was applied to education" (p. 493).

There was also great concern over U.S. ability to compete economically in the world market and U.S. students' achievement was compared to that of international students. "Popular dissatisfaction with the quality of American education is widespread" (Bell, 1988, p. 402). Two books published during this time, *The Closing of the American Mind* (Bloom, 1987) and *Cultural Literacy* (Hirsch, 1987), are typical descriptions of the public's disillusionment with the current public school system and their desire to return to the conservative traditional methods previously adhered to.

A Nation at Risk (National Commission on Education, 1983) called for major changes in U.S. public education. Like previous education reforms, this report insisted that the success of the U.S. economy and the preservation of the American way of life were closely tied to improving K–12 schooling. Fernandez (1985) reviewed 25 statements in *A Nation at Risk* and concluded there was an underlying assumption that, "people are steadfast in their belief that education is the major foundation for the future strength of this country" (p. 16). Again the commission spoke of quality education for all. "With rare exception, all students—regardless of race, ethnic background, economic circumstances, or handicapping condition—must complete the curriculum outlined above" (Bell, 1988, p. 403). Equal educational opportunity became more of a myth than a reality.

"Because advocates for poor and minority groups saw a class bias in the recommendations of these reports, there quickly followed a subset of reports arguing that the 'disadvantaged' should not be overlooked in the education reform movement" (Lytle, 1990, p. 199). There were four key advocacy reports. The first was *Barriers to Excellence: Our Children at Risk* (National Coalition of Advocates for Students (U.S.) Board of Inquiry Project, 1986). It was equally critical of the quality and kind of schooling being provided to poor and minority children and the failure of the United States as a nation to invest sufficiently in these young people. Two advocacy reports came out in 1988: *An Imperiled Generation: Saving Urban Schools* (Carnegie Foundation), and *America's Shame, America's Hope: Twelve Million Youth at Risk* (MDC, Inc.). "The plight of youth will not be remedied until the social insensitivities of the larger society are faced and eliminated" (Clark, cited in Lytle, 1990, p. 202). *Visions of a Better Way: A Black Appraisal of Public Schooling* appeared in 1989. These four advocacy reports make congruent recommendations for improving the education of the disadvantaged. Unfortunately their pleas have been ignored for the most part. *A Nation at Risk,* although it was highly publicized, did little to improve the status of LMS.

A Nation Prepared: Teachers for the 21st Century (1986) was issued by the Carnegie Forum on Education and the Economy's Task Force on Teaching as a Profession. This reform called for schools to meet far more demanding standards in the future. *A Nation Prepared* was an eight-point action plan that called for higher standards for entering teachers and at the same time cited the need to recruit more minority teachers. The fundamental issues of professional preparation, credentials, salaries, career opportunities, and working conditions were all addressed. In addition, the report targets the fact that there must not be a choice between equity and excellence.

Also appearing in 1986 was the Carnegie Forum's report that sought to empower practitioners. It was written in *A Nation at Risk,* and focused on what it claimed to be the link between education and the economy. "One of the problems with the Carnegie Report is that it accepts the view that there is a direct and linear relationship between the quality of schooling and the strength of the economy" (Darling-Hammond, 1987, p. 375).

The Carnegie Forum called for "taking steps to obtain teachers of high intellectual ability and with the skills needed for the future" (Raths, 1989, p. 263). They insisted that this is what counts as an improvement in the teaching force. It is estimated that there are 2.5 million teachers in the elementary and secondary public school systems in the U.S. "What would it take to increase the population of black and Hispanic teachers so that the proportion matched that of the national population (14.3%)? We would need to recruit roughly 130,000 minorities into teaching—the equivalent of roughly 5% of the teaching force" (Raths, 1989, p. 266).

Carnegie's trustees in endorsing the report indicate that they are "deeply troubled that a reform movement launched to upgrade the education of all students is irrelevant to many children—largely black and Hispanic—in our urban schools. . . . Many people have simply written off city schools as little more than human storehouses to keep young people off the streets" (Maeroff, cited in Lytle, 1990, p. 201).

Tomorrow's Teachers (1986) was produced by the Holmes Group in recognition of one of the assumptions held by many, that the people who were teaching in the United States were not the right ones. This reform dealt with the role of higher education in the preparation of teachers. It promoted a raise in standards and advised us to consider the issues confronting teachers and teacher education. *Tomorrow's Teachers* was dedicated not only to the improvement of teacher education, but also to the creation of a genuine profession of teachers (Sedlak, 1987, p. 315).

The Holmes Group's second major report, *Tomorrow's Schools*

(1987), "offers a radically different view on teachers and the role they might play in school reform" (Johnson, 1990, p. 581). This report is remarkably different in tone and content than *Tomorrow's Teachers* (Johnson, 1990; Soder, 1986). This time, they sought to reassert the primary role of university faculty in setting professional standards. According to this report, in 1990 teachers are renewed with greater respect and seen as potential colleagues in educational research. There was a different view of the classroom teacher, who was now seen as an essential and valuable colleague, and as someone who wants variety and great responsibility.

AMERICA 2000: AN EDUCATION STRATEGY

America 2000 is the latest federal initiative to improve the schools. In October 1989 President Bush, the self-described education president, and six governors started working on new educational goals for the 21st century; in April 1991, they published *America 2000: An Education Strategy.* Following a national conference in February 1990, George Bush and the governors announced six national goals for education. "America 2000 seems to follow the vein of recent reform efforts by continuing to exclude language minority students from its vision of the future" (McCollum & Walker, 1992, p. 183).

The major goals of the reform movement include higher academic standards and more demanding and uniform expectations; but there are no strategies to assist LMS to achieve them. Uniformity is often the proposed way to meet the goals of a newly restructured curriculum. What about students who need to learn curriculum in different ways? More time in school has been recommended, but if you just increase the time spent in school without increasing meaningful support, what's the point? (National Joint Committee on Learning Disabilities, 1991).

The 535 + new schools, one for each senator and representative, should be in place by 1996. Unfortunately, according to Houston (1992), "Our improvement has been incremental at a time when we live in an exponential environment" (p. 27). It will be difficult to show that the schools selected will reflect the diversity of the school-age population. In all of the America 2000 literature there are only two vague references to LMS. When referring to the first 535 New American Schools, it was stated that "the Governors and the Secretary will take added care to make sure that many such schools serve communities with high concentrations of 'at-risk' children" (p. 21). Under Goal 1, one of the objectives listed was: "All disadvantaged and disabled children will have access to high quality and developmentally appropriate preschool programs that help prepare children for school"

(*American 2000: An Education Strategy*, 1991, p. 37). This appears more like tokenism and public relations than substantive reform.

Eisner (1992) asked some puzzling and disturbing questions:

> Why do we think that all students should be measured by the same yardstick or that we will be able to calibrate the results of different tests in order to make them comparable? . . . Why do we believe that the most important aim of education is to get everyone to the same destination at the same time? . . . Why would a President who has made school choice the centerpiece of his platform for education reform support policies that prescribe a common set of education goals, a uniform assessment system, a national curriculum and a public report card? . . . What puzzles me even more is that such questions seem to puzzle policy makers so little. (p. 722)

It is clear that equity concerns take a back seat in America 2000. According to *America 2000: Where School Leaders Stand* (1991), the needs of LMS students should be directly addressed when the goals are set to meet diverse learning needs. Because the United States is a meritocracy, we have adopted standardization to judge merit.

> The fact that all children do not begin the race at the same place is apparently not something that the public or the education policy makers wish to consider. The fact that some children might be better served by running down a different course than others seems to concede too much to curricular differentiation, and differentiated programs are not tidy. (Eisner, 1992, p. 723)

But by trying to create equity, we are creating imbalance and inequity.

> Whereas federal policy prior to 1980 had emphasized equity, needs and access, social and welfare concerns, the common school, regulations and enforcement, federal intervention, and diffusion of innovations, the Reagan administration agenda included an emphasis on excellence and standards of performance, ability and selectivity, economic and productivity concerns, parental choice, institutional competition, deregulation, state and local initiatives, information sharing and exhortation. (Lytle, 1990, p. 213)

Raising educational standards without the needed support will increase the dropout rate. "Redirecting the curriculum away from vocational training or other endeavors and toward traditional academic subjects forces students to compete for credentials and jobs on a common standard" (Strike, 1985, p. 413).

RESTRUCTURING AND REFORM

According to Whichard-Morehouse and Elke (1992), the term *restructuring* is used to describe one method of affecting educational reforms and implies a fundamental change in the rules, roles, and relationships among schools, districts, and states. An adapted model based on organization development (OD) theory has been suggested as a viable way to help schools to achieve their restructuring goals.

In the Colorado School Restructuring Initiative, Whichard-Morehouse and Elke (1991) discussed the critical components of school reform/restructuring. In her presentation of the increasing diversity of the U.S. work force, Morehouse mentioned numbers from *Workforce 2000*, a report from the U.S. Department of Labor (1989). The work force will become older, more female, and more disadvantaged. According to the figures, in the year 2000, 61% of all women of working age will be in the work force, an increase of 29% of the new entrants into the labor force between now and the year 2000.

A CLOSER LOOK AT THE NATIONAL GOALS

Turning our attention once again to the National Goals, and to America 2000, it is our belief that these initiatives were also developed for political expediency and without adequate consideration of the student population of the 1990s, particularly that segment of the population labeled as language minority students. Further, during their development, little attention was paid to the sociocultural contexts of schools and the impact that context has on educational practice. In short, the goals have been built on questionable assumptions that create a mismatch between the goals and the students and schools they wish to reform.

School populations are changing dramatically, and schools of the 1990s are populated by students who are culturally, linguistically, and economically different than school populations of previous decades. The following statistics, reported by *Education Week* (May 14, 1986), illustrate some of these dramatic changes (see Hodgkinson & Migra, 1986):

1. By the year 2000, 48 out of 50 school districts in the United States will be majority/minority; that is, the number of ethnic minority students in these districts will outnumber White children.

2. Children now constitute one third of the 35 million Americans without health insurance. They are the poorest segment in U.S. society—poorer than the elderly. One in four school-age children now lives in poverty—for African Americans and Hispanics, the number approaches one in two.

3. In California, one in six of its public school students is now foreign born.

4. Fertility rates are higher for African-American and Hispanic families than for White families. African-American and Hispanic families now have 2.4 and 2.9 children, respectively, whereas White families have only 2.1.

These phenomena will make schools even more diverse in the 21st century. Further, there are now about 8 million school-age children who are language minority children and enter school speaking no English. That number is expected to increase by 35% by the year 2000 (Lyons, 1991).

It is interesting to note that no reference to this dramatic shift in school population was made in the framing of the national goals, nor was there reference to the need for school reform to consider student characteristics when making decisions regarding change. When one considers that the diversity of student backgrounds has been labeled the most serious and difficult issue with which our schools are now struggling (Howe, 1991; Ogbu, 1992), this oversight is a major one.

Failure to consider student needs and community characteristics as the center of this reform effort led researchers such as Cardenas (1991) and Ogbu (1992) to assert that these initiatives are not sufficient for the development of a comprehensive plan addressing current educational problems. Cardenas summarized these concerns by stating that they fail to address the most severe problems of the educational system: the perception of atypical students as being deficient, the inability to distinguish between lack of experiences and lack of capability, low levels of expectancy and incompatible materials and methodology between schools and students. If America 2000 does not provide direction, support, and resources to address these inadequacies in existing schools, efforts at reform will yield disappointing results.

A CRITIQUE OF GOAL 3

In the next few pages, we attempt to illustrate some of the issues related to the national goals and language minority students vis-à-vis examination of one of the most basic goals. The focus of the examination is National Goal 3. This goal was chosen as it relates directly to the school-age population and concerns itself with student achievement. Student achievement and literacy are considered to be inseparable and synonymous.

National Goal 3 calls for school reform efforts that will improve student achievement, particularly in literacy and math. Student achievement has long been a national concern for language minority students, but is now seen as a concern for all students. National Goal 3 states:

By the year 2000, Americans will leave grades 4, 8 and 12 having demonstrated competency in challenging subject matter including English, mathematics, science, history, and geography—and every school in America will ensure that all students learn to use their minds well so they may be prepared for responsible citizenship, further learning and productive employment in our modern economy (*America 2000: An Education Strategy*, 1991, p. 38)

Goal 3, as already stated, is rather like motherhood and apple pie. On the surface it is something everyone can agree on and it is difficult to argue against it. In fact, we would be hard pressed to find a community or school district in this country that would say that schools should be less rigorous in their academic endeavors or that student achievement is not important. However, as Passow (1984) stated, past experience with school reform has demonstrated to us that it is not enough to simply announce higher academic standards and expectations without solid implementation plans. With regard to Goal 3 and school reform, the overwhelming response to its implementation has been to demand a reinstatement of a core curriculum in U.S. schools (Bloom, 1987; Finn, 1989; Hirsch, 1987). The core curriculum is intended for all students. Interestingly, this core curriculum is not intended to change or reform the school, but simply to add to it (Ogbu, 1992). "Add-ons" include more math, science, English, geography, and history. This expanded curriculum is meant to create higher standards for schools and greater expectations for individual students that in turn will improve achievement (Ogbu, 1992). In spite of the obvious argument that more is not necessarily better, the assumptions of Goal 3 must be challenged on another level.

First, it is important to note that schools are being expected to implement all of the goals without additional federal money. In fact, the federal government currently pays for less than 8% of the nation's elementary and secondary school programs (Doyle, 1991). Second, there is an empathic message that more money for the schools is not the answer. As Secretary of Education Alexander said, "We're spending more money on education than ever in our history. As a nation, we now invest more in education than in defense. But the results have not improved. The challenge is how to do the job better with the same resources" (America 2000 Sourcebook, p. 15). Added to scarce federal resources to implement the national goals are the budget crises and short-falls currently being faced by many state and local governments (Doyle, 1991). The result is that, in order to implement Goal 3 with an expanded core curriculum, schools are being asked to do more with less money.

The issue of adding to the academic curriculum with fewer dollars creates an interesting dilemma for educators of language minority students. In order to partially meet the demands of Goal 3 via the implementation of additional core curriculum requirements, many school districts have had to reduce expenditures in other educational areas. Such reduction in services and programs have included: (a) guidance and counseling, (b) health programs and school nurses, (c) community liaisons, (d) extracurricular activities, (e) inservice education programs, and (f) in some cases, reduction of the teaching force itself (Howe, 1991).

It is important to once again state that the school population of the 1990s is increasingly non-English speaking, culturally diverse, and poor (Hodgkinson & Migra, 1986). However, none of the goals addresses these changing demographics in any way. It is our belief that failure to understand who our students are may mean that in order to implement the added curriculum requirements, we still have to eliminate the educational programs that are most needed to prepare language minority and other students to achieve academically.

Goals and standards, no matter how high, are meaningless if the intended beneficiaries, in this case the students, do not have the prerequisites to achieve them, or if the school does not have adequate resources to implement them. Consider a few examples. It has been well documented that lack of appropriate health care and nutrition for children create significant barriers to learning. Given the growing numbers of poor children in our schools, it is questionable that reducing the number of school nurses and cutting out health programs in order to add English classes or buy more copies of Shakespeare will result in improved academic achievement.

Furthermore, students from homes that are unfamiliar with the English language and dominant culture are unlikely to have access to information about colleges and careers other than through their school guidance counselors or through parent education and community involvement programs. Cutting guidance and counseling programs, and reducing community involvement in order to add more chemistry and calculus has several potentially negative consequences. First, it is not uncommon for high school guidance counselors to have case loads of 350 to 1. Under these circumstances, it is difficult to establish the personal relationships and rapport needed to effectively counsel students and their families. Second, in these cases, only students who become discipline problems find their way to the counselor's office. Counseling is reduced to disciplinary functions and students who are in the greatest need for information get the least.

In addition, although the ethnic, linguistic, and economic composition of the school population is changing dramatically, the teaching force is not. In 1989, fully 95% of the teaching force was White and had not been prepared to teach students who are culturally and linguistically diverse ("Tests Keep Thousands of Minorities Out of Teaching," 1989; Marcusson, 1992). Cuts in school in-service programs in order to add on to the curriculum exacerbate the problem of cultural conflict that exists between minority cultures as represented by the students and the U.S. mainstream culture as represented by the teachers (Ogbu, 1992). Moreover, failure to understand the cultural and linguistic backgrounds of their students will surely impede teacher efforts to improve the academic performance of the same students. We do not believe that only minority teachers should teach minority students or that White teachers cannot effectively teach students from different cultural and linguistic backgrounds. However, lack of opportunity to learn about cultural differences and how they influence learning can greatly impede the efforts of the most well-meaning teachers.

Research by Goldenberg and Gallimore (1991), Ogbu (1992), and Mehan (1992) concluded that school reform movements that do not consider the community or context in which they are being implemented are doomed to fail. Reforming schools depends on a thorough understanding of the interplay between local community knowledge and the schools, as well as an understanding of the social context of the school and the ways in which social class and ethnicity interact with language and culture. The key element in this interplay is the ability of the school staff to transform reform efforts to fit their particular context and students. Transformation is difficult if teachers and others in the school are unfamiliar with student cultural and linguistic backgrounds.

Within America 2000, Goal 3 is followed by five objectives. The first three outline more specifically how improved student achievement should be measured. The concerns raised previously with regard to Goal 3 and language minority students apply equally to the issue of measurement of achievement and thus will not be repeated. However, the final two objectives and their relationship to language minority students merit discussion. Objectives 4 and 5 are as follows:

The percentage of students who are competent in more than one language will substantially increase (p. 63).

All students will be knowledgeable about the diverse cultural heritage of the nation and about the world community (p. 63).

On the surface it would appear that these two objectives are those that would be the easiest to meet with regard to language minority students because they come to school with knowledge of other languages and cultural lifestyles. Ironically, however, school programs for language minority students often focus on teaching them English at the expense of their first language. In fact, 95% of federally funded bilingual programs during fiscal year 1992 (about $195 million) were spent on early-exit transitional bilingual programs that, by definition, are designed to transition language minority students from their native language to English "as quickly as possible" (McGroaty, 1992; Pease-Alvarez & Hakuta, 1992; Ruiz, 1988).

We see the dichotomy of the national agenda for school reform as it relates to language minority students. On the one hand, Goal 3 advocates the development of bilingualism for students in the nation and at the same time federal policy advocates that education for language minority students focus on English acquisition in order to "transfer" away from their native languages.

If Objective 4 of Goal 3 relating to bilingualism is to positively impact language minority students, other federal policies — such as Title VII — The Bilingual Education Act, will also have to change so that schools are encouraged to promote bilingualism as well as English acquisition in language minority students. With the current situation, language minority students have the greatest potential to achieve Goal 3, Objective 4, but none of the educational opportunities.

A similar phenomenon exists with regard to Goal 3, Objective 5. Language minority students do come to school with knowledge of a culture other than the dominant one. However, when students arrive at school, they are told in subtle and overt ways that they need to assimilate to a mainstream way of life (Cooper, 1989; Ruiz, 1988). As a result of these subtle and direct messages to assimilate, language minorities and other minority groups develop an additional cultural identity that is not just different from but in opposition to the social identity of the dominant group. They do so in response to their treatment by White Americans (Ogbu, 1992). The message that assimilation is the desired goal is one that is communicated to minority groups beyond the boundaries of a school. It extends into the entire economic, political, social, and psychological environment of the society (Ogbu, 1992).

The result of the interaction between historical treatment of minorities by the dominant society and the subsequent development of oppositional behavior in minority groups is that these groups experience greater difficulty in school. Ogbu (1992) stated that because of the negative relationship between minority cultures and the mainstream, minority students have great difficulty crossing cultural/language boundaries in school. Therefore, they resist the pressure to assimilate and struggle to maintain their cultural identity even if it means failing at school. Because of this relationship, then, language minority and other minority students do not embrace two cultural worlds. They cling to one and reject the other.

Ogbu (1992), Deyhle (1986), and Ruiz (1988) stated that it is possible for schools to overcome this cultural mismatch. Furthermore, they contended that many schools have tried to move away from their assimilationist policies toward policies embracing cultural diversity. However, each admitted that it will be difficult for interventionists and teachers without special training to detect problems related to cultural conflict and use this knowledge to help the students.

Lack of diversity of the current teaching force coupled with lack of preparation to deal with issues of cultural diversity (as discussed earlier) make it unlikely that Objective 5 of Goal 3 can be accomplished with regard to language minority students. Again tragically, language minority students have the potential to be the greatest beneficiaries of Objective 5, Goal 3. However, without meaningful school reform that directly addresses causes of cultural conflict and oppositional behavior, it is unlikely that language minority students will reap the intended benefits of these goals.

Howe (1991) summarized the concerns related to the national goals for language minority students with his observation that the most pressing issues in U.S. public education today were nowhere to be found in either the National Goals or America 2000. The most pressing issues are school finance and how to effectively finance school reform; growing poverty among children and youth; and cultural, linguistic, and racial diversity in U.S. society. What U.S. schools received as a result of this effort was greater pressure to produce but with no concrete support. U.S. schools have also been given implementation strategies that are far removed from the reality of today's schools.

IMPLICATIONS AND RECOMMENDATIONS

Language minority and culturally different students are the fastest growing group of students in the public schools today. As a group they are already the majority in more than 20 of our largest cities in this nation. This chapter argues that the literacy needs of these culturally and linguistically different students have not been given serious or sufficient attention in the many reform proposals and initiatives of the past 15 years. Not only have the educational and literacy needs of these students for the most part been ignored, but the many complex strategies and issues related to improving their educational experience have been largely ignored as well.

It has been pointed out that many of the basic assumptions of the various school reform proposals are no longer valid in today's society. Important paradigm shifts have been gradually occurring in all of the academic disciplines. These new theoretical perspectives have the potential of reconceptualizing and expanding our understanding of the nature of knowledge itself. It thus follows that our understanding of learning and schooling is also undergoing a transformation. As a result, we have gained a broader under standing of literacy within the public school curriculum and the range of models and strategies that can be successfully utilized to teach the literacy skills needed by today's diverse learners.

Put another way, today's students should no longer be instructed if they are a homogeneous group of learners. They should not be assimilated into a mainstream culture or standard lock-step curriculum. Instead, they should be acculturated into a multicultural and pluralistic school. Today's students are diverse in many respects, including language and culture. Schools, in effect, have perceived and thus treated these and many other differences as deficits. Two-way bilingual education programs that promote additive bilingualism and biliteracy could help reverse this current compensatory and remedial trend.

New and expanding insights into our understanding of the nature of knowledge, learning, and schooling demand that schools redefine a standard curriculum into various alternative curricula. Learning is more complex and occurs in more diverse ways than schools have acknowledged in the past. This will require that schools provide more choice for parents and students, including opportunities for service learning, cooperative learning, and experiential learning. These types of learning opportunities are considered highly effective for second language learners and literacy development. An additive form of bilingual education that promotes maximum cognitive and affective development as a top priority and biliteracy as an enabling objective should be the direction our schools should take for not only language minority students, but for all students. If this were to become a major part of educational reform, all students would have access to an optimal learning environment.

Parent and community involvement in the education of their children has become increasingly more important as a growing body of research emerges in this area. Most school reform proposals have not adequately addressed this critical need for English-speaking parents. To implement this critical strategy with non-English-speaking parents is even more important. Until school reform aggressively addresses this issue, it will continue to falter. Bilingual education, special education, Chapter I, and other special programs have much to offer regular education about this essential element of successful educational programs.

Site-based management and leadership appears to be a very promising administrative practice. In order for this important innovation to succeed, it must be made available and accessible to non-English-speaking parents and community members. Here again additive and effective two-way bilingual education programs have already demonstrated success in developing models and approaches for the positive involvement of non-English-speaking parents in the education of their children.

School organization models and service delivery designs should reverse the current decoupling of special need programs such as Chapter I, migrant education, special education, bilingual education, and so forth. Decoupled and pull-out programs not only send negative messages to students and parents, but weaken regular education students and teachers as well. Adopting a philosophy and practice of full inclusion can also help reverse the current remedial and student marginalizing trend so apparent in our schools today. Redefining and expanding the core curriculum to include bilingual and multicultural content as well as processes will enhance opportunities for increased levels of literacy among all students.

REFERENCES

American Association of School Administrators. (1991). *America 2000: Where school leaders stand*. Washington, DC: Author.

Bell, T. H. (1986, March). Education policy development in the Reagan administration. *Phi Delta Kappan*, 487–493.

Bell, T. H. (1988, February). Parting words of the 13th man. *Phi Delta Kappan*, 400–407.

Bloom, A. (1987). *The closing of the American mind: How higher education has failed democracy and impoverished the souls of today's students*. New York: Simon & Schuster.

Carnegie Corporation (1986). *A nation prepared: Teachers for the 21st century*. New York: Author.

Carnegie Foundation for the Advancement of Teaching. (1988). *An imperiled generation: Saving urban schools*. Princeton, NJ: Author.

Cardenas, J. (1991, June). Strategies for the education of the disadvantaged within our reach. *Intercultural Development Research Association Newsletter*.

Cooper, R. L. (1989). *Language planning and social change*. Cambridge, England: Cambridge University Press.

Darling-Hammond, L. (1987). Schools for tomorrow's teachers. *Teachers College Record, 88*(3), 354–377.

Deyhle, D. (1989). Pushouts and pullouts: Navajo and Ute school leavers. *Journal of Navajo Education, 6*(2), 36–51.

Doyle, D. (1991, November). America 2000. *Phi Delta Kappan*, 184–191.

Eisner, E. W. (1992, May). The federal reform of schools. Looking for the silver bullet. *Phi Delta Kappan*, 272–273.

Fernandez, E. (1985, January). Nation at odds—better description than nation at risk. *NASSP Bulletin*, 49–55.

Finn, C. E. (1989, July 16). Norms for the nation's schools. *Washington Post*, p. B7.

Goldberg, M. (1984, March). The essential points of a nation at risk. *Educational Leadership*, 15–16.

Goldenberg, C., & Gallimore, R. (1991, November). *Educational Researcher, 8*(20), 2–14.

Goodlad, J. (1984). *A place called school*. New York: McGraw-Hill.

Hirsch, E. D. (1987). *Cultural literacy: What every American needs to know*. Boston: Houghton Mifflin.

Hodgkinson, H. L., & Migra, T. (1986, May 14). Here they come, ready or not. *Education Week*, pp. 13–40.

Holmes Group. (1986). *Tomorrow's teachers: A report of the Holmes Group*. East Lansing, MI: Author.

Hornberger, N. H. (1992). Literacy contexts, continua, and contrasts: Policy and curriculum for Cambodian and Puerto Rican students in Philadelphia. *Education and Urban Society, 24*, 196–211.

Houston, P. D. (1992, April). What's right with schools? *American School Board Journal*, 24–27.

Howe, H., II. (1991, November). America 2000: A bumpy ride on four trains. *Phi Delta Kappan*, 192–203.

Johnson, W. R. (1990, Winter). Inviting conversations: The Holmes group and tomorrow's schools. *American Educational Research Journal, 27*(4), 581–588.

Lyons, J. (1991). The view from Washington. *NABE News, 14*(5), 1.

Lytle, J. H. (1990). Reforming urban education: A review of recent reports and legislation. *Urban Review, 22*(3), 199–220.

Marcusson, L. (1992). The Hispanic teacher: A dying breed? *NABE News, 15*(8), 15–16.

McCaslin, M., & Good, T. (1992). Compliant cognition: The misalliance of management and instructional goals in current school reform. *Educational Researcher, 21*(3), 4–15.

McCollum, P. A., & Walker, C. L. (1992). Minorities in America 2000. *Education and Urban Society, 24*(2), 178–195.

McGroaty, M. (1992). The societal context of bilingual education. *Educational Researcher, 21*(2), 7–15.

MDC, Inc. (1988). *America's shame, America's hope: Twelve million youth at risk.* Chapel Hill, NC: Author.

Mehan, H. (1992). *Sociological foundations supporting the study of cultural diversity.* Santa Cruz, CA: National Center for Research on Cultural Diversity and Second Language Learning.

National Coalition of Advocates for Students (U.S.) Board of Inquiry Project. (1986). *Barriers to excellence: Our children at risk.* Boston: Author.

National Commission on Excellence in Education. (1983). *A nation at risk: The imperative for educational reform.* Washington, DC: U.S. Department of Education.

National Joint Committee on Learning Disabilities. (1991). School reform: Opportunities for excellence and equity for individuals with learning disabilities. *Journal of Learning Disabilities, 25*(5), 276–280.

Ogbu, J. (1992). Understanding cultural diversity and learning. *Educational Researcher, 21*(8), 5–14.

Passow, A. H. (1984). *Equity and excellence: Confronting the dilemma.* Paper presented at the First International Conference on Education in the 1990s, Tel Aviv, Israel.

Pease-Alvarez, L., & Hakuta, K. (1992). Enriching our views of bilingualism and bilingual education. *Educational Researcher, 21*(2), 4–6.

Raths, J. (1989). Reformer's visions of tomorrow's teachers: A U.S.A. perspective. *Childhood Education, 65*(5), 263–267.

Reyes, M. de la Luz, & McCollum, P. M. (1992). Language, literacy and educational reform: Rethinking issues. *Education and Urban Society, 24,* 171–177.

Ruiz, R. (1988). Orientations in language planning. In S. L. McKay & S. Wong (Eds.), *Language diversity: Problem or resource?* Cambridge, MA: Newbury.

Sarason, S. (1990). *The predictable failure of school reform.* San Francisco: Jossey-Bass.

Sedlak, M. W. (1987). Tomorrow's teachers: The essential arguments of the Holmes Group report. *Teachers College Record, 88*(3), 314–325.

Strike, K. A. (1985). Is there a conflict between equity and excellence? *Educational Evaluation and Policy Analysis, 7*(4), 409–416.

Tests keep thousands of minorities out of teaching. (1989, Winter). *Fair Text Examiner,* pp. 8–9.

U.S. Department of Education. (1991). *America 2000: An education strategy.* Washington, DC: Author.

U.S. Department of Labor (1989). *Workforce 2000.* Washington, DC: Author.

Whichard-Morehouse, J. A., & Elke, D. L. (1992). *Restructuring: What is it and how is it done?* (Colorado School Restructuring Initiative, Paper No. 5). Denver, CO: Colorado Alliance of Business.

6

"Hispanic" Children: Effective Schooling Practices and Related Policy Issues

Eugene E. Garcia
University of California, Santa Cruz

The United States continues in a trend of ethnic and racial population diversification, a trend that inextricably and functionally ties the future of the United States as a whole to the future of the diverse populations of which it is comprised. This diversification is particularly pronounced among young and school-age children. Moreover, our next generation, in general, and ethnic and racial minority children, in particular, continue to be placed "at risk" in today's social institutions. The future lies in understanding and devising concrete measures that will enable people of diverse backgrounds to overcome this apparent state of adversity to attain social, educational, and employment competence.

The term *Hispanic* is a catchall label used by the U.S. Census Bureau to identify such varied populations as Mexicans, Mexican-Americans, Puerto Ricans, Cubans, Chicanos, and Latinos (see Table 6.1). The Hispanic population is representative of the U.S. demographic trend toward diversification in that:

1. There are 18.8 million Hispanics living in the continental United States.
2. The Hispanic population grew by 61% from 1970 to 1980 compared to an 11% growth in the general population.
3. Eleven million Hispanics report speaking Spanish in the home.

Unfortunately, Hispanics are also representative of the at-risk status of many minority peoples. Consider the following:

TABLE 6.1
Hispanic Demographic Synthesis

I. General Demographic Character
   A. Of the 18.8 million Hispanics in the continentual U.S., the following characterizes
      the population's ethnic diversity:

Country/Area of Origin	Number	Percent
Mexico	11.8 million	62.8
Puerto Rico	2.3 million	12.2
Central/South American	2.1 million	11.2
Cuba	1.0 million	5.3
Other	1.6 million	8.5

   B. 82% of this Hispanic population is found in eight states: Arizona (3%),
      California (31%), Colorado (3%), Florida (6%), Illinois (4%), New Mexico (3%),
      New York (11%), and Texas (20%).
   C. Average age of this population is 25.1 years (compared to 32.6 years for the
      general population).
   D. 200,000 Hispanics immigrate illegally to the U.S. yearly. (40% of all legal
      immigrants. An estimated 200,000 Hispanics immigrate illegally.)
   E. The Hispanic population grew by 61% from 1970 to 1980 compared to an
      11% growth in the general population.
   F. 11 million Hispanics report speaking Spanish in the home.
   G. 7% of Hispanics live in metropolitan areas; 50% in central cities.
II. Education
   A. 40% of Hispanics leave school prior to graduation (40% of these leaving do
      so by Grade 10).
   B. 35% of Hispanics are held back at least one grade.
   C. 47% of Hispanics are overage at Grade 12.
   D. 85% of Hispanic students are in urban districts.
   E. 70% of Hispanic students attend segregated schools (up to 56% in 1956).
   F. Hispanics are significantly below national norms on academic achievement
      tests or reading, math, science, social science and writing at Grades 3, 7, and 11,
      generally averaging 1–2 grade levels below the norm. At Grade 11, Hispanics
      average a Grade 8 achievement level on these tests.
III. Indices of "Vulnerability"
   A. Median family income has fluctuated for Hispanics (1972 – $18,880;
      1982 – $16,227; 1986 – $19,995), remaining below non-Hispanics (1972 – $26,261;
      1982 – $23,907; 1986 – $30,321).
   B. 29% of Hispanic families live below the poverty line, up from 21%
      in 1979. (10.2% of White families live below the poverty line.)
   C. 905,000 (23%) of Hispanic families are maintained by female head-of-household
      (up from 17% in 1970). 53% of these households live below the poverty line.
   D. 50% of Hispanic women are in the labor force.
   E. Hispanics are twice as likely to be born to an unmarried, teen mother compared
      to Whites.
   F. 56% of Hispanics are functionally illiterate compared to 46% for Blacks and
      16% for Whites.
   G. 65% of Hispanics hold unskilled and semiskilled jobs compared to 35% of
      non-Hispanics.

Note. Information taken from Bureau of the U.S. Census (1984, 1987); Change (1988,
May/June); Appleby, Langer, and Mullis (1988).

1. Twenty-nine percent of Hispanic families live below the poverty line, up from 21% in 1979 (10.2% of White families live below the poverty line).
2. Hispanics are twice as likely to be born to an unmarried, teen mother compared to Whites.
3. Sixty-five percent of Hispanics hold unskilled and semiskilled jobs compared to 35% of non-Hispanics.

Yet another aspect of vulnerability for this population centers on the deplorable status of Hispanic education in the United States:

1. Forty percent of Hispanics leave school prior to graduation.
2. Fifty-six percent of Hispanics are functionally illiterate compared to 46% for Blacks and 16% for Whites.
3. Hispanics score significantly below national norms on academic achievement tests, generally averaging one to two grades below the norm.

The future of the Hispanic population is particularly relevant to the state of California. Some 31% of the Hispanic population of the United States reside in this state. This of course directly impacts the demographics of California schools. Figure 6.1 illustrates the dramatic rise and projected increase of school-age Hispanic students over the next 40 years.

Recent research, however, has redefined the nature of this population's educational vulnerability. Stereotypes and myths have been destroyed and a new foundation on which to reconceptualize present educational practices and launch new initiatives has been laid. This foundation recognizes homogeneity/heterogeneity within and between Hispanic populations. No one set of descriptions or prescriptions will suffice. However, it is worth-

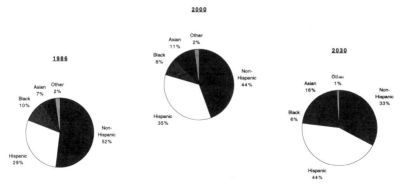

Fig. 6.1. California's school age population by race/ethnicity.

while to consider a set of intertwined commonalities that deserve particular attention such as the bilingual/bicultural and instructional circumstances of this population. The following discussion provides a brief overview of a 2-year study addressing the "effective" instruction of Hispanic students. The study paid special attention to educational issues of relevance to the growing number of Hispanic families and children in California. Particular emphasis was placed on instructional strategies and staffing characteristics of these schools.

EFFECTIVE INSTRUCTIONAL PRACTICES:
A CASE STUDY

The research reported here identified the specific school-related attributes of two elementary schools, Grades K–5, over a 2-year period. With a focus on academic learning, this research provided an in-depth investigation of schools serving Hispanic students effectively. The primary goal of the study was the documentation of organizational, instructional, and social charac- teristics of these effective schools, of their classrooms, and of their professional personnel. The research was conducted by an interdisciplinary research team utilizing multimethodological approaches that provided a broad (macro)analysis of the school environment and a more focused (micro)analysis of instruction. The research was carried out at the schools with the assistance and collaboration of the Pajaro Valley School District in Watsonville, California, and the Healdsburg School District, Healdsburg, California. The study owes a great deal to the students, staff, and parents of these communities for their patience and assistance.

The present study resets on the foundations established by recent research documenting educationally effective practices with Hispanic students in Carpenteria, California (Cummins, 1986); San Diego, California (Carter & Chatfield, 1986); Phoenix, Arizona (Garcia, 1988; Moll, 1988); and Northern California (Lucas, Henze, & Donato, 1990). These descriptive studies identified specific schools and classrooms serving Hispanic students that were particularly successful academically. That is, students scored at or above the national norms on norm-referenced tests of academic achieve- ment. The case study approach adopted by these studies included exami- nation of preschool, elementary, and high school classrooms. Teachers, principals, parents, and students were interviewed and specific classroom observations were conducted to assess the "dynamics" of the instructional process.

The study included the use of semistructured interviews as well as ethnographic descriptions of the school environment and the surrounding community. Program description developed by the school site or the district, in addition to actual inspection of curriculum materials, informed the research team with regard to the philosophy, goals, staffing, and implementation strategies. In addition, classroom instructional activities of teachers and students were systematically sampled utilizing audio- and videotaped segments of very specific small-group, large-group, teacher-led lessons (Garcia, 1988). Moreover, academic achievement data were obtained for the last two academic years for each student in the classrooms participating. Principals, classroom teachers, and a sample of parents were interviewed utilizing a previously developed interview protocol (Moll, 1988). These descriptive and interview data addressed: (a) instructional processes in literacy and math; (b) teacher and principal attitudes and instruction/organization philosophy; (c) parental attitudes/philosophy regarding educational materials, program alternatives, and their role in assisting their children with school work; and (d) student academic achievement.

The sites of the study included two elementary schools and six classrooms (average class size was 26–32 students) within those schools. Each school was selected because of its statewide reputation as an "exemplary" school. This designation was based on a California competition that acknowledges special achievement. Some 250 schools in the state receive this distinction each year. Moreover, these schools had demonstrated high academic achievement on standardized academic achievement measures: On average the students scored at or above the national norm over a consecutive 2-year period prior to this study. Each school was located in a semirural area and served a mixed population of students, approximately 50% to 60% Hispanic and 40% to 50% Anglo. Approximately 60% of the Hispanic students were identified as limited English proficient. Classrooms selected for intensive study included those with an equal mix of native Spanish- and English-speaking students, and those with a majority of students whose native language was English.

The results of the study provide important insights with regard to instruction, literacy development, academic achievement, and the perspectives of the students, teachers, administrators, and parents. With regard to instructional organization within classrooms, ethnographic descriptions of the classrooms indicated a high degree of common attributes:

1. Each classroom emphasized, more than might be expected in a regular classroom, the functional communication between teacher and students and students and teachers. Teachers were constantly checking in with students regarding the clarity of assignments and student roles in those assignments.

2. Classrooms were also characterized by a high (sometimes noisy) volume of communication emphasizing student collaboration on small-group projects organized around "learning centers." Such an organization

minimized individual work tasks (e.g., "worksheet" exercises), thus providing a very informal familylike social setting in which the teacher either worked with a small group of students (never larger than eight students and as small as one student) or traveled about the room assisting individual or small groups of students as they worked on their projects. Large-group instruction was rare, usually confined to start-up activities in the morning.

3. Instruction of basic skills and academic content was consistently organized around themes. These themes included "bears," "butterflies," or "dinosaurs" in the early grades and "pop music," "gardens," "pesticides," "peace/war," and so forth, in later grades.

4. In the majority of classrooms studied, the students actually selected the themes in consultation with the teacher either through direct voting or some related negotiation process. Teachers indicated that they followed this procedure to insure a "child-centered" curriculum approach that would enhance motivation for student learning.

In summary, these more global observations revealed that the teacher's responsibility was to insure that the instruction focusing on the chosen themes covered the content and skill-related goals and objectives for that grade level in that school district. This theme approach allowed the teacher to integrate content and skills. The major thrust in these classrooms was the appropriation of knowledge centered around these themes, realizing that basic skills were necessarily developed as a means to appropriate this knowledge. Students became "experts" in these thematic domains while also acquiring the requisite academic skills.

Analysis of audio- and videotaped instruction events in literacy and math following the instruction-response-evaluation (IRE) technique reported by Garcia (1988), along with qualitative analysis of actual writing and math products such as dialogue journals, learning logs, writing workshop publications, homework, student-conducted surveys, and so forth, reported by Moll (1988) indicated teachers organized instruction in a manner that required students to interact with each other utilizing collaborative learning techniques. It was during these student–student dialogues where most higher order cognitive and linguistic discourse was observed. Students asked each other "hard" questions and challenged each other's answers more readily than in their interaction with the teacher. Moreover, students were likely to seek assistance from other students and were successful in obtaining it. With regard to the language of instruction in these classrooms, lower grade teachers utilized both Spanish and English, whereas upper grade teachers utilized mostly English. However, although students were allowed to use either language, the same trend for limited English-speaking students was observed. With regard to the literacy development in non-English-speaking students, observations revealed: (a) a systematic progression of writing in the native language in the early grades shifting to English in the later grades; (b) writing in English emerged at or above the grade level of writing in Spanish; and (c) the quality of writing in various forms was highly conventional, with few spelling or grammatical errors, along with systematic use of "invented" spelling. Limited English-speaking students in these classrooms made the transition from Spanish to English without any detrimental effects.

Interviews with classroom teachers, principals, and parents revealed an interesting set of perspectives regarding the education of the students in these schools.

Teacher interviews that focused on first-grade, third-grade, and fifth-grade teachers indicated they were all bilingual and biliterate in English and Spanish. They had the prerequisite state teacher credentials and had graduated from specific bilingual, teacher-training programs. They had an average of 7.1 years experience as bilingual teachers. Therefore, these were not novice teachers with little general teaching or language minority teaching experience. In addition, they reported they routinely participated in staff development efforts, either taking courses or attending workshops on techniques they want to implement in their classrooms.

These teachers were quite knowledgeable and articulate with regard to the instructional philosophies guiding them. They communicated these quite coherently in their interviews. They never hesitated in addressing "why" they were using specific instructional techniques and usually couched these explanations in terms of a theoretical position regarding their role with regard to teaching and "how" students learn. Moreover, these teachers seemed to be quite competent in the content areas. For example, an upper elementary teacher had a solid and confident understanding of fractions, and therefore, did not seem to be "one step ahead of the students."

Despite their differing perspectives, the teachers demonstrated specific instructional skills. They used English and Spanish in highly communicative ways, speaking to students with varying degrees of Spanish and English proficiency in a communicative style requiring significant language switching. Direct translation from one language to another was a rarity, but utilization of language switching in contexts that required it was common. These teachers felt strongly that classroom practices reflecting the cultural and linguistic background of minority students were important ways of enhancing student self-esteem. They reported that part of their job was to provide the kind of cultural and linguistic validation that is missing in the local community known for deprecating the Latino culture and Spanish language. According to these teachers, learning Spanish and learning about Latino culture benefits Anglo students as well as Latino students.

Latino culture was reflected in the content of the curriculum in various ways. The two primary grade teachers, who organized their curriculum around a variety of student-generated themes, addressed cultural experiences of Latino students within the themes. For example, in a unit on monsters, they highlighted Latino legends and folktales that deal with the supernatural.

Most significant was the teachers' affinity toward their students:

> These students are like my very own children.

> I love these children like my own. I know that parents expect me to look after their kids and to let them know if they are in trouble.

> When I walk into that classroom I know we are a family and we're going to be together a whole year. . . . I try to emphasize first that we are a family here. . . . I tell my students, "You're like brothers and sisters and some students even call me Tom or Tia. It's just like being at home here."

Each teacher spoke of the importance of strong and caring relationships among class members and particularly between the teacher and the students.

Parents also reported a similar feeling. They directly referred to the teachers in the interviews as an extended family member, someone to be trusted, respected, and honored for their service to their children. Principals (average administrative experience of 11.7 years) tended to be highly articulate regarding the curriculum and instructional strategies undertaken in their schools:

1. They were highly supportive of their instructional staff, taking pride in their accomplishments.
2. They reported support of teacher autonomy although they were quite aware of the potential problems regarding the pressure to strictly conform to district policies regarding the standardization of curriculum and the need for academic accountability (testing).

Parents (average schooling of 7.1 years) expressed a high level of satisfaction and appreciation with regard to their children's education experience in these schools. All indicated or implied that academic success was tied to their child's future economic success. Anglo parents and Hispanic parents were both involved in the formal parent support activities of the schools. However, Anglo parents' attitudes were much more in line with "child advocacy," somewhat distrustful of the school's specific interest in doing what was right for their child. Conversely, Hispanic parents expressed a high level of trust or the teaching and administrative staff.

POLICY ISSUES

This research specifically addresses some significant policy questions regarding effective academic environments for Hispanic students:

1. *What role did native language instruction play?* These "effective" schools considered native language instruction a key in the early grades (K–3).
2. *Was there one best curriculum?* No common curriculum was identified. However, a well-trained instructional staff, implementing an integrated student-centered curriculum with literacy pervasive in all aspects of instruction, was consistently observed across grade levels. Basals were utilized sparingly and usually as resource material.
3. *What instructional strategies were effective?* Consistently, teachers organized so as to insure small collaborative learning activities requiring a high degree of heterogeneously grouped student-to-student social (and particularly linguistic) interaction. Individual instructional activity such as worksheets/workbooks was limited as was individual competition as a classroom motivational ingredient.
4. *Who were the key players in this effective schooling drama?* School administrators and parents played important roles. However, teachers were the key players. They achieved the educational confidence of their peers and supervisors. They worked to organize instruction, create new instructional environments, assess effectiveness, and advocate for their children. They were proud of their students, academically reassuring but consistently demanding. They rejected any notion of academic, linguistic, cultural, or intellectual inferiority regarding their students.

In summary, the effective instructional strategies and an effective instructional staff that we observed recognized that academic learning has its roots in language experiences and processes of communication. This "effective" schooling provided abundant and diverse opportunities for speaking, listening, reading, and writing along with native language scaffolding to help guide students through the learning process. A focus on communication encouraged students to take risks, construct meaning, and seek reinterpretations of knowledge within compatible social contexts. Within this knowledge-driven curriculum, skills were tools for acquiring knowledge, not a fundamental target of teaching events (Gallimore & Tharp, 1989; Garcia, 1988).

CONCLUSION

If the aforementioned set of data can be perceived as a preliminary look at the effective academic instruction of Hispanic students, then the following are specific derived principles that the research team developed as a result of the descriptions and analyses for the growing Hispanic population and the general increasing number of classrooms where cultural and linguistic diversity is the norm:

1. Any curriculum, especially one for "diverse" children, must address all categories of learning goals. We should not expect "less" for this student population.

2. The more diverse linguistically and culturally the children we teach, the more content must be related to the child's own environment and experience.

3. The more diverse the children, the more integrated the curriculum should be. Children should have opportunities to study a topic in depth, to apply all kinds of skills they have acquired in a variety of home and school contexts.

4. The more diverse the children, the more the curriculum should address learning through active endeavors rather than passive ones, particularly informal social activities such as group projects in which students are allowed flexibility in participating with the teacher and other students in engaging academic material.

5. The more diverse the children, the more important it is for the curriculum to offer opportunities to apply what they are learning in a meaningful context (worksheets are not meaningful).

6. The more diverse the children, the more likely it is that excessive practice and drill that focuses only on skill development will endanger the disposition to use those skills.

7. In general, the more the curriculum emphasizes performance goals rather than learning goals of relevance to the student, the more likely it is that students will distance themselves from the school. Performance goals rely on the pressure to get the right answer, as opposed to learning goals that emphasize how much one can learn.

8. Educational professionals must grasp the significance of these new understandings and challenges. Present principles and practices of teaching and learning must be accommodated to the linguistic and cultural diversity of a growing Hispanic student population.

REFERENCES

Appleby, A. N., Langer, J., & Mullis, I. J. S. (1988). *The Nation's Report Card: NAEP.* Princeton, NJ: Educational Testing Service.

Bureau of the U.S. Census (1984). *Conditions of Hispanics in America Today.* Washington, DC: U.S. Government Printing Office.

Bureau of the U.S. Census (1987). *The Hispanic Population in the United States: March 1986 and 1987.* Washington, DC: U.S. Government Printing Office.

Carter, T. P., & Chatfield, M. L. (1986). Effective bilingual schools: Implications for policy and practice. *American Journal of Education, 95*(1), 200–234.

Change (1988, May/June). Washington, DC: American Association of Higher Education.

Cummins, J. (1986). Empowering minority students: A framework for intervention. *Harvard Educational Review, 56*(1), 18–35.

Gallimore, R., & Tharp, R. G. (1989). *Challenging cultural minds.* London: Cambridge University Press.

Garcia, E. (1988). Effective schooling for language minority students. In *National clearing house for bilingual education* (New Focus) (pp. 1–43). Arlington, VA: National Clearing House for Bilingual Education.

Lucas, T., Henze, R., & Donato, R. (1990). Promoting the success of Latino language minority students: An exploratory study of six high schools. *Harvard Educational Review, 60,* 315–334.

Moll, L. (1988). Educating Latino students. *Language Arts, 64,* 315–324.

II

LITERACY AND COGNITION

7

Critical Thinking and Literacy

Nancy J. Ellsworth
Fordham University

Today a redefinition of literacy is in process that will incorporate the broader understandings and competencies needed in our changing society. An important component of this redefinition consists of critical thinking skills that underlie social competence and reading comprehension. One purpose of this chapter is to explore the rationale for the changing view of the requirements for literacy. The second is to describe an initial study designed to evaluate an instructional program to teach students with learning disabilities to improve their ability to solve real-life problems by thinking critically. Students generated a general problem-solving schema that consisted of a series of questions to be asked in making a decision. They then applied the schema to problems presented in short narratives; these problems were similar to those they were experiencing in their own lives.

What accounts for the redefinition of literacy that is currently in process? In large part, it stems from the increasing need of society for a more educated citizenry, and this need is reflected in a steady decline of employment for blue-collar workers. The ability to comprehend new problems and to solve them appropriately may be among a person's most valuable educational assets. Critical thinking, creative thinking, and problem solving may be even more important than the traditional three Rs. In earlier times, literacy meant little more than being able to read and write one's name. Today, however, expectations are higher, and a "literate" person would be expected to read widely with understanding of the meaning, or identifying the barriers to understanding. The ability to comprehend written text is only one of the components of literacy as we now view it, and increasingly attention is being turned to the thinking skills that enable one to utilize knowledge to reach good decisions. Teaching critical thinking skills to students in classrooms is the major concern of this chapter.

The relationships between critical thinking, creative thinking, and problem solving are complex, at best. According to Jones, Palincsar, Ogle, and Carr (1987), the "dimensions of thinking" include areas such as "problem solving and decision making, critical and creative thinking, and metacognition" (p. ix). Ruggiero (1988) included both critical and creative thinking as parts of the problem-solving process. Their interrelatedness was emphasized by Wales, Nardi, and Stager's statement (1986) that critical thinking and problem solving represent "the enabling skills" (p. 41) required for decision making, although in a different work they stressed that in the process of decision making, students "learn how to think critically" (Nardi & Wales, 1985, p. 223). In summary, Beck (1989) concluded that "the terms higher order thinking, critical thinking, problem solving, and reasoning are virtually synonymous. So while we can't define the abstraction precisely, we know it when we see it, and it is highly valued and important for learning and living" (p. 676).

As changes in the demographics of the student population accelerate, many are not succeeding in the mainstream, and conceptualization of the skills students need to have in order to function both in and out of school is being broadened. Increasing numbers of children do not come to school ready to learn; economic and societal deprivation already has taken a heavy toll. Poverty is the norm for a large percentage of children, especially the 25% living in single-parent families (Children's Defense Fund, 1992). In addition, with over half the mothers of very young children and two thirds of the mothers of all school-age children employed (Children's Defense Fund, 1990), much of the nurturing of young children has been shifted to a succession of surrogate caretakers. This shift of mothers into the labor force usually results from the need for income, rather than from choice. The high percentage of low-income working mothers is notable in minority families, the poorest in the nation.

In parts of the United States, the multicultural minority has become the "emergent majority." Hayes-Bautista (1992) reported that already over 60% of the residents of Los Angeles County are Hispanic, Asian, and Black, and in the state of California the European population will cease to be the majority group around 1997. With 18% of all children living in poverty, according to the 1990 census, and a poverty rate for Hispanics of 32% and for African Americans of 40% ("Making Schools Work for Children in Poverty," 1993), it is no wonder that many children do not come to school ready to learn.

Compounding this poverty, just under 2 million U.S. children—about

5% — were receiving services as learning disabled in the 1988–1989 school year (U.S. Department of Education, 1990), almost double the figures of a decade earlier. Students with learning disabilities have greater difficulty achieving in school than others. They perform poorly in comprehension and critical thinking in comparison with nondisabled students (Williams & Ellsworth, 1990), and they experience frequent academic failures over long periods of time and across a variety of tasks and teachers. For example, the U.S. Department of Education reported in 1990 that over one third of secondary students with learning disabilities who remained in school received a failing grade in one or more courses in the previous school year. Not only do these students have difficulty with reading and writing, but they are less able than nondisabled students to apply strategies in solving arithmetic problems (Fleischner & Garnett, 1987). Indeed, learning disabilities may be viewed as a problem-solving difference affecting how behavior is organized, that is, information-processing deficits may hinder the formation and use of efficient strategies (Parrill-Burnstein, 1981).

Far from being a condition to be "outgrown," learning disabilities can affect education, self-esteem, socialization, and daily living activities throughout life. For adolescents with learning disabilities, the challenges of both school and work are considerable, and in adulthood these problems often cause serious difficulties in vocational adjustments (Lerner, 1993). As the needs of employers change and there are fewer jobs for blue-collar workers, young people will need greater competence in order to take their places in the adult world.

The cognitive strategies that are an important component of appropriate behavior and personal problem solving are often poorly developed in students with learning disabilities (Ellsworth, 1989), and their peer status is often low (Wiener, 1987). The notion that students with learning disabilities do not meet expected social norms is bolstered by research showing negative evaluations by strangers with no prior knowledge of the specific child (Perlmutter & Bryan, 1984). More recent studies suggested that mildly disabled and nondisabled students can be classified accurately on the basis of social skills measures alone (Gresham & Reschly, 1988). It is interesting to note that there is no evidence that students with learning disabilities are socially withdrawn; indeed, in school settings they participate as much as their nondisabled peers. On the whole, studies show that students with learning disabilities do not differ from nondisabled peers in their knowledge of social norms, but they may be more willing to engage in social behaviors considered less desirable. Investigations such as these have resulted in a number of efforts to provide social skills training for children with learning disabilities, with varying results. Many of these efforts are reviewed by Bryan and Lee (1990) and Vaughn, McIntosh, and Hogan (1990).

One type of social skills instructional program focuses on teaching the personal problem-solving strategies essential to building social competence. In evaluating these, Hughes (1986) reported that only 8 of the 32 studies she reviewed met the important criteria of social validity and individualization. Social validity refers to the relationship between the skill being taught and outcomes that are important to that student. To be of benefit, instruction must be focused on acquiring competencies that will achieve improved functioning within the individual's own social milieu. Unfortunately, there is little evidence that greater attention is paid today to the validation of strategies being taught for building social competence than there was in the past.

Recent findings have demonstrated that students with learning disabilities can behave strategically if they have been taught how to do so (Borkowski, Johnston, & Reid, 1987; Palincsar & Brown, 1987). Effective strategy instruction supports the learner's development of new skills and abilities. It also bridges the gap between the learner's actual level of development and the level needed for independent problem solving, the gap that Vygotsky (1978) alluded to as the zone of proximal development. Additional investigation is needed to determine the most promising specific methods of instruction. Because the critical thinking skills utilized to solve social problems are essential to being able to learn and to function well in society, they are an important component of a redefinition of literacy.

Schools are being challenged to create educational environments in which, as students acquire knowledge, they also acquire the cognitive strategies that will allow them to apply that knowledge better. In the past, classroom instruction to improve problem solving has been notable for its absence. Schools have not been well equipped for this task. They have been more inclined toward remediation of specific skills, although it is clear that students with learning disabilities, given appropriate instruction, can acquire the knowledge and skills necessary to execute a strategy efficiently. Today, however, instructional materials and methods that incorporate schema-general and problem-specific questions to improve critical thinking are becoming an increasing focus of schools. This change is based on recent theoretical investigations of intelligence, the structure of acquired knowledge, and the underlying skills of learning and problem solving.

Earlier efforts to teach thinking and problem solving focused on having students learn abstract, content-free strategies applied to formal problems (de Bono, 1985; Feuerstein, Jensen, Hoffman, & Rand, 1985; Lochhead, 1985; Nisbett, Fong, Lehman, & Cheng, 1987). Sternberg and Martin (1988) suggested that when students have not learned how to use the skills they have acquired because the problems on which they were trained were not well connected to their real worlds, their knowledge is "inert" rather than "active," and instructional efforts are likely to fail. Whereas it was hoped that content-free strategies would generalize to other spheres, evidence of such transfer has not been demonstrated (Adams, 1989; Bransford, Sherwood, Vye, & Rieser, 1986; Groteluschen, Borkowski, & Hale, 1990; Manning, 1984; Polson & Jeffries, 1985). The generalizeability of cognitive training appears to be constrained by the strategies specific to a particular training task, so a schema approach that incorporates many individual applications in the context of specific domains of knowledge is more likely to produce transfer.

SCHEMA-BASED INSTRUCTION

A cognitive schema was selected as the instructional model for the following study for two reasons. First, the recent research suggests that focus on schema shows promise when incorporated into curriculum practices. Second, because cognizance of schema underlies reading comprehension and writing as well as thinking skills, integrating instruction in all three areas within the existing language arts curriculum seems desirable.

An understanding of cognitive schema and its application to curriculum and instruction underlies envisioning the integration suggested earlier. A schema is a representation of a basic information structure from the perspective of the participant (Kintsch & van Dijk, 1978). As differentiated from text structure, the schema of the problem solver is the process or procedure used to construct a mental model that integrates the problem solver's own knowledge structures with the problem introduced. When a problem is presented in written form, the text is encountered first. In addition to literal information, descriptive information about the antecedents of the problem and the action that initiates the problem event provides a context for understanding the problem. Presentation of the goal, obstacles, alternatives, and priorities trigger problem-solving operations. The structure of the text can affect the way the problem is represented in the readers' mind, for readers must relate this textual information to their own background knowledge in order to construct a framework or schema for understanding the problem that has been formulated in the text (van Dijk & Kintsch, 1983).

Personal and social problems have traditionally been viewed as ill structured (Halpern, 1989; Simon, 1980); indeed, one focus of counseling and psychotherapy has been to provide help in structuring problems more clearly so that alternatives may be evaluated and solutions arrived at. The relatively greater success of problem solving in more highly structured disciplines such as arithmetic (Kintsch & Greeno, 1985) may reflect the clearer problem representation schemata in these disciplines. Because text can present inherently ill-structured problems in a well-structured form, introducing personal or social problems in a structured narrative can facilitate learning the critical thinking and problem-solving skills needed to reach appropriate decisions.

Similar principles apply to reading comprehension as well as to problem solving, for comparable cognitive processes underlie both finding the main idea and solving personal problems. As comprehension consists of an interaction between the resources of the reader and the characteristics of the text (Adams, 1990; Perfetti, 1985), so the critical thinking needed to solve real-life problems appears to consist of an interaction between the resources of the individual and the characteristics of the specific problem (Gick, 1986). Three similarities are of particular interest. First, appropriate prior knowledge must exist as a basis for understanding in both cases. For example, if one does not know the rigors of the social convention of returning what is borrowed, one is less likely to understand Maupassant's "The Necklace;" and if one does not know this convention, one cannot intelligently address the real-life problem of what to do when a borrowed item is lost. Second, knowledge of a general cognitive schema is helpful to both reading comprehension and problem solving. When reading a story, the scenario or expectations in the reader's mind will, in part, determine the reader's understanding and interpretation. Many preschool children, told that a story begins with "Once upon a time . . . ," can predict the expected ending spontaneously. Their comprehension skills are enhanced by familiarity with the genre because they will know what to look for as they read, and they are more likely to generate germane questions. Similarly, a general schema assists in personal decision making when it structures defining the problem, generating alternatives, obtaining needed information, and evaluating alternatives before arriving at a solution. Third, text-specific or problem-specific questions that focus on the immediate situation must be derived from the general schema. For example, given knowledgeable expectations of fairy tales in general, the reader must apply text-specific questions to understand what happened to Cinderella as compared to Snow White. Likewise, to apply "Stop, look, and listen" effectively in an emergency, one must move to problem-specific questions or remain immobilized. In summary, we now know that reading comprehension and problem solving are facilitated by understanding a problem both as a general cognitive structure and as a series of specific cognitive operations.

A variety of applications of a schema approach can be found in the clinical and educational literature. The studies that influenced the present investigation were patterned after the principles described by Adams (1989) in that they employed a general schema for problem solving, coupled with applications of this strategy to solve specific problems. In the area of clinical therapy, Janis (1982) employed a schema approach in individual counseling to teach clients to make effective life decisions. Janis found that by learning a general schema for decision making and then applying it to specific problems, people could improve decision making. Five steps are incorporated into Janis' schema: (a) appraising the challenge; (b) reviewing alternatives; (c) weighing alternatives; (d) decision making; (e) verification. Larson and Gerber (1987), working in the field of learning disabilities, developed a social metacognitive program that they used successfully with delinquent youths living in a residential facility in California. The program involved the application of a seven-step general problem-solving strategy. Larson and Gerber are among the few investigators who focused their work on teaching learning-disabled and emotionally disturbed adolescents strategies for personal decision making (see also the work of Schumaker, Deshler, & Ellis, 1986; Vaughn, 1987). Thus a range of investigations has examined applications of schema, but little focus has emerged. The problem-solving schema employed in the following study comes from a variety of traditions, both clinical and educational.

AN INSTRUCTIONAL PROGRAM

This program was designed to teach adolescents with learning disabilities to understand and solve personal social problems by identifying a general problem-solving schema and applying it to specific problem situations presented in short narratives to reach appropriate decisions. Intact resource room classes participated in the instruction.

The narratives, written by the investigator, utilized a structured, predictable schema based on the model described by Williams (1988). They portrayed bipolar problems, each pole presented in a separate paragraph, and they implied the need for more facts and for the investigation of alternative solutions. Each narrative depicted an adolescent trying to solve a problem similar to those experienced by the students themselves. The problems revolved around school, employment, peer pressures, and family, and the student in the story was always uncertain of what to do.

Two examples of the narratives follow. "Joe" was used on the posttest, and a modification of "Joe" was included on the pretest. The problem situations in the pretest, posttest, and the initial instructional sessions were suggested as being typical of adolescent students' concerns by 12 learning disabilities specialists who were individually interviewed; the resulting narratives were then piloted and refined.

JOE

Joe is a junior in high school. He works afternoons during the week at McDonald's. His boss is pleased with his work and wants to promote him. With the new promotion he would be in charge of the kitchen, which is a more responsible job. Joe would also earn a higher salary, and he needs the extra money he would take home each week. If Joe takes this job, he will have to work Friday and Saturday nights.

Joe has a girl friend. They have been going out on Friday and Saturday nights every weekend for the past two months. He especially likes going to the movies. He likes her more than he has any other girl, and he's afraid of losing her because she is very popular. If he takes the promotion, they will not be able to get together on weekend nights any more.

Joe is not sure what he should do.

While "Joe" was written in preparation for the study, the problem situations in almost all of the narratives were student generated, which helped ensure their social validity. The instructor encouraged such contributions, commenting that "made-up problems are interesting, but our own and our friends' real problems are very interesting!" About 25% of the participants volunteered the problem of a "friend" during the course of the instruction, which was unexpected given such brief contact with the investigator. The resulting stories commanded a high level of student interest, and this use of students' own problems in the instructional materials seemed to create greater commitment to the program. The following narrative about Trina is typical.

TRINA

Trina has been cutting classes with her friends for a long time. In fact, it's Trina's best friend who started it. All her friends are doing it now. Lately they've been cutting school and going to the movies, but three of the kids were suspended last week. Her best friend just called and wants her to go up to the arcade tomorrow to play video games. She says everyone is going, and it sounds like fun.

Trina is 17, but she's only in 10th grade. Yesterday her counselor told her that she isn't going to pass this year if she keeps cutting. She really doesn't want to drop out of school like her older sister did, and she likes some of her classes when she goes to them. Her sister is working as a waitress. Trina is scared to cut any more, but she's also afraid of losing her friends if she starts going to class.

Trina isn't sure what to do.

After a problem was presented in a narrative like "Trina," students applied a general problem-solving schema that triggered problem-specific questions.

The problem-solving schema was a sequence of general questions designed to clarify problem identification and solution. The investigations of Janis (1982), Singer and Donlan (1982), and Williams (1988) were important influences in constructing the schema. The students applied this general schema to all problems we discussed. The schema included eight questions:

1. What is the main problem?
2. What alternative solutions are there?
3. What additional information is needed in order to make the best decision? How could it be obtained?
4. What are the advantages and disadvantages of each alternative?
5. What is the best decision? Why? Is it appropriate?
6. What would be a good back-up decision?
7. What could the person do in implementing this decision to improve the chances of success?
8. What could the person do to improve the chances of adhering to this decision despite some initial negative feedback? What problems might be encountered?

Students were taught this schema through an instructional method that employed an inductive teaching approach and was based on Vygotsky's (1962) model. The investigator modeled the critical thinking skills that she herself used in making decisions. As students gained confidence and their thinking skills improved, the investigator gradually withdrew support and students functioned more independently. This process has been described by a number of researchers (Beyer, 1987; Halpern, 1989; Jones et al., 1987; Nickerson, 1989).

The instructional activities for each class session included:

1. *Motivation.* During the initial session the investigator gave an example of a young person in the current news who faced an important decision, and she passed around the actual newspaper account with pictures. She and the students discussed implications of a good or a poor decision for the person featured in the story. During the second session, the investigator shared with students a decision she faced because of a disagreement with her teen-age daughter; she posed the questions, "How can I reach a good decision? What should I do?" Students suggested alternatives, facts needed, and the schema was worked through together. A week later, when the difficulty was resolved, she reported back to them what had happened. Subsequently, students asked the investigator to write stories based on problems they volunteered so they could discuss their own concerns in class. These narratives formed the focus of instruction from then on. Later in the program, when students were more competent in using the problem-solving schema, they tried applying the schema in their personal decision making outside of class, reporting back on what had happened. The personal

commitment of both the investigator and students was important to motivation.

2. *Prereading preparation.* The investigator reviewed the purpose of the instructional program and introduced the day's problem narrative.

3. *Reading the narrative.* Students read the narrative together, following in their own copies of the text while the investigator read aloud. This ensured that limited reading skills would not hinder comprehension.

4. *Inductive generation of the schema.* Students inductively created the general schema in response to the investigator's question: "What questions should you ask yourself when you need to make a tough decision?" The investigator recorded the components of the schema on the chalkboard as students contributed them. By the end of the third session all instructed groups had formulated all eight questions of the schema, but with slightly different wording. For instance, one group's wording of Question 2 was "What are all the possible decisions?" instead of "What alternative solutions are there?"

5. *Application of the schema.* The investigator guided the group, again using the chalkboard, in applying the schema to the problem presented in the narrative. Students learned to ask problem-specific questions as they moved through the eight general questions in the schema. The investigator began by saying, "What's the real problem here?" (Question 1 of the schema), and continued until the group reached a decision and planned for implementation and contingency planning. At times students worked in pairs in applying the schema, and then returned to the larger group to pool their ideas.

6. *Conclusion.* The investigator closed each session with a discussion that recognized students' progress in learning to make better personal decisions. For example, she might ask what insights from that day's work students could apply to their own lives. The ensuing comments would provide the framework for the investigator to suggest that students try applying this critical thinking strategy and report back on what happened.

EVALUATION OF THE PROGRAM

A pretest–posttest design was employed. The investigator administered the pretest and posttest, as well as planning and providing the instruction. All 92 students in 20 resource room classes for mainstreamed students with learning disabilities completed the pretest. These students were enrolled in two large, heterogeneous, urban public high schools with an average dropout rate of 52% of entering students. In 10 of the classes, all students who were attending ($N = 35$) were instructed. From the students in the remaining classes, comparison groups were formed to match each instructed group on the basis of size, grade level, reading level, and ethnicity. The mean age of these 70 students was 16.5 years (*SD* = .9), and they were enrolled in Grades 9-12. Their mean reading level, measured by the Wide Range Achievement Test (WRAT-R, 1984, Level 2), was a grade equivalent of 7.6 (*SD* = 1.1). The students faced a number of important personal decisions in their lives. Some had children of their own; others had criminal records or histories of alcohol or drug abuse. All had been survivors in school, so far.

The pretest consisted of an individual, audiotaped interview in which students were asked to describe the steps to be taken in reaching a decision (i.e., to identify a general problem-solving schema), to recall two problem narratives, and to answer eight specific questions that required them to apply the general schema to each of these two problem narratives. During the instructional part of the study, instructed groups participated in seven training sessions of 40 minutes each. Comparison groups received their regular language arts program taught by the resource room teachers; comprehension, writing, and critical thinking were a part of their program, but without a schema focus. The posttest was the same as the pretest except for minor modifications. Posttest narratives followed the same structure and posed the same problems to be solved as pretest narratives, but names and locations were changed, as were other minor details.

Comprehension, measured by recall of the narratives, was over 97% in both the instructed and comparison groups. This was important, for it ensured that lack of understanding of the narrative would not affect the decision-making task.

Five measures evaluated students' ability to identify and apply the general schema. *Schema identification* reported how many (0-8) of the parts of the general problem-solving schema students could name. The following four measures of *schema application* utilized two problem narratives such as "Joe":

1. *Solution generation* reported the number of acceptable alternative solutions the student generated.
2. *Fact finding* was the number of additional pieces of information that the student identified as being needed in order to reach the best decision.
3. *Implementation planning* measured whether or not the student devised an acceptable plan to increase the probability of successfully implementing the decision the student had chosen.
4. *Contingency planning* reported whether the student stated a plan that could improve the likelihood of adhering to the decision chosen.

For these last two measures, answers were judged to be either successful or not successful, and the score for the group was the proportion of students who succeeded. Because we could not evaluate the personal appropriateness of the decisions proposed, the other applications of the general schema were not scored. To assess reliability of scoring from the audiotapes, a second scorer rescored about 20% of the tapes; interscorer agreement was .95.

To create a scoring key for the four items measuring application of the schema, all student responses were listed and three resource room teachers determined independently whether or not each response was acceptable. If the decisions were not unanimous, they were discussed and consensus was reached. The scoring key to the solution generation question for the narrative about Joe follows.

SCORING KEY: SOLUTION GENERATION, JOE

Acceptable Answers:

Take the promotion and:

- Talk to the girlfriend.
- Send a friend to talk to the girlfriend for him.
- Convince the girlfriend to see him another time.
- Get the girlfriend a job with him at McDonald's.
- Drop the girlfriend if she doesn't understand.
- Get a new girlfriend if she doesn't understand.
- Talk to his boss; compromise re: Friday/Saturday nights.
- Switch shifts with a friend at work.
- Try out the new job for a short time, then decide.
- Look for a different job with better hours.

Refuse the promotion and:

- See the girlfriend as usual.
- Look for a different job with better pay and good hours.

Unacceptable Answers:

Think it over.

- Ask a friend/parents what to do.
- It depends on the relationship.
- Call her from work on Friday/Saturday nights.
- Have the girlfriend visit him Friday/Saturday during breaks at work.
- Work fast so he can get off earlier (unacceptable because employed on an hourly basis).
- Give her money to go out without him Friday/Saturday.
- Quit job (unacceptable because could just refuse promotion).
- Lie to girlfriend; say he is helping his family these nights.

This scoring key reveals the breadth of alternative solutions generated by the students.

Separate analyses of covariance were conducted on the posttest scores of the five measures of schema identification and application, using the pretest score as the covariate. Data was analyzed using the instructed group with its comparison group as the unit of analysis; the main findings are presented in Table 7.1.

Data were also analyzed using the individual student as the unit of analysis; the results of the two sets of analyses showed remarkably similar effects (Ellsworth, 1989). To summarize the findings, on all five measures the instructed groups performed significantly higher (at the .01 level or better) on the posttest than did the comparison groups. These findings support the view that instruction in application of a general schema to specific problems can improve critical thinking and decision making.

It is interesting that whereas students in the instructed groups worked together to generate and apply the schema to solve problems, the posttest interview required each individual to pursue the process independently, creating a progression from group to individual application. Informal analysis of a videotape of one training session supported the hypothesis that the structured group interaction was an important part of the instruction.

Future investigation would help clarify some of the issues raised by this study. How would the intervention compare with others such as bibliotherapy or interactive group therapy? Might it be more productive to employ a broader range of instructional media and materials? For instance, videotaping the students role-playing alternative solutions could highlight the need to investigate a wide range of possible solutions before selecting one. This line of inquiry is appealing because, at the beginning of the study,

TABLE 7.1
Means and SDs on All Posttest Measures

	Instructed Groups		Comparison Groups	
	Mean	(SD)	Mean	(SD)
Schema identification[a]				
Mean no. of components repeated	6.25	(1.44)	.35	(.39)
Solution generation[a]				
Mean no. of solutions generated	5.15	(.80)	2.85	(.39)
Fact finding[a]				
Mean no. of additional facts identified	2.77	(.70)	.77	(.32)
Implementation planning				
Proportion of students with satisfactory plan	.73	(.32)	.36	.20)
Contingency planning				
Proportion of students with satisfactory plan	.63	(.27)	.31	(.15)

[a]Adjusted scores

impulsive acceptance of the first alternative solution that came to mind was characteristic of a majority of the participants. Searching for a range of alternative solutions is the cornerstone of successful application of the schema, for the other parts are dependent on this step.

Perhaps the most important suggestion for future investigation is that we attempt to determine which aspects of the instructional program caused the improvement and whether this improvement will carry over to the critical thinking and decision-making skills of students in their own lives. Learning a general schema and applying it to relevant problems, as was done in this study, is only the beginning; however it was a necessary first step.

CONCLUSION

Including students with learning disabilities and students of differing cultural and linguistic backgrounds in regular education classrooms is an important thrust in public education today. One of the requirements for successful inclusion of these students is a curriculum that is appropriate for all. Because critical thinking and personal problem solving are essential components of academic and social learning for all students, focus on instruction in these areas is important. Finding practical means to implement these objectives has been a logistical challenge.

The economy and simplicity of incorporating schema-based instruction in critical thinking into the existing language arts curriculum is appealing. In this study the instruction was included in the remedial component of the resource room curriculum. To introduce a new area of instruction is impractical, given current limits to the school day, and the bridge that the focus on schema provides has been recognized only recently.

An understanding of schema can improve academic achievement in writing, as well. We now know that a schema approach can alter organizational strategies, and as early as 1981 the National Assessment of Educational Progress (NAEP) reported that the problem with student writing lies more in the quality of organization and thinking than in the mechanics. Students with learning disabilities have particular needs in this area, for recent studies confirm that these students have little awareness of the techniques for performing the writing process (B. Y. L. Wong, R. Wong, & Blenkisop, 1989). A range of investigation has been conducted on the teaching of writing. For instance, Englert (1990) and Scardamalia and Bereiter (1986) reported successful applications of formal prompts to help students carry out sophisticated writing strategies. Following the investigation reported here, we undertook pilot work on a schema approach to teaching writing. Students wrote narratives depicting the problems with which they and their friends were confronted, and this instruction generated active, enthusiastic student participation and productivity.

Using students' own problems to which they seek solutions as the focus of instruction provided compelling motivation for them to participate. Adolescents have often viewed classroom instruction as "boring"; however, their personal concerns are obviously of interest. As we seek ways to capture students' attention with a curriculum that is relevant to their needs, the personal involvement of the students in this study is promising.

The students also enjoyed working together. Informal analysis of a videotape of one training session supported the hypothesis that structured group interaction was an important part of the learning. In addition, a beginning effort was made in the direction of working in cooperative learning groups.

Students responded positively to working in pairs rather than as a larger group, saying they liked it because they had the opportunity to talk more and because the students were in charge. In a related area of instruction, Flynn (1989) noted that cooperative learning facilitates developing "critical thinking through discussion, negotiation, clarification of ideas, and evaluation of others' ideas" (p. 666). Along similar lines, a number of researchers have successfully applied cooperative learning procedures to instruction to improve both comprehension and problem-solving skills (Kuhrt & Farris, 1990).

In the study reported in this chapter, urban, minority adolescents with learning disabilities showed significant gains in the critical-thinking skills needed to make better decisions. The instructional program provided ample practice in applying a general problem-solving schema to the kinds of decisions that students were facing in their own lives. The fact that instruction was not heavily dependent on reading comprehension made success more achievable by all, an important characteristic as educators strive to provide for a broad range of individual differences within the context of their classrooms.

As we reexamine our notions of literacy and incorporate the needs of tomorrow's adults, the increased competence in critical thinking that underlies making good decisions is an essential component of the new definition. Effective instructional programs in schools that will meet the needs of all students to achieve in this area is indeed a worthy objective.

ACKNOWLEDGMENTS

The study reported in this chapter is an unpublished doctoral dissertation. Its design and execution was made possible through the advice and support of my mentor, Joanna P. Williams.

REFERENCES

Adams, M. J. (1989). Thinking skills curricula: Their promise and progress. *Educational Psychologist, 24,* 25–77.

Adams, M. J. (1990). *Beginning to read: Thinking and learning about print.* Cambridge, MA: MIT Press.

Beck, I. L. (1989). Reading and reasoning. *The Reading Teacher, 42,* 676–682.

Beyer, B. K. (1987). *Practical strategies for the teaching of thinking.* Boston: Allyn & Bacon.

Borkowski, J. G., Johnston, M. B., & Reid, M. K. (1987). Metacognition, motivation, and controlled performance. In S. J. Ceci (Ed.), *Handbook of cognitive, social, and neuropsychological aspects of learning disabilities* (Vol. 2, pp. 147–173). Hillsdale, NJ: Lawrence Erlbaum Associates.

Bransford, J. D., Sherwood, R., Vye, N., & Rieser, J. (1986). Teaching thinking and problem solving. *American Psychologist, 41,* 1078–1089.

Bryan, T., & Lee, J. (1990). Social skills training with learning disabled children and adolescents: The state of the art. In T. E. Scruggs & B. Y. L. Wong (Eds.), *Intervention research in learning disabilities* (pp. 263–278). New York: Springer-Verlag.

Children's Defense Fund. (1990). *Children 1990: A report card, briefing book, and action primer.* Washington, DC: Author.

Children's Defense Fund. (1992). *Vanishing dreams: The economic plight of America's young families.* Washington, DC: Author.

de Bono, E. (1985). The CoRT Thinking Program. In J. W. Segal, S. F. Chipman, & R. Glaser (Eds.), *Thinking and learning skills: Vol. 1. Relating instruction to research* (pp. 363–388). Hillsdale, NJ: Lawrence Erlbaum Associates.

Ellsworth, N. J. (1989). *Using a cognitive schema to teach problem-solving skills to urban, learning-disabled adolescents.* Unpublished doctoral dissertation, Teachers College, Columbia University.

Englert, C. S. (1990). Unraveling the mysteries of writing through strategy instruction. In T. E. Scruggs & B.Y.L. Wong (Eds.), *Intervention research in learning disabilities* (pp. 186–223). New York: Springer-Verlag.

Feuerstein, R., Jensen, M., Hoffman, M., & Rand, Y. (1985). Instrumental enrichment, an intervention program for structural modifiability: Theory and practice. In J. W. Segal, S. F. Chipman, & R. Glaser (Eds.), *Thinking and learning skills. Vol. 1. Relating instruction to research* (pp. 43–82). Hillsdale, NJ: Lawrence Erlbaum Associates.

Fleischner, J. E., & Garnett, K. (1987). Arithmetic difficulties. In K. Kavale, S. Forness, & M. Bender (Eds.), *Handbook of learning disabilities: Vol. 1. Dimensions and diagnosis* (pp. 189–209). Boston: Little, Brown.

Flynn, L. L. (1989). Developing critical reading skills through cooperative problem solving. *Reading Teacher, 42,* 664–668.

Gick, M. (1986). Problem-solving strategies. *Educational Psychologist, 21,* 99–120.

Gresham, F. M., & Reschly, D. J. (1988). Issues in the conceptualization, classification and assessment of social skills in the mildly handicapped. In T. R. Kratochwill (Ed.), *Advances in school psychology* (pp. 203–247). Hillsdale, NJ: Lawrence Erlbaum Associates.

Groteluschen, A. K., Borkowski, J. G., & Hale, C. (1990). Strategy instruction is often insufficient: Addressing the interdependency of executive and attributional processes. In T. E. Scruggs & B.Y.L. Wong (Eds.), *Intervention research in learning disabilities* (pp. 81–101). New York: Springer-Verlag.

Halpern, D. F. (1989). *Thought and knowledge: An introduction to critical thinking.* Hillsdale, NJ: Lawrence Erlbaum Associates.

Hayes-Bautista, D. E. (1992, October 28). Academe can take the lead in binding together the residents of a multicultural society. *Chronicle of Higher Education,* pp. B1–2.

Hughes, J. N. (1986). Methods of skill selection in social skills training: A review. *Professional School Psychology, 1,* 235–248.

Janis, I. L. (1982). *Counseling on personal decisions.* New Haven, CT: Yale University Press.

Jones, B. F., Palincsar, A. S., Ogle, D. S., & Carr, E. G. (Eds.) (1987). *Strategic teaching and learning: Cognitive instruction in the content areas.* Alexandria, VA: Association for Supervision and Curriculum Development, in cooperation with the North Central Regional Educational Laboratory.

Kintsch, W., & Greeno, J. G. (1985). Understanding and solving arithmetic word problems. *Psychological Review, 92,* 109–129.

Kintsch, W., & van Dijk, T. (1978). Toward a model of text comprehension and production. *Psychological Review, 85,* 334–394.

Kuhrt, B. L., & Farris, P. J. (1990). Empowering students through reading, writing, and reasoning. *Journal of Reading, 33,* 436–441.

Larson, K. A., & Gerber, M. M. (1987). Effects of social metacognitive training for enhancing overt behavior in learning disabled and low achieving delinquents. *Exceptional Children, 54,* 201–211.

Lerner, J. W. (1993). *Learning disabilities* (6th ed.). Boston: Houghton Mifflin.

Lochhead, J. (1985). Teaching analytic reasoning skills through pair problem solving. In J. W. Segal, S. F. Chipman, & R. Glaser (Eds.), *Thinking and learning skills: Vol. 1. Relating instruction to research* (pp. 109–131). Hillsdale, NJ: Lawrence Erlbaum Associates.

Making schools work for children in poverty. (1993, January 13). *Education Week,* pp. 46–51.

Manning, B. H. (1984). Problem-solving instruction as an oral comprehension aid for reading disabled third graders. *Journal of Learning Disabilities, 17,* 457–461.

Nardi, A. H., & Wales, C. E. (1985). Teaching decision making with guided design. In A. L. Costa (Ed.), *Developing minds: A resource book for teaching thinking* (pp. 220–223). Alexandria, VA: Association for Supervision and Curriculum Development.

National Assessment of Educational Progress. (1981). *Reading, thinking and writing: Results from the 1979–80 National Assessment of Reading and Literature* (Report No. 11-L-01). Princeton, NJ: Educational Testing Service.

Nickerson, R. S. (1989). On improving thinking through instruction. In E. Z. Rothkopf (Ed.), *Review of research in education* (Vol. 15, pp. 3–57). Washington, DC: American Educational Research Association.

Nisbett, R. E., Fong, G. T., Lehman, D. R., & Cheng, P. W. (1987). Teaching reasoning. *Science, 238,* 625–631.

Palincsar, A. S., & Brown, D. A. (1987). Enhancing instructional time through attention to metacognition. *Journal of Learning Disabilities, 20,* 66–75.

Parrill-Burnstein, M. (1981). *Problem solving and learning disabilities: An information processing approach.* New York: Grune & Stratton.

Perfetti, C. A. (1985). *Reading ability.* New York: Oxford University Press.

Perlmutter, B., & Bryan, J. H. (1984). First impressions, ingratiation and the learning disabled child. *Journal of Learning Disabilities, 3,* 157–161.

Polson, P. G., & Jeffries, R. (1985). Instruction in general problem solving skills: An analysis of four approaches. In S. F. Chipman, J. W. Segal, & R. Glaser (Eds.), *Thinking and learning skills* (Vol. 1, pp. 417–455). Hillsdale, NJ: Lawrence Erlbaum Associates.

Ruggiero, V. R. (1988). *Teaching thinking across the curriculum.* New York: Harper & Row.

Scardamalia, M., & Bereiter, C. (1986). Written composition. In M. Wittrock (Ed.), *Handbook of research on teaching* (3rd ed., pp. 778–803). New York: Macmillan.

Schumaker, J. B., Deshler, D. D., & Ellis, E. S. (1986). Intervention issues related to the education of LD adolescents. In J. K. Torgesen & B. Y. L. Wong (Eds.), *Psychological and educational perspectives on learning disabilities* (pp. 329–365). New York: Academic Press.

Simon, H. A. (1980). Problem solving and education: Issues in teaching and research. In D. T. Tama & F. Relif (Eds.), *Problem solving and education: Issues in teaching and research* (pp. 81–96). Hillsdale, NJ: Lawrence Erlbaum Associates.

Singer, H., & Donlan, D. (1982). Active comprehension: Problem-solving schema with question generation for comprehension of complex short stories. *Reading Research Quarterly, 17,* 166–185.

Sternberg, R. J., & Martin, M. (1988). When teaching thinking does not work, what goes wrong? *Teachers College Record, 89,* 555–578.

U.S. Department of Education. (1990). *Twelfth annual report to Congress on the implementation of the education of the handicapped act.* Washington, DC: Government Printing Office.

Van Dijk, T. A., & Kintsch, W. (1983). *Strategies of discourse comprehension.* New York: Academic Press.

Vaughn, S. R. (1987). TLC—Teaching, learning, and caring: Teaching interpersonal problem-solving skills to emotionally-disabled adolescents. *Pointer, 31,* 25–30.

Vaughn, S., McIntosh, R., & Hogan, A. (1990). Why social skills training doesn't work: An alternative model. In T. E. Scruggs & B.Y.L. Wong (Eds.), *Intervention research in learning disabilities* (pp. 279–303). New York: Springer-Verlag.

Vygotsky, L. (1962). *Thought and language.* Cambridge, MA: MIT Press.

Vygotsky, L. (1978). *Mind in society: The development of higher psychological process* (M. Cole, V. John-Steiner, S. Scribner, & E. Souberman, Eds. and Trans.). Cambridge, MA: Harvard University Press.

Wales, C. E., Nardi, A. H., & Stager, R. A. (1986). Decision making: New paradigm for education. *Educational Leadership, 43,* 38–41.

Wide Range Achievement Test—Revised Edition, Level 2 (1984). Wilmington, DE: Jastak Associates.

Wiener, J. (1987). Peer status of learning disabled children and adolescents: A review of the literature. *LD Research, 2*(2), 62–79.

Williams, J. P. (1988, November). *Teaching problem-solving skills to learning-disabled adolescents.* Paper presented at the Division of Learning Disabilities Conference, CEC, Purdue University.

Williams, J. P., & Ellsworth, N. J. (1990). Teaching learning disabled adolescents to think critically using a problem-solving schema. *Exceptionality, 1,* 135–146.

Wong, B. Y. L., Wong, R., & Blenkisop, J. (1989). Cognitive and metacognitive aspects of learning-disabled adolescents' composing problems. *Learning Disabilities Quarterly, 12,* 300–323.

8

Visual Thinking and Literacy

Carolyn N. Hedley
W. Eugene Hedley
Anthony N. Baratta
Fordham University

THE VISUALIZATION OF IDEAS

The human need to order the flow of experience, to reshape it, or simply to remember it, requires a multiplicity of means, and among these, language and imagery are of particular interest. Both of these processes assist the individual in bridging the personal and social aspects of experience. . . . Language is a highly conventionalized form of expression, but images—the constituent forms of visual thought—are hard to standardize or to define. There is no dictionary of images, or thesaurus of photographs and paintings. Imagery and visual expressions reflect the uniqueness of an individual's life.

—V. John-Steiner, 1985

Visual Thinking

There are two modes we use for thinking as we understand it: verbal thinking and visual thinking or imagery. We often think in terms of the pictures in our mind. We visualize circumstances and events: We hypothesize, daydream, and plan based on these visual images. Much of our thought occurs as imagery, as visually recalled memory, and as visually perceived experience. For example, we visualize or realize an experience of going to a New Year's party; afterward, we put into words an orderly description of what took place. We have converted experience into a manageable linear order, and it has fewer of the dimensions of the experience itself.

Television, often lamented because it proselytizes the learner as a distraction from reading, is currently challenging notions of how we learn. TV provides a fuller, more emotional, more complete visual experience for the observer and learner. In contrast, a book containing the same information is often perceived as dry, overly rational, with no heart. Reading, especially reading expository text, has often become antiseptic and boring. How can we reclaim some of the elliptical, holistic, experiential, affective, and emotional sense of the visual experience (including its verbal dimensions) as a vital learning experience for students?

We give a great deal of attention to verbal communication in classrooms, but very little to visual learning and thinking. Verbal thinking promotes linear, logical thinking useful in the achievement of educational tasks involving reading and writing. Visual thinking, on the other hand, tends to be more mosaic, more holistic, and more complex, promoting different orders of complex thinking. Much instruction in classrooms involves the regurgitation of verbally structured, linear knowledge of facts and concepts. Thus, we learn to think in this same linear, memorizing mode.

Visual thinking requires us to think like an artist, a dancer, a musician, "in what Copland calls the *languages of emotion* or the thoughts that are realized in music and in choreography" (John-Steiner, 1985, p. 9). Drama, music, and the dance are the forms that move us from our isolation. Even Einstein found that words were inadequate to his thinking and his discovery. "The words of the language as they are written or spoken, do not seem to play any role in my mechanisms of thought. The physical entities which seem to serve as elements in thought are certain signs and more or less clear images which can be voluntarily reproduced or combined" (Einstein, 1945, in response to a questionnaire by Jacques Hadamard). Other well-known scientists have reported their reliance on visual forms to order their thought, as stated in the quote at the beginning of this chapter.

John-Steiner (1985) summarized her perceptions in her chapter on visual learning:

> In this study of visual thinking, I have relied in particular on the insights of those who have linked the internal forms of visualization to a mastery of graphic, plastic, or cinematic language because no direct observation of inner visualization can be done. The easy availability of images was frequently mentioned both by artists and scientists whom I had talked with, or whose written works I had searched for a description of their own thought processes. These individuals share with others outside their professions a reliance upon mental pictures as a record of their past, and the reliance upon more generic images as kernels of their understanding of biological and physical processes. But productive thinkers use their stubborn patience to work with these images to go beyond the representational function of visual thought. They find new thoughts hidden as metaphors in their reflections, as did the young Einstein

while riding on his wave; these images lead them to new generative synthesis. (p. 109)

For decades, students have been taught linear outlining as the principal representation and organization of information in a chapter. This made sense because it was assumed that reading, writing, and perhaps even thinking proceeded in a sequential, linear fashion. Visual knowledge often involves the restructuring of knowledge and thinking using metaphor and analogy. Thinking for one's self, reasoning imaginatively, originally, and creatively is facilitated by tasks with specific characteristics (Smith, 1990).

Smith's (1990) definition of thinking and the thinking processes that occur during a learning experience, explains that there are not exclusive and alternative modes of thought. There are not different kinds of thinking; there are different kinds of tasks that call for judgments in thinking or choosing among alternatives. The kinds of thinking that are engaged often simultaneously are dependent on the prior knowledge of the thinker relative to the task and the perceived demands of the task.

> The elements of thinking critically and creatively are in everyone's behavioral and cognitive repertoire. People may not appear to be thinking critically or creatively because the situation does not permit or call for critical or creative behavior. This does not mean that some individuals are totally incapable of thinking critically or creatively, or that they lack the training. It is just that they are not thinking in those ways, for one reason or another. (Smith, 1990, pp. 101–102)

Perhaps we may not be thinking visually because we are unaware of the possibilities of visual thinking and unaware of using imagery as a dominant means for creative thinking and problem solving.

> Provided we know enough we are always capable of thinking. . . . If we can make no sense of what we are trying to think about, then critical [and creative] thinking is impossible. Critical thinking [including visual thinking] does not demand a complex array of learned skills, but competence in whatever you are thinking about. If you understand cooking, you can be critical of the way in which a meal is being prepared. If you are not able to criticize or think analytically about such things, it will not be because you cannot think critically, but because you lack the experience to make a critical judgment. (Smith, 1990, p. 103)

Thinking in its various aspects depends on the idiosyncratic thinking processes individuals bring to the task as they perceive it. Some of these strategies should include visual thinking or combinations of visual, verbal, and other constructs for thinking that may never be defined. Finally, these processes probably engage simultaneously, not sequentially or hierarchically.

AN OVERVIEW OF VISUAL THINKING

Until recent times, visual images were thought of as pictures of reality. The model often used to explain the creation of visual images was that of the camera: the eyes serving as lenses, the visual cortex serving as a photographic plate. Today, it is well accepted that the visual cortex is much more than a passive "recorder" of light patterns transmitted from the "lenses." Visual imagery is as much a product of the internal state of the human body as it is of the light received from an external source. Both deep memory and working memory, general and specific emotional states, chemical balances and imbalances, and a myriad of other factors can and do play a role in the creation of visual images. Visual images, then, are not merely a recording but are images created by the individual. Consider some of the roles played by visual images in the process of thinking.

Visual Thinking and Ancient Man

"Thinking" refers to any number of mental processes such as remembering, extrapolating, interpolating, speculating, and so on. Most of these processes are initiated by the confrontation of some kind of problem or exigency requiring an individual response. (The *problem* could simply be one of boredom.) Without delving into mental processes, it may be assumed that ancient man was involved in thinking as a primary means of problem solving. *Ancient man* refers to humans who had developed a rudimentary form of oral language, but who had not yet developed a written form. *Ancient man* existed for some 10,000 to 100,000 years prior to the development of written language. Demonstrably, he was a good problem solver, surviving against great odds. The type of thinking and problem solving used by ancient man was visual. Two ways of establishing this fact help clarify the notion of visual thinking.

Survival

First, consider the survival needs of ancient man. Born into a "buzzing, blooming confusion" of an often hostile world, he had to actively create a vision of the world, not unlike what a modern child must do. As young children create now, his world was created out of the light, dark, color, sounds, tastes, smells, and the feel of an external *something*. Increasingly, this world became peopled with objects that became more precisely distinguished and accessible to memory over time. To function in a world containing other beings, the objects of a child's world must come to correspond to objects already present in the world of others, especially adults. In this conformed understanding of objects, the role of a spoken language becomes essential.

The language of earliest man must have been quite childlike. Words were used as prompts to generate visual images, especially those essential to physical survival. Man's language might never have developed beyond the need to signal, adequate for other animals, if he had been physically capable of surviving by either flight or fight. This was not the case; man had not only to be warned of a predator's presence, but of what kind of predator. A tall tree may serve as an escape from a lion, but not from a leopard. Initially words had to function as a generator of visual images. The generated image could identify a predator as well as suggest possible escape possibilities. In short, the more detailed the image, the more valuable it became as a source of thinking and problem solving.

Group Survival

As ancient man moved beyond the problems of mere survival, his language became more and more complex. However, language remained visually oriented. Language developed from and contributed to visual thinking. The problem of survival was moved to a different level. Now, the problem became one of group survival. For group survival to occur, the group must have an identity and the individual must have an identity within the group. The response to the survival problem resulted in the elaborate mythologies generated by ancient man, present today in primitive tribes and cultures and, to some extent, in our own.

Myth and Visual Imaging

These myths were communicated by means of dramatic presentations and by music, usually with audience participation. This insured common or shared group visual imaging securing both group and individual identities from generation to generation—the oral tradition. Products other than spoken languages emerged from ancient visual thinking. Most of these products—such as cave paintings, pottery, bas relief, statuary, carvings, and others (such as weaving) that perish with time—we classify as works of art. Today we recognize symbolic forms of art and myth as products of visual thinking. Creativity is highly dependent on visual thinking; its major linguistic tools are metaphor and analogy.

Consider the needs of man and the difference between visual and nonvisual thinking. The introduction of written languages had a profound effect on the thinking processes of man. Thinking became more verbal and less visual over time. However, the young child is no less dependent on the creation of a visual image of the world today. We are not suggesting that we have any fewer visual images; in fact we may have more. It is being asserted that we are no longer very dependent on visual imagery for our thinking and problem solving. Nonvisual thinking has come to dominate modern cultures. In any case, once a language becomes a written language, a whole new form of thinking becomes not only possible, but necessary. Survival, group survival, is still probably the ultimate motivator. The need to secure increasingly large populations into the group and provide for individual identities requires new forms of communication. That is, we need communication that is less subject to interpretation of an increasing number of participants.

In a word, the stabilization of meanings shared by the culture was achieved by reading and writing. One of the most dramatic examples of the difference in thinking that results from the development of a written language can be found in a comparison of Homer and Thucydides. The tales of the battle of Troy found in Homer existed long before Greek became a written language. The tales of Homer were known to all Greeks. Learned and relearned in song, they are essentially poetry. On the other hand, the history of the Peloponnesian War described by Thucydides is a classic example of descriptive prose.

Visual Thinking and Modern Man

A written language requires a set of highly specific rules—a grammar for the structure of a written sentence. It also requires rules for the structure of thoughts, a logic. A written language is linear and provides the best means for detailed descriptions. Precise quantitative measurements become a part of a written language, increasing further the accuracy and precision of description and thought. The development of a written language corresponds with the development of prose styles, both in writing and in speech, but also in thinking. Protagoras, in the 5th century B.C., is credited with remarking on the difference between the then traditional poetic or mythical form of speech and the new emerging prose style: When a man learns to speak correctly, he will then learn to think correctly, and as a result, see the world differently. A written language enormously facilitates verbal thinking, that is, thinking with words about words. This permits the development of increasing levels of abstract thought, thoughts totally devoid of visual imagery—except, of course, the symbols themselves.

Roughly speaking, there are two basic modes of thinking: verbal and visual. Whereas the two are not mutually exclusive and may occur simultaneously, they do each possess distinct characteristics. Verbal thinking is linear, logical, and analytical. Visual thinking is holistic, nonlinear, and synthetic. Since the advent of written languages, verbal thinking has come to dominate Western culture. This has been due to the outstanding success of this mode of thought in solving problems associated with an external world. It has brought us to a culture dominated by the values of science and technology. It provides us with labor saving technologies, rapid transportation, rapid information processing, medical and nutritional improvements, and so forth. These successes have forced visual thinking to occupy a very secondary role. The Western world has spent the past two centuries in a sometimes frantic effort to continually expand verbal thinking into all areas of human endeavor. Successes have continued to mount. However, it is becoming increasingly clear that the success of verbal thinking has been limited primarily to areas of the physical and biological sciences and their resulting technologies. No great successes are encountered in the social, psychological, or political domains. Ideologies and personal and social values have been little affected. Visual thinking — associated with myth and poetry — has not received the attention or the development that might have been expected.

Even in today's high-tech society, the need to translate verbal thinking into visual thinking is becoming evident. In the world of computers, the epitome of linear, logical, verbal thinking, the speed and quantity of information that can be processed is truly astounding. Unfortunately, the human user of this technology cannot possibly absorb, use, or make sense of this deluge of information. Computer programmers are more and more concerned with developing programs that will present information to the user in visual form: a form that will condense large amounts of information into a visual picture. The world of computer graphics for accommodating this need is still in its infancy.

Importance of Visual Literacy

The importance of visual thinking to our contemporary society needs to be appreciated in relation to a number of problem areas. First, a need to improve our skills at personal problem solving exists. Personal problems — for example, learning how to network within a profession with the myriad skills and relationships necessary — are not simple and are seldom fully understood by linear analysis. Visual thinking that integrates into a single visual image the factors relevant to comprehending a personal problem forms the best basis for imagining the coordinated pattern of acts that could lead to a resolution of the problem.

In the early stages of thinking and development, the foundations of both personal and social identities are formed. Early visual thinking forms the ongoing basis from which we derive our subsequent personal and social values. The extent to which visual thinking results in shared visual images is the extent to which our personal value system becomes a shared social value system. From the beginning of life to its end, individuals are dependent on visual thinking for their personal identity—visual imaging that is continually increasing in complexity. From the pool of visual images and through visual thinking grows the security of the individual about "who and why" they are. The personal relationships of the individual with others and with society are better understood through visual experience.

Society needs to continually form and renew its own identity as well. When an individual's visual images are understood as being held in common with the group, personal and group identity is formed and validated. We find ways to communicate about such views; from communicated and shared images a community is affirmed. Society constantly reintegrates its resources, human and others, to focus on common problems. What is required for such integration is, quite literally, the "vision thing." The better a society is at visual thinking, the easier it becomes to deal with social problems. And the better society's chance of civilized survival.

Educational Implications

An important consideration of our discussion is the role of visual thinking in terms of education. For the development of the human organism and the evolution of the species, it must be recognized that infant and early childhood learning is concerned almost exclusively with visual thinking. As language develops, its first function is that of naming categories within a visual field. Later on, the development of verbal thinking becomes a significant factor in our problem-solving capacity. These two kinds of thinking, visual and verbal, can present a paradox to the learner. But it is paradox that is resolved by integrating the visual experience with the verbal one.

Teaching science in the elementary and secondary schools is a prime example of the problems associated with the two modes of thinking. Attempting to teach science as science, we are teaching a form of verbal thinking. Young children and early adolescents are still dependent for problem solving on visual thinking and imagery. When teachers present science in its verbal form, its use as a basis for problem solving for young children often reduces to nonsense. The visual images of the physical and biological world built by children are usually based on their experiences and are not the result of instruction. For them, the earth is flat and static, and the sun does rise and set. A child may come to memorize and dutifully recite scientifically correct answers. However, when confronted with a new problem, the child will call on visual, not verbal images to derive a solution. In such cases, the result is not always failure. We encounter little problem with our visual image of the sun's rising and setting. We speak of the sun rising and setting in our everyday visualization. But when we are asked more difficult questions about the sun, such as the derivation of our year, different seasonal changes, or the changing length of the days, our visual thinking fails to provide answers; we realize that the sun's action can only be explained by the rational physics of the earth's rotating on its own axis while revolving about the sun. It takes many graphic diagrams and visual experiences to learn the concept of the rotating earth. Teachers must find the time and the means to incorporate visual thinking into the curriculum so that children can call up appropriate visual images to assist them in solving problems related to science and other subjects. Visual thinking accounts for many of the creative insights that have advanced the disciplines. Those rare moments of synthesis, the "Aha" experience, which lead to scientific discoveries have their origin in visual imagery and visual thinking.

What seems lacking in our time is a new mythology or a new set of myths. The old, preliterate myths are meaningful only in the context of visual thinking. Visual thinking as a developing process has made but little advancement since ancient times. The processes involved in visual thinking need attention for those processes to be improved. Updating old myths with sensitized cognitive verbal processes is not sufficient. A new set of myths, accessible by visual thinking and consistent with the available electronic knowledge and information as a result of verbal thinking is essential. Better, we need myths that integrate both visual and verbal forms of thinking.

A case of the lack of such integration is that of the creation myths. The big bang myth, a visual image generated by verbal thinking within science, envisions an image of implosion followed by explosion. In contrast, a myth or visual image of modern biological evolution has not been generated for our time. However, such myths do predate modern science. For example, the creation myths of the Australian aborigines are evolutionary. What results when an ancient creation myth, such as the Christian one, attempts to incorporate within itself the contents of scientific verbal thinking is that it simply does not "compute." In the case of "creationism" the attempt at effective imagery and subsequent myth destroys the visual impact of the original and renders illogical or "unscientific" the verbal part. Clearly, a no-win situation!

To summarize, verbal thinking seems to have eclipsed visual thinking in modern times. Yet, visual thinking is an essential part of the human mental apparatus. Its value in ancient times as the exclusive means of problem solving and of survival is paralleled today in the way that children learn and think. It becomes evident that improved understanding of this process is called for so that a new set of myths can be generated. These new myths could serve to integrate the two forms of thinking in ways that will enable society to resolve social conflicts more effectively and insure the continued survival of society itself.

LEARNING THROUGH IMAGERY AND IMAGINATION

Smith (1990) made clear how imagery and imagination are related:

> Imagining is something else that the brain does continually. Far from being an escape from reality, imagination makes reality possible. For once, the dictionary provides a reasonable description of what the brain is doing when imagination is defined as the forming of mental concepts of what is not actually present to the senses, the mental consideration of actions or events not yet in existence, and the conception of the absent as if it were present. In short, imagination is the creation of possible realities, including the reality we actually inhabit. . . . The brain has no direct contact with the physical world in which we live; the world is never actually present to the senses. . . . The brain does not respond to react to the world, it creates the world. Whatever is "out there" receives its form and substance from the brain itself. All texture and meaningfulness that we perceive in the world around us are put there by the brain, order imposed on chaos. The brain paints the images we see, composes the sounds that we hear, and shapes the substances that we feel. The brain creates the world we call reality. (pp. 45–46)

From this quotation it is clear that Smith is talking about imagery, about sensory and visual thinking regarding a physical world. Why has visual thinking about that world become so important? As Smith (1990) pointed out, the imaginative sweep that creates reality, also creates fantasy. "We live in the present and in the future, both products of our imagination, as we constantly revise our own history and anticipate what is to come. . . . We would not have reality without fantasy; reality is a fantasy that works" (p. 46). To create a future, we clearly need imagination, an imagination that derives from sensory input.

Visual thinking has become important as a result of the successes of verbal thinking. The analytic, two-dimensional linear operation of verbal thinking, demonstrated by computer technology, has produced enormous quantities of detailed information and continues to do so at incredible speeds. Were we to confine our structuring of reality to this flow of information, we would be banishing ourselves quite literally to a *Flatland*. Visual thinking provides us with a four-dimensional reality: three spatial dimensions and a temporal dimension. Information and the reality we construct from it is enhanced by the addition of color. Verbal thinking only describes motion; visual thinking creates it.

Computer sciences are creating a need to better understand the working of visual thinking. Verbal thinking is restricted in both the amount and kind of information it can handle in a reasonable amount of time, more time than it takes a computer to produce the information. In the early days of computer science, computer graphics consisted primarily in putting data in two-dimensional graphic form—bar graphs, pie charts, and so forth. Today, we are provided with three-dimensional graphs that can be rotated through 360 degrees. Not only graphs, but computer-created objects are viewed in three dimensions and can be rotated and moved in a holographic fashion. Color is used to enhance and add to the information produced. And this is not the end of the matter! The future will see not only high-definition video screens, but the inclusion of holography—a true three-dimensional form of representation.

In the foreseeable future we will be able with the help of interactive computer/TVs to create virtual realities on the screen—realities created from our own visual thinking. These realities may be shared with others in all their details, dimensions, motion, and color. A new, more inclusive social reality has been created; an ever-evolving reality via technology integrates information produced by verbal thinking to visual thinking. The culminating result is a visual reality realized from and through verbal input to which everyone can relate.

We need to give visual imagery more consideration. We cannot escape our imagination, because it invariably comes into play. According to Smith (1990), "Distraction is the imagination going off on its own . . . because these alternative worlds have a compelling reality for us" (pp. 47–48).

To the extent that we can learn to integrate the information produced by the verbal thinking of science and technology, our visual "alternative worlds" become effective tools in helping the individual to solve both personal and social problems. The more alternative worlds individuals create, the more options for action can be recognized in their social reality. In other words, the more and better the alternative worlds we create, the more effective we become at surviving in our social reality.

Everyday Imagery for the Classroom

At quite another level, images and their use in thought enable us to use the metaphor to be creative, to be constructive, and to be emotive. The forms of imagery allow us to experience reality in plays, books, movies, art, and personal fantasy. We experience imagination in many possible worlds and it brings vitality to living—generating not only new possibilities and new realities, but new feelings and understandings.

Visual thinking, imagery, and imagination foster social life and cultural values. We must consider how rich these visual experiences can be, how, according to Smith (1990):

[the] worlds of art: music, dance, painting, sculpture, literature, poetry, drama, cinema, and the realms of human ingenuity, like architecture (from garden sheds to ocean liners), design (letterheads to landscapes), and fabrication (clothing to cuisine)—all "crafts" and "trades" as well as the "arts" are created in chiefly visual formats. (p. 72)

Practically speaking, for many of us these visual experiences are presented in television or screen format. When McLuhan (cited in McLuhan & Carpenter, 1960) stated that we are becoming a global village with oral traditions, he was speaking of the impact of television on the thinking of many of us. As an example, TV was modified from a cinematic format, because it was demonstrated that people wanted to be talked to in their living rooms, not lectured. Thus, a more neighborly manner and presentation were developed for TV. Now interactive media, the combination of live television from every part of the world with faxes, reciprocal television, and call-ins by phone and E-mail is demonstrating that electronics is changing our thinking once again. In this year of 1993, we see that the newscaster of old is irrelevant; the commentator seems like a crank. We can see and talk with the principals (President Clinton, our congressperson, other representatives); we do not need to have government interpreted for us. We have become impatient with the assumptions and patronage of pompous news analysts, when we can get so much more for ourselves off CNN (Cable News Network). And yet, the primetime newscasters "don't get it"; they are being challenged about their basic beliefs and their roles. And they have not found a way to make themselves relevant.

We are moving toward electronic communications; the computer screen is crowded with print, but visuals, graphics, maps, and pictures are being presented with greater regularity. It is clear that as we retrieve information from the screen, we will become more visual as we combine technologies to provide film and television interspersal. There is a clear need to elicit and combine all forms of thinking, because thinking in all forms can and does occur simultaneously. How can we promote the kind of learning that does not inhibit thinking in all of its forms; how can we encourage the use of multiple means of learning?

Returning to our television example, children can be found in front of the set on the average of two to three hours a day. For the most part, educators lament this overuse of TV. We note that educational television—the news programs, cinema verite, and documentaries, "Sesame Street," math programs, selected videocassettes, classical films—are of benefit, except that the students view these experiences so passively (though often with great attention). Relating these sometimes moving and rich experiences to the verbal communications that we emphasize in schools has not been a preoccupying thrust of teachers. For example, we show videocassettes on science, have follow-up discussions, go back to the prescribed curriculum and teach for the test, almost as if the film were a diversion from learning. How can we learn from the new texts described by Venezky in a previous chapter? How can we more effectively combine the visual experience with the verbal, logical linear experience and make them both relevant and exciting to learners? We need to work on socializing learners; we need to develop their creative and problem-solving skills; we need to capitalize on their preoccupation with the electronic media; we need to develop clear, verbal forms of communication with students; and we need to find new forms of assessment for evaluating these functions. Forms that show promise for promoting visual thinking in terms of the needs listed earlier are cognitive apprenticeships, cooperative learning, graphic organizers, problem-based learning, and new means for interfacing electronic media and print media.

LEARNING TASKS THAT FOSTER VISUAL THINKING

We summarize the arguments for visual thinking: It develops imagination and creativity; it encourages a departure from the linear logic of print; it elicits emotions and feelings as a kind of "language of emotion"; it fosters cultural values and socialization. What, then, are contexts, strategies, and tasks that will foster the appreciation and integration of imagery, visual thinking, and verbal thinking in schools?

Cognitive Apprenticeships

Cognitive apprenticeships, a visual demonstration of how one learns or proceeds, is one method of implementing visual learning. The notion of cognitive apprenticeships derives from notions of how one learns in the trades (especially current in Germany today and with great success). Using visual presentations, one has a master builder, the journeyman, and the apprentice. The apprentice works with the master, or perhaps the journeyman, and to some extent models his behavior. The first attempts of the apprentice are filled with mistakes and awkwardness. Eventually under the teaching and modeling of the master builder, using scaffolding and coaching, while providing limited frameworks, the apprentice becomes a journeyman and later a master, who may excel his former mentor. For our purposes, the theory gains currently from Vygotsky (cited in Rieber & Carton, 1987) and his notion of zones of proximal development (ZPD), which indicates modeling cognitive processes for others to learn as they are helped. The following steps summarize the method of cognitive apprenticeship:

1. *Demonstrate* what you are trying to get the learners to do or to think or to work on. Provide the best model that you can.

2. *Model* desired behavior with the learners participating in a limited way.

3. *Promote observation* on the part of the learners; in like manner, teachers are observers. The learners are observing to learn more; teachers are observing to perfect their method and performance for learner progress.

4. *Scaffolding* provides learners with the opportunity to practice their new ability in a simplified framework during particular instances of the experience.

5. *Coaching* occurs during analysis and performance. Once learning has been initiated, refining and expanding performance continues.

6. The *fading process* begins when learners have mastered the processes and content of learning in a particular area. The master is no longer needed and learners assumes responsibility for their own professionalism, at least in the area designated for learning.

Cooperative Learning

A second component fostering visual thinking and verbal thinking integration is cooperative learning. Experts have come to the conclusion that one does not learn well apart from verbalization and internalization of knowledge and ideas in a social context. Indeed, current psychological theory, vis-à-vis Vygotsky and Bruner, suggests that unless some kind of verbalization, transaction, and visualization occur with text and/or knowledges in a social context, little knowledge is assimilated in any long-term way.

> Cooperative learning seems to affect such outcomes as: motivation, interest, and persistence in completing tasks; more positive attitudes toward subject matter, classmates, teachers and the school; higher levels of self-esteem, and psychological health; greater use of inferential and critical thinking; improved relations among students, across ethnicities and learning abilities; and increased time on task and greater academic achievement. (Whisler & Williams, 1991)

The use of graphic organizers as a part of the dynamic of task demand and social learning in groups is one way to visualize the outcomes of such discussion. The graphics presented by Calfee (chapter 2) demonstrate such visual thinking growing from group processes.

Problem-Based Learning

Closely related to cooperative learning is problem-based learning. There are numerous world-based problems for students to solve. For instance, a study of garbage, the community construction of a meeting area for teenagers, the creation of a local art show, are real issues that students can address. In the *before* phase of this process, they focus, set goals, review prior knowledge, ask questions, and predict outcomes. *During* the process of problem-based learning, students read, find out, discuss, and think about how to solve the problem. *After* learning, students reflect on what they have learned and apply knowledge to problem solution. In this phase, assessment of learning and problem solving can occur. Graphic organizers (discussed later) are particularly useful in problem-based learning. Solutions do not always result in a practical outcome, but the problem has made learning more real. To solve the problem, all of the resources of the mind, unifying visual and verbal learning, have been activated; moreover, these problem-solving and social skills have been activated as a group function. Problem-based learning is a kind of learning we are going to have to practice in the 21st century.

The Use of Graphics and Graphic Organizers

> Graphic organizers are being examined as valuable, nonlinear ways of representing information, matrically, cyclically, and temporally. Such graphic organizers better reflect the structure of information, making the relationships among the ideas and concepts clearer, thus making information more meaningful and memorable. . . . Teacher constructed organizers seem to work less well than when students construct their own or completely partially constructed organizers. Moreover, teacher modeling [vis-à-vis, the method of cognitive apprenticeships] for constructing organizers in cooperative groups students select graphic organizers without great prompting. (Jones, Tinzmann, & Pierce, 1990, pp. 20–21)

Graphic organizers have the greatest single advantage that they foster the integration of visual thinking and verbal thinking. The group of students who watch TV or a videocassette or a graphic on computers can analyze the visual input from these sources into graphic forms for story grammars, factual analysis, comparative analysis, character analysis, synthesis of ideas, and so on, using this information to create verbal or visual presentations. The student learns to move from visual learning to verbal creation and back again. As the use of visual and graphic media grows, as students create electronic visual presentations as well as verbal ones, literacy will be defined by knowledge of its graphic, pictorial forms as well as its verbal one.

Mandalas and Maps

Clagett (1993) suggested other ways of fostering visual thinking and analysis as a response to literature is through the use of the graphic mandala, a kind of circle with intersecting lines that weaves sun and shadow metaphors into sentences that frame the drawing. The design uses functions of imagine, feel, observe, and analyze. Students draw to answer such questions as:

What animal are you most like?
What plant are you most like?
What color are you most like?
What shape are you most like?
What number are you most like?
What mineral or gem are you most like?
What natural element are you most like: air, earth, fire, or water?

From there she developed other forms of graphic thinking such as graphic maps, concrete abstractions, surrealistic games, group graphics, and literary mandelas. At a very personal, almost mystic level she asked learners to look to themselves for interpretations and reflect on the basic forms of thought from which they derive. These are the kinds of graphics that speak to our emotion and our inner selves.

Knowledge restructuring does not seem to occur spontaneously. Rather, tasks that require a different format, which aid in the assimilation and accommodation of knowledge, can be created through visual thinking that utilizes graphic organizers. These graphically organized tasks must be meaningful, complex, and long-term in nature. For this reason, the graphic organizer, with its visual mosaic of interweaving information aids in the restructuring and critical thinking task. Graphic organizers:

Mimic semantic memory structures, more like what the brain actually does.
Illustrate and explain often complex relationships on a single page.
Depict key skills and ideas with task demands.
Promote clear understanding of content.
Serve as "mental maps" to depict complex relationships.
Serve as a tool for transfer of a thinking process to other lessons featuring the same relationships.
Allow for many higher level kinds of analysis.
Model the habit of critical, analytical, creative thinking about concepts in the process of learning.
Foster clarity, objectiveness, and interaction.
Show information as part of a *system* or as contrasting concepts.
Serve as notations and maps for writing on a topic.
Record information for more abstract examination, discussion, and evaluation.
Help students think and rethink possible solutions.
Aid in the solution of real-world problems.

May be used to analyze TV and film presentations.

Aid in *writing* of essays, reports, and oral talks.

Can be used in a read-depict-write format.

Aid in cooperative learning, reciprocal teaching, inquiry learning, and individual study.

Help prepare effective lectures and demonstrations.

Are highly adaptable to all content areas.

Are highly adaptable to all grade levels.

Aid organization of lecture discussions.

What may be said for graphic organizers may be cited as a benefit for developing visual literacy. Developing visual literacy in literature has become a concern for teachers. Short (1993) gave a lengthy list of children's books to develop just such sensitivity; each entry specifies particular means for giving children insight into beauty, aesthetics, form, and color. This compendium of materials forms the basis for teaching for visual literacy.

We can summarize our thinking by citing Arnheim (1969), who closes his work, and ours, with this statement.

> What is needed it seems to me is the systematic training of visual sensitivity as an indispensable part of an educator's preparation for his profession. The difference between a picture that makes its point and one that does not can be discerned by anybody whose natural responses to perceptual form have been cultivated rather than stifled.
>
> The experimental and theoretical basis for visual education is being developed in psychology. Practical experience is best provided by work in the arts. It is not good strategy, however, to label perceptual sensitivity as artistic or aesthetic, because this means removing it to a privileged domain, reserved for the talents and aspirations of the specialist. Visual thinking calls, more broadly for the ability to see visual shapes as images of the patterns of forces that underlie our existence—the functioning of minds, or bodies or machines, the structure of societies or ideas.
>
> Art works best when it remains unacknowledged. It observes that shapes and objects and events, by displaying their own nature, can evoke those deeper and simpler powers in which man recognizes himself. It is one of the rewards we earn for thinking by what we see. (p. 315)

REFERENCES

Arnheim, R. (1969). *Visual thinking*. London: Faber & Faber Ltd.

Claggett, F. (1993). *Drawing your own conclusions*. Portsmouth, NH: Heinemann.

John-Steiner, V. (1985). *Notebooks of the mind*. New York: Harper & Row.

Jones, B. V., Tinzman, M. B., & Pierce, J. (1992). How thoughts are made. In C. Collins & J. Mangiere (Eds.), *Teaching thinking*. Hillsdale, NJ: Lawrence Erlbaum Associates.

McLuhan, M., & Carpenter, E. (1960). *Explorations in communication.* Boston: Beacon.

Rieber, R. W., & Carton, A. S. (Eds.). (1987). *The collected works of L. S. Vygotsky.* New York: Plenum.

Short, K. G. (1993). Visual literacy: Exploring art and illustration in children's books. *Reading Teacher, 46*(6), 506–517.

Smith, F. (1990). *To think.* New York: Teachers College Press.

Whisler, N., & Williams, J. (1990). *Literature and cooperative learning.* Sacramento, CA: Literature Coop.

9

Cooperative Learning and Literacy Instruction

Robert J. Stevens
Pennsylvania State University

Cooperative learning has become a significant and widely used method for restructuring classrooms and schools over the past 15 years. What started as a means for improving interpersonal relations between students, giving them ways to interact and develop social skills, has grown into a national restructuring movement led by both teachers and researchers who want students to become more actively engaged in and take more responsibility for their own learning. Cooperative learning has helped to transform classrooms in elementary schools, secondary schools, and universities from passive learning situations with the teacher dominating the instructional conversation into engaging environments where students are active co-participants in the learning process.

HISTORICAL BACKGROUND

Cooperative learning is not a new idea to the theory or practice of education. Early uses of cooperative learning certainly occurred in one-room schoolhouses, where one teacher was forced to teach students with a very wide range of abilities. A natural to the problems caused by that diversity was to have older or more proficient students tutor younger or less proficient students. Students teaching students and students learning from one another is a philosophical idea, and probably an instructional technique that goes back much further. Some of the earliest references to learning through peer collaboration are in the writings of Quintilian (1st century AD), Comenius (17th century), and Dewey (early 20th century), all of whom recommended the potential benefits of students teaching and being taught by each other (D. Johnson, R. Johnson, & Holubec, 1991).

Social-Psychological Roots of Cooperative Learning

The more recent history of cooperative learning can be traced to two primary sources: Allport's social contact theory and Deutsch's studies on cooperation versus competition. Allport's (1954) work addressed the issues surrounding prejudice and his concern for understanding how prejudice can be reduced and interpersonal relations improved. In his study of social groups that had lower levels of racial prejudice, Allport found that there were a few common constructs: close social contact, common group goal, and equal status contact. From this evolved his social contact theory that prejudice could be decreased and interpersonal relations improved if people of different kinds were put into situations of close social contact where all members were given equal status and the group interacted in order to achieve a common goal.

Deutsch was a contemporary of Allport and was also interested in the dynamics of group interaction, primarily with respect to the group processes resulting from cooperative and competitive situations. Deutsch conceived of group dynamics as directly related to the goal structure and how the success of the participants are interrelated. "In a cooperative situation the goals are so linked that everybody sinks or swims together, while in the competitive situation if one swims the other must sink" (Deutsch, 1949b, p. 129). A cooperative goal structure was one where one individual's success was dependent on the success of the other. In a competitive goal structure an individual's success reduced the chance of others being successful.

Based on this theoretical notion, Deutsch studied the processes, interactions, and outcomes of cooperative and competitive groups. He found that students who worked in cooperative settings had more positive peer relations, more frequent and more positive communication among one another, and higher group productivity (Deutsch, 1949a). Students who worked in competitive settings were more self-centered in their work and had more aggressive communications about their work with their peers. The work by Deutsch, and others who elaborated upon his theory (e.g., Grossack, 1954), provided the foundation for our understanding of the dynamics of cooperation and the potential benefits of cooperative learning in terms of interpersonal relations. This provided the empirical research substantiating Allport's social contact theory.

These social-psychological developments were of particular interest in the educational setting in the late 1960s and the 1970s when desegregation was a major issue facing many schools. Schools often became desegregated by court order and used a variety of processes like redistricting and busing to achieve the desired racial balance. However, even though schools were racially desegregated, studies found that within the schools students segregated themselves, thus minimizing the intended social contact and any positive effect it would have on prejudice (Gerard & Miller, 1975; St. John, 1975). Simply putting students of different races together in the same physical location did little to influence interracial relationships and prejudice.

Cooperation and Interracial Relations

In an attempt to help desegregated schools achieve their goal of improved racial relations and decreased racial prejudice, educational psychologists and educational sociologists integrated the ideas of Allport's social contact theory with Deutsch's research on cooperation and competition in developing cooperative learning instructional models for schools (e.g., Jigsaw by Aronson & Bridgeman, 1981; Teams-Games-Tournaments by DeVries & Edwards, 1973).

Over the last 20 years there has been a great deal of research on the effects of cooperative learning on students' peer relations and interracial friendships. Generally, these studies have shown that when students work on heterogeneous learning teams to achieve a group goal students develop more positive peer relations, more positive attitudes toward peers of a different race or ethnic group, and more interracial friendships (Sharan, 1980; Slavin, 1990). These studies have covered most grade levels from elementary school through secondary school, have used a variety of content areas, and have been conducted in a variety of countries (including Canada, Israel, and the United States).

The dynamics of the classrooms and the breadth of these sociological results directly addressed the issues related to effectively desegregating schools. The social contact initiated in the cooperative learning setting was not limited to only the situations where cooperation was implemented. D. Johnson and R. Johnson (1981) found that students in classes that used cooperative learning had significantly more interracial interactions both in the classroom and outside of the classroom during their free time. This positive transfer of the effects of cooperative learning on students' social relations was also seen in their friendships. Hansell and Slavin (1981) found that cooperative learning not only encouraged more interracial friendships, but that many of those friendships were very close and reciprocal. Further, Slavin (1979) found that the effects on students' friendships remained after their cooperative learning experience was over. A year after being in cooperative learning classes students still listed more interracial friends than did their peers who had been in traditionally taught classes. Cooperative learning clearly helped restructure desegregated schools to accomplish their goal as set out in Allport's theory, close contact of equal status to achieve a common goal significantly reduces prejudice. The cooperative processes and the kinds of interactions in which students engage have the potential to alter racial attitudes and prejudices and to greatly improve all peer relations in schools.

Cooperative Learning Effects on Achievement

As cooperative learning research expanded in the educational setting there became an increased concern for academic outcomes as well as social relations outcomes. During the 1970s generic cooperative learning models (e.g., Jigsaw, Student Teams Achievement Division—STAD, Learning Together) became more integrated with academic content and the teacher's instructional objectives. Implicit in this connection was that students could improve their social relations and social skills while learning content and mastering objectives that were central to the curriculum. With this additional academic emphasis in cooperative learning, studies began to investigate the effects on academic as well as social outcomes.

By the 1980s there were a number of different types of cooperative learning. The research literature contained a large number of studies on the effects of these models in a variety of content areas and at a range of grade levels. In order to compile these results and to summarize them adequately, reviews and meta-analyses were done to determine the effects of cooperative learning (e.g., Sharan, 1980; Slavin, 1983, 1990). At first the effects on students' achievement seemed inconclusive and even somewhat contradictory. However, Slavin (1983, 1990) considered the constructs of the various models and found that there was a pattern of results related to whether the models included two specific components: a group goal and individual accountability. Cooperative learning models that had both constructs indicated fairly consistent average effects on achievement of approximately one third a standard deviation on all outcome measures (effect size[1] of +.30), and nearly a quarter standard deviation on standardized achievement tests (effect size = +.21) (Slavin, 1990). Cooperative learning models

---

[1]An effect size is a metric to determine the magnitude of effect an experimental treatment has as compared to the control group, as measured in standard deviations (Glass, McGaw, & Smith, 1981). An effect size is the difference between the experimental group mean and the control group mean divided by the control group standard deviation. In educational research effect sizes of approximately +.25 are considered educationally significant; however the measures used and the characteristics and length of the study can influence the effects. For example, standardized achievement tests tend to be more stable and typically produce smaller effect sizes.

without one or both of those constructs had small and insignificant effects on the average.

Group goals and individual accountability are two components that transcend all cooperative learning models and are linchpins to their effectiveness. The group goal gives the students a *reason to cooperate* and gives students a reason to communicate on an equal and meaningful basis. With a group goal the students need to integrate and coordinate their activity in order to attain the goal. The group goal creates interdependence between the members of the group. They can only succeed as a group if each of them is successful.

The individual accountability gives each student a *reason to learn* the content. In the cooperative learning group it helps prevent students simply "going along for the ride" and letting all of the other members do the work. With individual accountability there is a way for the teacher to make sure everyone meets the instructional objective and it gives the clear expectation that each student must learn.

When the two components are put together the individual accountability can help the group attain the group goal. For example, the group goal may be measured by summing or averaging the group member's score on the individual accountability assessment. The sum or average can then be compared to a preestablished criterion to determine goal attainment. In such a case, the group's success directly depends on the success of each person. Upon recognizing that interdependence, students respond accordingly by teaching, motivating, and monitoring one another as they work on mastering the academic content.

Mainstreaming Special Education Students with Cooperative Learning

During the past decade there has been a great deal of interest and research on the issue of mainstreaming special education students. The goals of mainstreaming are to improve the social acceptance and increase the achievement of handicapped students (W. Stainback & S. Stainback, 1984; Will, 1986). Furthermore, federal legislation (PL 94-142) has mandated that handicapped students be educated in the least restrictive environment possible as a means of attaining these goals. However, the results of mainstreaming have been slow to show significant effects on either of these goals, and often the results have been contradictory (D. Fuchs & L. Fuchs, 1991). Some research suggests that simply putting academically handicapped students in regular education classes is not sufficient to produce significantly better achievement or student attitudes (Marston, 1987). Instead, effective mainstreaming seems to require a significant degree of school restructuring to provide programs and support for the instructional needs of academically handicapped students (W. Stainback & S. Stainback, 1991).

Cooperative learning is a model that has been used to facilitate main-streaming and to provide the additional support needed to successfully accommodate academically handicapped, or learning-disabled, students in the regular classroom. A review of this research has found results similar to those general results already cited: When cooperative learning models include group goals and individual accountability, and when the studies last at least 4 weeks, cooperative learning has a significant positive impact on the achievement of mainstreamed learning disabled-students (Stevens & Slavin, 1991b). The magnitude of these effects was substantial, averaging +.48 standard deviations. Studies have also documented that handicapped students mainstreamed in classes using cooperative learning are also more socially accepted by their regular education peers (R. Johnson & D. Johnson, 1981; Slavin, 1984) and that learning-disabled students have more friends and are selected as friends more frequently by regular education students in cooperative learning classes (Stevens & Slavin, 1992). Thus cooperative learning has shown some effectiveness as a vehicle to facilitate mainstreaming mildly handicapped students and attaining the academic and social goals desired.

Cooperative Learning and Gifted Students

Despite the well-documented advantages of cooperative learning described previously, there has remained significant concern about the impact of cooperative learning on academically gifted students, students typically in the top 5% on standardized achievement measures. Parents, gifted educators, and some researchers have voiced concern that cooperative learning has gifted students teaching slower students in the class at the expense of their own learning (Allan, 1991; Willis, 1990).

Although there are very little data evaluating the effects of cooperative learning on gifted students, one study at the elementary school level does suggest that these fears are unwarranted. A study of schoolwide use of cooperative learning in second through sixth grade compared gifted students who remained in cooperative learning classes to gifted students in traditional schools who were in pull-out gifted education programs. The results indicated that gifted students in cooperative learning gained significantly more on standardized measures of reading and mathematics achievement than did their peers who received specialized gifted education (Slavin, 1991; Stevens & Slavin, 1992). The magnitude of the effects for cooperative learning ranged from +.32 to +.96 in reading and +.19 to +.62 in mathematics.

These results suggest that common conceptions about gifted students in cooperative learning and the effects of cooperative learning on gifted students may not be accurate. It seems that cooperative learning may not only be beneficial for gifted students, but they may in fact reap the greatest academic benefits from it. However, these results are limited to one study and there is clearly a need for more research on the effects of using cooperative learning with gifted students, both in heterogeneous classes and with accelerated gifted programs, to determine its effects on gifted students' achievement, attitudes, and relations with their peers.

Cooperative Learning and Cognitive Psychology

The Nature of the Cooperative Dialogue.   Research into the nature of students' dialogue during cooperative learning activities and cognitive psychological theories of learning helps us better understand how and why cooperative learning works. Webb and her associates (Webb, 1985; Webb & Kenderski, 1984) studied the dialogue of students working in groups where one condition used individual rewards (individualistic structure) and the other used group used rewards based on individual scores (cooperative structure). They found very different types of communication patterns in the two kinds of structures. In the individualistic structure students often made errors without receiving feedback and when they did get feedback it was most often terminal feedback (answers rather than explanations). In the cooperative structure the students more frequently asked questions and more frequently received explanations in response to those questions. Similarly, in cooperative structures students' errors were corrected more frequently and the corrections were typically in the form of explanations of how to arrive at correct answers.

There were also significant relationships between these interactions and students' achievement. They found that terminal feedback and no feedback on errors or in response to questions was consistently negatively correlated to achievement. However, receiving explanations was often highly correlated with achievement and giving explanations was consistently highly correlated with achievement (Webb & Kenderski, 1984). Although there are benefits for students who receive explanations, the results suggest that the largest impact of cooperative learning on achievement is for those students who give elaborative explanations to others in the cooperative setting.

Cognitive Learning Theory.   Cognitive theories of learning help explain the results described by Webb. As students interact cooperatively they explain strategies to one another in their own words, helping them further process the complex cognitive activity or content (A. Brown & Campione, 1986; Wittrock, 1986). "Understanding is more likely to occur when a student is required to explain, elaborate, or defend his or her position to theirs; the burden of explanation is often the push needed to make him or her evaluate, integrate, and elaborate knowledge in new ways" (A. Brown & Campione, 1986, p. 1066). Collaborative activity requires students to reflect on their knowledge to make generalizations and elaborations that they can convey to their peers. Making generalizations and elaborations requires students to understand the cognitive relations of the new knowledge and to relate it to their prior knowledge, which is an effective way to improve their "depth of processing" of the information (A. Brown & Campione, 1986; Wittrock, 1986). Thus when students explain to one another they become more actively engaged in learning and constructing meaning from what has been presented.

Vygotsky (1978) also suggested that the importance of collaborative learning and interaction with peers during the learning process may go beyond the effects due to the elaboration processes, particularly as is relevant for the student who receives the explanations and who is not elaborating. Observing others and practicing with peer support and dialogue helps learners internalize the cognitive functions they are attempting to master, those within their "zone of proximal development" (Vygotsky, 1978). Particularly when learning complex cognitive tasks, such as reading comprehension or writing, it may be particularly important for students to engage in the collaborative dialogue to improve the efficiency and effectiveness of the learning process.

Cognitive Apprenticeship.   The notion of a cognitive apprenticeship has evolved in part from Vygotsky's (1978) notion of socially shared cognition. Just as a traditional apprenticeship involved a learner or an apprentice studying with a master craftsperson to learn a craft, so too does a cognitive apprenticeship involve learners observing and interacting with experts or more proficient peers about cognitive processes (Collins, J. Brown, & Newman, 1989). A cognitive apprenticeship uses social experience to shape the learning and integration of cognitive processes. An apprenticeship notion of learning begins with the students observing models from those who are experts or are more proficient in the cognitive task, such as the teacher or more proficient peers. This is followed by coaching or guiding the initial practice as learners make their initial attempts with the new process. Part of the coaching involves getting feedback from the "master," prompts or cognitive supports that help the learner do the process (i.e., guides for the process). Initially the prompts provide a scaffold that aids students in their use of cognitive process. Gradually the scaffold is reduced by fading the prompts and instructional support. This helps learners gradually take on more responsibility for the cognitive activity and to rely less on external support. Eventually the supports are completely removed and learners engage in the processes independently. Finally, learners also engage in self-reflection following their completion of the process. During self-reflection students critically assess their use of the process and the quality or appropriateness of the resulting product. The goal is not only to evaluate the use of the process, but also to understand the relationship between the use of the cognitive process and the product of the process (Collins et al., 1989).

One of the important aspects of a cognitive apprenticeship is that it externalizes or attempts to make overt cognitive processes. This is particularly important for learning cognitively complex activity because it typically is not bound by explicit rules that are easily taught. Instead we use heuristics or strategies that are often ambiguous and need to be applied flexibly. Part of this flexible use of the strategies involves learners focusing primarily on the use of the processes more so than on the product of the processes. This is further emphasized during the apprenticeship's self-reflection on the learner's use of the processes. By reflecting on their use of the processes learners get a better understanding of how to use the processes, how to monitor their use, and how to correct errors or revise the use of the processes if necessary.

Well-structured cooperative learning seems to be just such a cognitive apprenticeship. As students explain to one another they are essentially acting as mentors in the learning process, giving explanations of how they engage in the process, acting as another model, and giving apprentices feedback and guidance as they attempt to implement the new cognitive process.

Application of Cognitive Apprenticeship to Teaching Literacy Skills.   A cognitive apprenticeship approach to instruction may be particularly important when teaching content that is not well structured, like reading comprehension, math problem solving, creative writing, and drawing. These ill-structured domains of knowledge have similar characteristics in that the cognitive processes are not rule based. Instead the processes are less prescriptive and use strategies or heuristics that often lack specific, well-defined steps. For example, in creative writing we give students some strategies for writing better, but we cannot actually tell them to do Step 1, then Step 2, and so on, and they will successfully master the process. Another characteristic of ill-structured domains is that there is a wider range of acceptable products for the process, whereas well-structured domains tend to have a narrow range of acceptable answers or even one correct answer. For example, there are a number of ways readers can state their summary of a paragraph, a summary that represents the information in the paragraph. Finally, in an ill-structured domain the process used for arriving at the answer or product is as important as, or more important than, the product itself. For example, how students arrive at their comprehension of the paragraph's main ideas is as important as the student's summary of them.

As a result of these characteristics of ill-structured domains, they place unique demands on the teaching and learning process. Because the rules and processes are rather vague and primarily covert, the presentation phase of teaching, where the teacher tells students "how to do it," is particularly weak. The best that teachers can do is give students an introduction to and a model of the strategic processes. However, students need to learn how and when to use the strategies. That puts more pressure on other components of the teaching–learning process. When students initially practice their use of the strategic processes, they need additional support and guidance to help them learn to use the processes and to correct errors or misconceptions that have resulted from the inherent lack of explicitness in them. A cognitive apprenticeship, such as cooperative learning with its added support, focuses on the cognitive processes and provides the guided practice necessary for novices to learn the processes imbedded in these ill-structured domains.

THE CIRC PROGRAM

The Cooperative Integrated Reading and Composition (CIRC) program (Stevens, Madden, Slavin, & Farnish, 1987) is a cooperative learning approach to teaching elementary reading and language arts. The program applies recent findings from research on cognitive psychology, reading instruction, writing instruction, teacher effectiveness, and cooperative learning in a comprehensive model for literacy instruction. The CIRC program consists of three main elements: story-related activities, direct instruction in comprehension strategies, and integrated writing and language arts. The cycle of instruction in reading and language arts uses a cooperative learning type of cognitive apprenticeship described previously.

The instruction begins with the teacher presenting the new information or strategies through models and explanations. The students receive cognitive support during the initial phase of practice in the form of collaboration with their peers and teacher guidance and feedback. Gradually the cognitive support is diminished by reducing the guidance from the teacher while allowing the peers to work closely with partners. Eventually the support is reduced to the point where the students work independently and receive occasional feedback from their peers or the teacher.

Students are assigned to heterogeneous-ability teams in which they collaborate on structured follow-up activities. Cooperative activities are reinforced through group goals and recognition based on the points that team members receive for their individual performance on all quizzes and compositions. Teams that meet a minimum average criterion of 90% on the week's activities are designated "superteams" and receive attractive certificates in recognition of their performance; those averaging 80% to 89% are designated greatteams" and those averaging 70% to 79% are designated "goodteams," and these teams receive less elaborate certificates as recognition. As noted, previous research has established the instructional effectiveness of the use of heterogeneous teams that receive recognition on the basis of individual team members' performance (Slavin, 1983, 1990).

Story-Related Activities

Students use their basal readers as an anthology of stories. Stories are introduced and discussed in teacher-led reading groups, which meet for about 20 minutes each day. During reading groups the teacher introduces the new vocabulary, sets the purpose for reading, discusses the story after the students have read it, and so on.

After the stories are introduced, students are given a series of cooperative learning follow-up activities to do as teams or partners. The seatwork activities are directly related to the teacher-directed instruction of the reading group and to the basal stories, with the added cognitive support of working cooperatively with peers while completing the activities. The goal is to make the activities more engaging and useful. The activities are as follows (see also Stevens et al., 1987):

Partner Reading.   Students read the story silently first, then orally with their partners. During partner reading the partners take turns reading aloud, alternating after each paragraph. This repeated reading of the story gives the students significantly more practice decoding words in context than is found in the quantity of oral reading in traditional reading lessons (Thurlow, Groden, Ysseldyke, & Algozzine, 1984). Repeated oral reading has been found to significantly contribute to students' decoding ability and reading fluency (Allington, 1984; Dahl, 1979; Samuels, 1979; Shany, 1992). Recent research has also shown that oral reading may have a more significant positive effect on students' reading comprehension ability than does silent reading (Wilkinson, Wardrop, & Anderson, 1988). The goal of partner reading was to provide students with both an opportunity to read the story silently and to read a significant portion of the story orally with the hopes of building decoding, reading fluency, and reading comprehension as a result.

Treasure Hunts.   The goal of the treasure hunts was to improve students' comprehension and understanding of the story they have read and to give students an understanding of the structure of stories so they become sensitive to top-level structure and use it to improve their comprehension.

Students are given questions related to the story that focus on understanding what happened in the story. The treasure hunts use questions related to the story structure or story grammar of the selection. Story structure questions help students improve their comprehension of the specific story and teach students a top-level structure that can help improve their ability to comprehend new stories with similar structures (Fitzgerald & Spiegel, 1983; Meyer, Brandt, & Bluth, 1980; Short & Ryan, 1982).

Students were also asked to predict how the characters might solve problems that occurred in the story and to clarify why the characters behaved in a particular way. Research has shown that prediction and clarification questions improve students' comprehension of what they have read, and increase their cognitive processing of the information presented in the story (Palincsar & A. Brown, 1984).

Words Outloud.   Students' comprehension of a story is in part related to their ability to decode the words quickly and accurately. When students lack automaticity in decoding, comprehension suffers (LaBerge & Samuels, 1974; Perfetti, 1985). The CIRC materials provide students with a list of the new vocabulary for the story. These new words are introduced by the teacher in the teaching group and students practice them prior to reading the story. Students also practice the new words with their partners as a follow-up activity as a way of distributing the practice on the words. The goals of the words outloud practice is for the students to develop automaticity on the new vocabulary and for them to retain their recognition of those words for subsequent stories.

Word Meaning.   Research has shown that students' knowledge of vocabulary and their ability to quickly access that knowledge can have a significant impact on their reading comprehension (Beck, Perfetti, & McKeown, 1982). Thus effective vocabulary instruction is a critical component of reading instruction. However, simply teaching students the meaning of new words is not sufficient for improving their ability to know the words or to improve their comprehension (Mezynski, 1983). Effective reading instruction develops the understanding of the meaning of the word through using the word in meaningful context and linking the meaning of the word to the learner's prior knowledge.

In CIRC students were asked to write the meaning of the new vocabulary word and to use it in a meaningful sentence that provided sufficient context to tell what the word meant. The goals were to get the students actively engaged in thinking about and using the word and to get the students to use their relevant background knowledge in writing the sentence to help them learn the meaning and to link the vocabulary word to a meaningful context.

Story Retelling.   After reading the story and discussing it in their reading groups with the guidance of the teacher, the students summarize the main events in the story to their partners. The goal of the activity is for the students to briefly describe the event in their own words to help them further process what has happened in the story, and to help them practice recalling important information. Summarizing and paraphrasing information that has been read helps students generate relations among the information presented in text and relate it to their prior knowledge (Wittrock, 1986). The story retelling activity engaged students in actively making these relations in order to improve their comprehension of the story that had been read, and it was hoped that this skill would generalize to other reading tasks so students would learn to actively generate these relations without being prompted to do so.

Story-Related Writing.   After reading the story and completing the aforementioned activities, the students are given a writing topic that relates to the theme or events in the story. The students are asked to write a few paragraphs in response to the prompt. Typically the prompts ask students to elaborate on what has happened in the story or to relate an event or events in the story to their own experiences. The goal of this activity, like that of story retelling, is to actively engage students in generating relations between the information they have read and their prior knowledge and experience (Wittrock, 1986). Previous research with elementary school children has shown that writing stories about text improves students' comprehension of that text and their ability to make inferences based on that text (Paris, Lindauer, & Cox, 1977).

Quizzes.   At the end of the activity cycle for a story students are given a comprehension quiz about the story, are asked to write meaningful sentences for vocabulary words, and are asked to read the new vocabulary aloud to the teacher. The students complete these quizzes independently. The goal of the quizzes is to provide accountability for all students to insure that they master the new vocabulary and comprehend the story. Previous research on cooperative learning has shown that individual accountability is an important component of cooperative learning programs that are effective in producing achievement gain (Slavin, 1983, 1990). The quiz scores are used as points for the individuals in determining the team scores, as described previously. In this way the team score, and the resultant group goal, is based on individual accountability. This connects the success of the group with the success of *each* of the individuals in the group and motivates the group members to help one another.

Independent Reading

Students were also asked to spend 20 minutes reading silently from a trade book of their choice each evening as their reading homework. The goals of this activity were: (a) to increase the time that students spent in sustained silent reading, which has been shown to be strongly related to the development of reading comprehension abilities (Anderson, Hiebert, Scott, & Wilkinson, 1985; Anderson, Wilson, & Fielding, 1988), and (b) to encourage students to engage in reading as an independent activity. Parents were asked to monitor the independent reading and to encourage students to read for at least the prescribed time. Students were required to complete a book report on a trade book every 2 weeks as a means of accountability for this independent reading. Students who read more than one trade book in 2 weeks were encouraged to do an additional book report and earned bonus points for their team score.

Explicit Instruction in Comprehension Strategies

One day each week students received explicit instruction in specific reading comprehension strategies, such as strategies for identifying main ideas, strategies for making inferences, and strategies for drawing conclusions about what they have read. The strategic instruction included providing students with comprehension-fostering strategies, metacognitive self-regulation strategies, and strategic awareness about the importance of and appropriate use of the strategies.

Recent research in applying cognitive psychology to reading instruction has consistently supported the effectiveness of providing explicit instruction in reading comprehension strategies. Strategic instruction has been found effective across a variety of skills, including summarizing (Day, 1986), identifying main ideas (Baumann, 1984; Stevens, 1988; Stevens, Slavin, & Farnish, 1991), answering literal questions (Raphael, 1980), predicting and clarifying (A. Brown & Palincsar, 1982; Palincsar & A. Brown, 1984), and making inferences (Dewitz, Carr, & Patberg, 1987).

Much of the research in reading comprehension has included not only the "how to" of comprehension strategies but also self-regulation skills and strategic awareness. Self-regulation is an important metacognitive skill that helps students monitor and control their use of comprehension strategies, which is important for effective use of strategies (A. Brown, Campione, & Day, 1981). Similarly, strategic awareness provides the student with situational knowledge about when to use strategies and their usefulness. Strategic awareness has been found to be a useful component when training students in new reading comprehension and metacomprehension strategies (Paris, Cross, & Lipson, 1984; Paris & Jacobs, 1984).

Integrated Writing and Language Arts

During language arts time the teachers used a writing and language arts curriculum that uses a process approach to writing instruction. Students spent approximately 3 days a week engaged in the steps of the writing process: planning, writing drafts, revising, editing, and making a final draft (see Calkins, 1983; Graves, 1983). During each of the steps of the writing process the students get consultation from their peers to help them plan and revise what they are writing. The other 2 days of the week the students receive instruction in specific language mechanics and language usage skills that are related to their writing. Each skill lesson concluded in an applied activity where students use the skill in writing.

In a writing process approach to language arts instruction students spend significantly more time in extended writing activities than in traditional language arts instruction (Bridge & Hiebert, 1985; Graves, 1978). Previous research on writing process models has found that a sequence of planning, drafting, revising, and editing that uses peer responses and feedback produces significantly better students' process approaches and yields significant results on language expression achievement measures, as well as on measures of writing performance, without any decrement in students' language mechanics achievement (Hillocks, 1984; Stevens et al., 1987).

ACADEMIC, SOCIAL, AND AFFECTIVE
OUTCOMES OF CIRC

Previous studies have documented that the CIRC program can produce positive effects on third- and fourth-grade students' reading and language achievement (Stevens et al., 1987). However, these studies were of relatively short duration (12 and 16 weeks) and were limited to two grade levels. However, questions remained: How applicable was CIRC and the processes and activities in CIRC to other elementary grade levels? How much impact would CIRC have in long-term implementations (e.g., a year or longer) where CIRC was treated as the school's literacy program rather than an experimental intervention?

Description of the Study

In order to answer the questions presented previously, a long-term investigation of the effects of CIRC was planned (Stevens & Slavin, 1991a). For 2 years three elementary schools implemented the CIRC program as their reading and writing/language arts programs. The CIRC program was used in second through sixth grades in 31 classes in the schools. The CIRC schools were matched with four nonexperimental schools with similar socioeconomic makeups and similar levels of initial achievement. The student populations were primarily from working class suburbs in Maryland, and ranged from 0% to 10% minority students ($M = 5.2\%$) and from 6% to 13% disadvantaged students ($M = 9\%$).

The seven schools used similar reading and language arts curricula, as mandated by the school district, although the CIRC school materials were altered as described earlier in the description of the program. All of the schools also had similar amounts of time allocated for reading and language arts, typically 60 to 90 min daily for reading and 45 min daily for language arts, again as mandated by the school district.

Traditional Literacy Instruction.   The nonexperimental schools used fairly traditional methods and curricula for literacy instruction. Reading generally consisted of using a basal series from the district's adoption list with two or three reading groups. Instruction in the reading group consisted of vocabulary instruction, story discussion, and a brief opportunity for oral reading turns. Following the reading group the students worked independently to read the story silently, answer a few questions about the story, and complete seatwork activity provided by the basal series or written by the teacher. Language arts instruction usually involved the teacher providing whole-class instruction on mechanics skills. Approximately once a week the teacher provided writing instruction and had the students engage in an independent writing activity.

Cooperative Learning Literacy Instruction.   The three experimental schools used the CIRC program, as described here, for their literacy instruction. As with the nonexperimental classes, the CIRC classes used basal series selected from the district's adoption list with two or three reading groups. However, the instructional activities and follow-up materials were those of the CIRC program. The language arts instruction used a writing process approach, as described in the CIRC program description.

Training CIRC Teachers.   All of the teachers in the school, including special education teachers, were trained in the CIRC program for 2 days (1 day for reading and 1 day for language arts). During the training, teachers were given explanations of how to do classroom processes and what the rationale was behind them. Program elements were simulated during the training, with the trainer acting as the "teacher" and the teachers acting as the "students." The teachers were also given a detailed manual for the CIRC program.

During the initial 6 weeks of implementation, the project staff observed the experimental teachers three or four times a week to monitor their implementation. The staff coached the teachers by providing feedback on the implementation and answering their questions about the CIRC program. The implementation of the cooperative learning processes and the teacher-led direct instruction were emphasized as critical elements. Also of concern was mainstreaming academically handicapped students into the regular classrooms and integrating them in the cooperative learning teams and activities, as well as the special education teachers' implementation of the CIRC model. Periodically the project staff held afterschool meetings to provide further feedback and discussions of implementation issues with the teachers. As the teachers became more proficient with CIRC the observations occurred less frequently and at more random intervals.

Most of the teachers remained in the CIRC schools throughout the 2-year period, but at the end of the first year one retired, three transferred, and one teacher moved out of state. To maintain the implementation of CIRC in all of the classes, we held a 2-day training in CIRC for the new teachers in the summer between the first and second years of the study. That training followed the same procedure as described here, and we monitored and coached the new teachers just as we had the teachers the previous year.

Mainstreaming of Academically Handicapped Students. One of the goals of the CIRC program was to provide an instructional system that facilitates mainstreaming of academically handicapped students. In CIRC the special education teachers discontinued pull-out remedial reading instruction for learning-disabled students. Instead of pulling learning-disabled students from different classrooms and taking them to the resource room for reading instruction, the special education teachers went into the regular classroom with the learning-disabled students and team taught with the regular education teacher. In this way it was possible to give the academically handicapped students the additional instructional support they required. The mainstreamed students received reading instruction in an ability-level reading group often comprised of both handicapped and nonhandicapped students. Typically the regular education teacher provided the reading group instruction for the students. The special education teacher provided follow-up on and an extension of the instruction the regular teacher had provided. The special education teacher provided more support for the learning-disabled students by giving additional instruction related to what was covered in the reading group, or by guiding them and giving them feedback during their initial practice activities.

Typically, the special education teacher was in the classroom for about 30 min per day, which was approximately half of the total time allocated for reading instruction and was similar to the amount of time the special education teachers in the control schools spent using a "pull-out" model.

The mainstreamed learning-disabled students also were integrated into the cooperative learning teams within the class, distributing the special education students among the teams with the nonhandicapped students. The mainstreamed students interacted with the other students on academic tasks as they worked on the cooperative learning teams, giving the learning-disabled students all of the potential cognitive advantages of cooperative learning described previously. The cooperative learning processes also provided a way for the special education students to become socially mainstreamed through academic interactions with their nonhandicapped classmates.

Measures

Achievement Tests. Students' scores on the California Achievement Test Form C were obtained from the school district's records and used as a pretest to determine if the treatment groups were equivalent. The district administered achievement tests during the fall of third and fifth grade, so third- and fifth-graders' pretests were recent whereas fourth-graders' scores were a year old. The school district did not test the second graders, so we had the teachers administer Form C to their students each fall as a pretest for second grade. Because the initial cohort of sixth-graders were not going to be in the CIRC program during the second year, we did not include them in the analyses, although their teachers did implement CIRC in their classrooms.

In May 1988 and May 1989 (the end of the first year and the end of the second year, respectively) all of the teachers administered the California Achievement Test Form E, using appropriate levels for their grades. Students were given the reading comprehension, reading vocabulary, language mechanics, and language expression subtests.

Metacognition Measure. Improved metacognition is often the goal of instructional interventions but it is seldom measured as an outcome. Instead the researcher infers differences in metacognition through measures of reading comprehension, an inference that may not be warranted (Paris, Wasik, & Turner, 1991). In an attempt to measure students' knowledge of their reading processes and strategies more directly, Jacobs and Paris (1987) developed an informal assessment of metacognition called the Index of Reading Awareness. The index measures students' awareness of comprehension strategies, their knowledge of which strategies are appropriate for specific situations, and their knowledge of what to do if their comprehension is flawed. These constructs of metacognitive control have been described in previous research and are part of effective and efficient reading comprehension (Jacobs & Paris, 1987).

The index is composed of 20 multiple-choice questions, each with three responses. The responses are scored as 0, 1, or 2, indicating increasing levels of metacognitive awareness (see the questionnaire and response values in the appendix). Previous research has shown that the Index of Reading Awareness is an effective measure of changes in metacognition resulting from instruction and also shows sensitivity to developmental differences in metacognition (Jacobs & Paris, 1987). Although the index is still an indirect and inferential measure of students' metacognitive processes, it adds an important facet to our measures of students' reading ability and it could provide some evidence that CIRC materials and processes affect more than students' ability to answer multiple-choice questions found on achievement tests. We chose not to use the index with second-grade students due to the readability level of the instrument.

Attitude Measure.   The students were also given a rating form to assess their attitudes toward and their perceived abilities in reading and language arts. They were asked to list their three favorite subjects and the three subjects in which they were the most able. This was followed by asking the students to rate how much they liked their five major subjects (reading, language arts and writing, math, science, and social studies) on a three-point scale ("I like it a lot," "I like it a little," and "I don't like it").

RESULTS

Implementation

During the first 6 weeks of the implementation the teachers were observed frequently by the project staff and coached to improve the quality of their implementation. Following that time, the teachers were observed periodically, a minimum of once every 2 weeks, to monitor the fidelity of the program. The special education teachers were also observed to monitor their implementation of CIRC and the mainstreaming of the academically handicapped students and to assist them in working out specific problems they might encounter.

In monitoring the CIRC implementation we accepted and encouraged some degree of variation in the teachers' presentation of instruction (e.g., new vocabulary, story discussion, writing activities) provided that the adaptations met the goals of the CIRC materials and processes outlined in the teacher's manual. We asked, however, that the teachers use the cooperative learning processes described for each of the program components. These expectations were made clear during the training and subsequent observations indicated that teachers did vary some of the instructional procedures, but the prescribed cooperative learning interactions were evident in each of the components.

Analyses

The analysis of the data from this study is complicated by the fact that the students are from intact classes and are nested within class, the classes are nested within schools, and the schools are nested within treatment. This problem of the different levels of potential units of analysis and this nested design make it difficult to disentangle the effects of schools or teachers on student growth relative to the experimental interventions (Burstein, 1980; Raudenbush & Bryk, 1988). The data were analyzed using the hierarchical linear model (HLM; Bryk, Raudenbush, Seltzer, & Congdon, 1988) to resolve the problems related to multilevel data. Because the study lasted for 2 years, the data were analyzed and reported separately for each year.

Initially grade-by-treatment interactions were conducted to test for differential effects of the treatment at different grade levels. No significant interactions were found in these class-level analyses of the achievement or attitude measures. Because there were no significant grade-by-treatment interactions we converted the achievement test scores to z scores so we could collapse the data across grade levels to increase the power of the analyses and simplify the discussion of the results. We also investigated the possible impact of the different schools on the impact of the program (school-level effects) but we found no significant effects attributable to the schools on any of the outcome measures ($t < 1.0$). There were, however, significant pretest differences on reading and language arts measures (see Table 9.1 and Table 9.2), so students' total reading and total language scores were used as covariates in the HLM analyses.

TABLE 9.1
Students' Achievement After First Year: Means, Adjusted Means, Analyses,
and Effect Sizes

Collapsed Across Grades		CIRC			Control			t^a	Effect Size[b]
		M	(SD)	Adj M	M	(SD)	Adj M		
Pretest:	Reading	−.11	(.96)		.13	(1.03)		3.06**	
	Lang. Arts	−.09	(.98)		.10	(1.01)		2.62*	
Posttest:	Read. Voc.	.03	(.97)	.11	−.03	(1.03)	−.12	2.06*	+.22
	Read. Comp.	.04	(.96)	.12	−.05	(1.04)	−.13	2.06*	+.22
	Lang. Mech.	.01	(.97)	.04	−.01	(1.03)	−.07	<1.0	+.11
	Lang. Expr.	−.03	(.99)	.01	.04	(1.00)	−.03	<1.0	+.04
	N	502			498				
	N of Classes	25			25				

[a]Levels of significance: *$p < .05$. **$p < .01$.
[b]Effect size equals the difference in the adjusted treatment means divided by the unadjusted control group standard deviation.

TABLE 9.2
Students' Achievement After Second Year: Means, Adjusted Means, Analyses,
and Effect Sizes

Collapsed Across Grades		CIRC			Control			t^a	Effect Size[b]
		M	(SD)	Adj M	M	(SD)	Adj M		
Pretest:	Reading	−.12	(.96)		.14	(1.04)		3.71**	
	Lang. Arts	−.11	(.98)		.13	(1.01)		3.54**	
Posttest:	Read. Voc.	.06	(.97)	.09	−.05	(1.02)	−.11	2.18*	+.20
	Read. Comp.	.09	(.97)	.12	−.08	(1.02)	−.15	2.27*	+.26
	Lang. Mech.	.00	(1.00)	.05	.01	(1.00)	−.08	1.12	+.13
	Lang. Expr.	.03	(.99)	.12	−.11	(1.02)	−.16	2.35	+.26
	N	635			664				
	N of Classes	31			32				

[a]Levels of significance: *$p < .05$. **$p < .01$.
[b]Effect size equals the difference in the adjusted treatment means divided by the unadjusted control group standard deviation.

Achievement Posttests After the First Year.   The analyses after the first year of the study indicate significant effects favoring the experimental classes on measures of reading vocabulary, $t(47) = 2.06$, $p < .05$, and reading comprehension, $t(47) = 2.11$, $p < .05$. There were no significant effects on language mechanics ($t < 1.0$) or language expression ($t < 1.0$). The means, adjusted means, analyses, and effect sizes are presented in Table 9.1. The magnitude of the significant experimental effects, as indicated by the effect sizes, were +.22 for vocabulary and +.24 for comprehension.

Achievement Posttests After the Second Year   The analyses of the second year data indicate significant positive effects for the experimental treatment on three of the four achievement measures. There were positive effects on reading vocabulary $t(60) = 2.13$, $p < .05$, reading comprehension $t(60) = 2.27$, $p < .05$, and language expression $t(60) = 2.35$, $p < .05$. There were no significant effects on language mechanics achievement ($t = 1.12$). The means, adjusted means, analyses, and effect sizes for the second year are presented in Table 9.2. The magnitude of the significant experimental effects, as indicated by the effect sizes, were +.20 for vocabulary, +.26 for comprehension, and +.26 for language expression.

Metacognition Measures.   There were no significant differences between the treatment groups on the initial measures of the students' level of metacognitive knowledge as measured by the Index of Reading Awareness. The analysis of covariance ANCOVA indicated a significant posttest difference on the metacognition score in favor of the experimental treatment $F(1, 944) = 10.9$, $p < .01$. There were no significant grade-by-treatment interactions on the metacognition measure so the data were collapsed across grades for the analyses (see Table 9.3). Inspection of the

TABLE 9.3
Index of Reading Awareness: Means[a] and Standard Deviations

Grades	CIRC	Control
Collapsed		
Premeasure	26.58 (4.6)	26.95 (4.1)
Postmeasure	29.40 (4.5)	27.99 (4.6)
N	462	485
Third Grade		
Premeasure	22.68 (4.6)	22.95 (4.3)
Postmeasure	27.24 (5.3)	25.58 (4.6)
N	131	160
Fourth Grade		
Premeasure	27.32 (4.7)	26.76 (3.8)
Postmeasure	29.22 (4.5)	27.38 (4.4)
N	120	123
Fifth Grade		
Premeasure	27.70 (4.3)	28.18 (4.2)
Postmeasure	30.10 (5.0)	38.91 (4.7)
N	69	54
Sixth Grade		
Premeasure	27.97 (4.9)	39.34 (4.1)
Postmeasure	30.64 (3.8)	29.77 (4.7)
N	142	148

[a]The questionnaire consists of 20 questions each with three alternative choices. The choices are scored from 0 to 2 points, depending on the level of metacognitive awareness exemplified in that choice, as described in Paris and Jacobs (1987). The total scores ranged from 0 to 40.

means in Table 9.3 does, however, reflect a developmental trend with older students scoring higher than younger students.

Attitude Measures. There were no significant pretest or posttest differences between the treatment groups on measures of students' attitudes toward reading or writing before or after the study.

Academically Handicapped Students

The data for students who received special education or remedial reading services, as identified by the school, were analyzed separately to determine the impact of mainstreaming them in the CIRC program. Most of these students were diagnosed as learning disabled. In the experimental schools, the academically handicapped students were kept in the regular classroom for their reading instruction, as described earlier. In the control schools, the academically handicapped students received their instruction through pullout instruction in a separate room with the remedial reading teacher for approximately 30 min.

Pretests.   There were no significant pretest differences between the two treatment groups in this subsample.

Achievement Posttests After the First Year.   As with the analyses for the entire sample, we initially tested for grade-by-treatment interactions. There were no significant interactions, so the data were collapsed across grade levels to simplify the presentation of the results. The multiple analysis of covariance (MANCOVAs) of the achievement data for academically handicapped students indicated significant positive effects for the experimental group on measures of reading vocabulary $F(1, 118) = 4.46, p < .05$ and reading comprehension $F(1, 118) = 4.11, p < .05$. There were no significant differences for language mechanics $F(1, 118) = 1.26$ or language expression $(F < 1.0)$. The means, adjusted means, analyses, and effect sizes are presented in Table 9.4. The magnitudes of the significant effects were $+.40$ for reading vocabulary and $+.31$ for reading comprehension.

Achievement Posttests After the Second Year.   The analyses of the second year data indicated significant positive effects for the experimental group on measures of reading vocabulary $F(1, 134) = 4.58, p < .05$, reading comprehension $F(1, 134) = 3.98, p < .05$, and language expression $F(1, 134) = 4.32, p < .05$. There was no significant difference on language mechanics achievement $F(1, 134) = 1.98$. The means, adjusted means, analyses, and effect sizes are presented in Table 9.5. The magnitudes of the significant effects were $+.37$ for reading vocabulary, $+.32$ for reading comprehension, and $+.36$ for language expression.

TABLE 9.4

Academically Handicapped Students' Achievement After First Year: Means, Adjusted Means, Analyses, and Effect Sizes

Collapsed Across Grades		CIRC			Control			t^a	Effect Size[b]
		M	(SD)	Adj M	M	(SD)	Adj M		
Pretest:	Reading	-1.42	(.59)		-1.36	(.85)		<1	
	Lang. Arts	-1.38	(.74)		-1.45	(.94)		<1	
Posttest:	Read. Voc.	-1.11	(.62)	-.02	-1.41	(.90)	-.38	2.46*	+.40
	Read. Comp.	-1.19	(.62)	-.07	-1.34	(.80)	-.32	4.11*	+.31
	Lang. Mech.	-1.09	(.61)	-.14	-1.37	(.80)	-.32	1.26	+.23
	Lang. Expr.	-1.29	(.94)	-.34	-1.38	(.97)	-.36	<1	+.02
	N		68			53			
	N of Classes		25			25			

[a]Levels of significance: *$p < .05$. **$p < .01$.
[b]Effect size equals the difference in the adjusted treatment means divided by the unadjusted control group standard deviation.

TABLE 9.5

Academically Handicapped Students' Achievement After Second Year: Means, Adjusted Means, Analyses, and Effect Sizes

Collapsed Across Grades		CIRC			Control			t^a	Effect Size[b]
		M	(SD)	Adj M	M	(SD)	Adj M		
Pretest:	Reading	−1.35	(.61)		−1.32	(.86)		<1	
	Lang. Arts	−1.38	(.73)		−1.44	(.90)		<1	
Posttest:	Read. Voc.	−1.03	(.62)	−.01	−1.28	(.87)	−.33	4.58*	+.37
	Read. Comp.	−1.14	(.65)	−.10	−1.28	(.75)	−.34	3.98*	+.32
	Lang. Mech.	−.86	(.60)	−.02	−1.08	(.78)	−.24	1.98	+.28
	Lang. Expr.	−1.34	(.86)	−.20	−1.48	(.74)	−.47	4.23*	+.36
	N	68			53				
	N of Classes	25			25				

[a]Levels of significance: *$p < .05$. **$p < .01$.

[b]Effect size equals the difference in the adjusted treatment means divided by the unadjusted control group standard deviation.

Attitude Measures. There were no significant differences between the treatments in special education students' pre- or postattitudes toward reading and language arts.

CONCLUSIONS

The results of the study presented here support the effectiveness of the CIRC program as a multifaceted, cooperative learning approach to literacy instruction. The results show that students' literacy skills can be positively effected by a multifaceted program that includes the following:

- Reading activities and discussions that focus on understanding the information in the story and its relation to the student's prior knowledge.
- Reading activities that focus on higher level comprehension and appreciation of the stories as literature.
- Repeated readings of the story.
- Meaningful use of the new vocabulary words.
- Activities that make connections between reading and writing.
- Explicit instruction in generalizable reading comprehension strategies.
- A writing process approach that integrates writing and language arts.
- Cooperative learning processes that actively engage the students in the learning activities and encourage them to help and mentor one another as they learn.

In the study there was no attempt to disentangle the relative effects of each or any of these elements. Instead we have relied on a large body of previous research about these elements and their effectiveness to build a model for elementary literacy instruction and investigate its impact. This study shows that the CIRC model had a positive impact of approximately one-quarter standard deviation on achievement measures of vocabulary, comprehension, and language expression.

A second important finding of this study is that the positive impact of CIRC on students' achievement was maintained over 2 years. This suggests that the positive results are more likely to be due to the CIRC program, and less likely to be due to a Hawthorne effect resulting from the novelty of the experimental treatment. As such, these results become more ecologically valid and meaningful because CIRC became "normal" reading instruction to the teachers and students.

The study also gives an interesting look at the developmental effects of CIRC over the 2 years on reading and language arts achievement. In reading after the first year there were significant effects on vocabulary and comprehension, effects that were maintained during the second year. Maintaining the level of effect in reading is important because it implies continued improved performance of students in CIRC. As students get older the variance in their achievement increases; thus differences between the experimental and control groups must increase to maintain an effect size of one-quarter standard deviation.

In language arts there were no significant differences after the first year, but after the second year CIRC students had significantly better language expression achievement. This suggests that although the CIRC program and its writing process component can improve students' achievement in language expression, the improvement is more difficult and slower to obtain. The lack of positive effects on language mechanics, on the other hand, is most likely due to the curricular emphasis on writing and the expression of ideas inherent in a writing process model. Traditional instruction in language arts focuses mostly on mechanics and usage skills, whereas a writing process approach focuses on the expression of ideas with integrated mechanics skills instruction to support and the written expression of ideas. It is interesting to note that the control treatment, which emphasized mechanics skill instruction, produced no better outcomes on the language mechanics measure.

This study also investigated the effects of using the CIRC program with different grade levels than those in the previous studies. In this study CIRC was expanded to include second, fifth, and sixth grades. The results show no significant grade-by-treatment interactions on any of the outcome measures, suggesting that CIRC had similar effects across all five grade levels. The results of this study are also very consistent with the results previously found in studies with third- and fourth-graders (Stevens et al., 1987). Thus the CIRC seems to have a comparable impact on students at all grade levels from second through sixth and the components and processes in the CIRC model seem applicable to the abilities and needs of all these levels of students.

Another goal of this study was to investigate the impact of CIRC on the way students think about the process of reading. Although it is important for students to have improved academic achievement, it was also our objective to increase students' knowledge about and control over their comprehension processes. In doing so, CIRC would develop students' metacognitive abilities and develop more effective independent readers. Much of the research in reading comprehension purports to have an impact on both students' measurable comprehension abilities and their metacognition, or their knowledge of reading and reading processes. However, most of this research assumes improved metacognition when improved reading comprehension is measured or observed (Paris et al., 1991). In this study we used the Index of Reading Awareness (Jacobs & Paris, 1987) as a means to assess the impact of CIRC on students' knowledge and awareness of their own reading processes. We found that CIRC students had significantly higher levels of awareness of their own reading processes. Although this measure is only a proxy for cognitive activity we cannot observe, the result is important as the students were not explicitly taught metacognitive awareness. Instead, CIRC students' increased awareness seems to be the result of strategic instruction they received and their successful application of it to the story-related activities in CIRC.

When taken together, the achievement and metacognitive results suggest that the instruction and practice in CIRC improve students' ability to use and monitor their own comprehension strategies. This improves not only their ability to answer discrete questions about what they have read, but also increases their knowledge about how to control their reading processes.

Finally, this study supports the notion that cooperative learning can indeed function as a cognitive apprenticeship model for teaching complex cognitive tasks such as those in reading comprehension and writing. Just as an apprentice learning a craft from a master, students in cooperative learning can rely on their peers as mentors when learning literacy skills. First the teacher provides the support and expert guidance for students in the learning process. Gradually that responsibility is shifted to learners in their collaborative dialogues. Working together collaboratively at first allows the students to provide cognitive support and guidance to one another. As they become more proficient with newly learned skills, the learners take on more responsibility for their own activity and rely on their peers and the teacher for increasingly infrequent support, guidance, and feedback. Eventually the students develop proficient use of the new cognitive strategies and become able to monitor and evaluate their use of these processes.

APPENDIX:
Index of Reading Awareness

DIRECTIONS: Read each of the questions and answers that follow them. CIRCLE the letter of YOUR ANSWER to each question.

1. What is the hardest part about reading for you?
   a. Sounding out the hard words.
   b. When you don't understand the story.
   c. Nothing is hard about reading for me.

2. What would help you become a better reader?
   a. If more people would help me when I read.
   b. Reading easier books with shorter words.
   c. Checking to make sure I understand what I've read.

3. What is special about the first paragraph in a story?
   a. The first paragraph always begins with "Once upon a time. . . ."
   b. The first sentences are the most interesting.
   c. They often tell what the story is going to be about.

4. What is important about the main character in the story?
   a. The main character is the one who solves the problem of the story.
   b. The main character is the person or animal the story is mostly about.
   c. The main character is the hero of the story.

5. How can you tell which sentences are the important ones in the story?
   a. They're the ones that tell the most about the characters and what happens.
   b. They're the most interesting ones.
   c. All of the sentences are important.

6. If you could only read some of the sentences in the story because you were in a hurry, which ones would you read?
   a. Read the sentences in the middle of the story.
   b. Read the sentences that tell you the most about the story.
   c. Read the interesting, exciting sentences.

7. When you tell other people about what you've read what do you tell them?
   a. What happened in the story.
   b. The number of pages in the story.
   c. Who the characters are.

8. If the teacher told you to read a story to remember the general meaning, what would you do?
   a. Skim through the story to find the main parts.
   b. Read all of the story and try to remember everything.
   c. Read the story and remember all of the words.

9. Before you start to read, what kinds of plans do you make to help you read better?
   a. You don't make any plans. You just start reading.
   b. You try to remember the meaning of the new vocabulary.
   c. You think about what the story is going to be about.

10. How does knowing the new vocabulary words help you read the story?
    a. Knowing the new vocabulary words helps you understand the parts of the story that use the new words.
    b. Knowing the new vocabulary words helps you predict what will happen in the story.
    c. Knowing the new vocabulary words helps you predict what will happen in the story and helps you understand the story.

11. What would you do if you couldn't answer a question about the story?
    a. Ask your partner what the answer is.
    b. Talk to your partner and skim the story to find the answer.
    c. Skip that question and then discuss it in reading group.

12. Why would you go back and read things over again?
   a. Because it is good practice.
   b. Because you didn't understand it.
   c. Because you forgot some words.
13. What do you do if you come to a word and you don't know what it means?
   a. Use the words around it to figure it out.
   b. Ask someone else.
   c. Go on to the next word.
14. What do you do if you don't know what a whole sentence means?
   a. Read it again.
   b. Sound out all of the words.
   c. Think about the other sentences in the paragraph.
15. If you were reading silently and didn't understand a paragraph, what would you do?
   a. Read the next paragraph to help you understand the last one.
   b. Reread the paragraph before going on to the next paragraph.
   c. Read to the end of the story before rereading parts of the story.
16. If you are reading a story for fun what would you do?
   a. Look at the pictures to get the meaning.
   b. Read the story as fast as you can.
   c. Imagine the story like a movie in your mind.
17. If you were reading a factual story, what would you do to remember the information?
   a. Ask yourself questions about the important ideas.
   b. Skip the parts you don't understand.
   c. Reread the whole story.
18. If you are reading for a test, which would be the most helpful?
   a. Read the story as many times as possible.
   b. Talk with somebody to make sure you understand it.
   c. Say the sentences over and over.
19. If you are reading a library book to write a book report, which would help you most?
   a. Sound out the new words.
   b. Write it down in your own words.
   c. Skip the parts you don't understand.
20. Which of these is the best way to remember a story?
   a. Say every word over and over.
   b. Think about remembering it.
   c. Write it down in your own words.

REFERENCES

Allan, S. (1991). Ability-grouping research reviews: What do they say about grouping and the gifted? *Educational Leadership, 48,* 60–65.

Allington, R. (1984). Oral reading. In P. D. Pearson (Ed.), *Handbook of reading research* (Vol. 1, pp. 829–864). New York: Macmillan.

Allport, G. (1954). *The nature of prejudice.* Cambridge, MA: Addison-Wesley.

Anderson, R., Hiebert, E., Scott, J., & Wilkinson, I. (1985). *Becoming a nation of readers: The report of the commission on reading.* Washington, DC: National Institute of Education.

Anderson, R., Wilson, P., & Fielding, L. (1988). Growth in reading and how children spend their time outside of school. *Reading Research Quarterly, 23,* 285–303.

Aronson, E., & Bridgeman, D. (1981). Jigsaw groups and the desegregated classroom: In pursuit of common goals. In E. Aronson (Ed.), *Readings about the social animal* (pp. 329–340). San Francisco: WH Freeman.

Baumann, J. (1984). The effectiveness of a direct instruction paradigm for teaching main idea comprehension. *Reading Research Quarterly, 20,* 93–115.

Beck, I., Perfetti, C., & McKeown, M. (1982). The effects of long-term vocabulary instruction on lexical access and reading comprehension. *Journal of Educational Psychology, 74,* 506–521.

Bridge, C., & Hiebert, E. (1985). A comparison of classroom writing practices, teachers' perceptions of their writing instruction, and textbook recommendations on writing practices. *Elementary School Journal, 86,* 155–172.

Brown, A., & Campione, J. (1986). Psychological theory and the study of learning disabilities. *American Psychologist, 14,* 1059–1068.

Brown, A., Campione, J., & Day, J. (1981). Learning to learn: On training students to learn from texts. *Educational Researcher, 10,* 14–21.

Brown, A., & Palincsar, A. (1982). Inducing strategic learning from text by means of informed self-control training. *Topics in Learning and Learning Disabilities, 2,* 1–17.

Bryk, A., Raudenbush, S., Seltzer, M., & Congdon, R. (1988). *An introduction to HLM: Computer program and user's guide.* Chicago: University of Chicago, Department of Education.

Burstein, L. (1980). The analysis of multilevel data in educational research and evaluation. In D. Berliner (Ed.), *Review of research in education* (Vol. 8, pp. 158–233). Washington, DC: American Educational Research Association.

Calkins, L. (1983). *Lessons from a child: On the teaching and learning of writing.* Exeter, NH: Heinemann.

Collins, A., Brown, J., & Newman, S. (1989). Cognitive apprenticeship: Teaching the crafts of reading, writing and mathematics. In L. Resnick (Ed.), *Knowing, learning, and cognition: Essays in honor of Robert Glaser* (pp. 453–494). Hillsdale, NJ: Lawrence Erlbaum Associates.

Dahl, P. (1979). An experimental program for teaching high-speed word recognition and comprehension skills. In J. Button, T. Lovitt, & T. Rowland (Eds.), *Communication research in learning disabilities and mental retardation* (pp. 33–65). Baltimore, MD: University Park Press.

Day, J. (1986). Teaching summarization skills: Influences of student ability level and strategy difficulty. *Cognition and Instruction, 3,* 193–210.

Deutsch, M. (1949a). An experimental study of the effects of co-operation and competition upon group processes. *Human Relations, 2,* 199–229.

Deutsch, M. (1949b). A theory of cooperation and competition. *Human Relations, 2,* 129–151.

DeVries, D., & Edwards, K. (1973). Learning games and student teams: Their effects on classroom processes. *American Educational Research Journal, 10,* 307–318.

Dewitz, P., Carr, E., & Patberg, J. (1987). Effects of inference training on comprehension and comprehension monitoring. *Reading Research Quarterly, 22,* 99–119.

Fitzgerald, J., & Spiegel, D. (1983). Enhancing children's reading comprehension through instruction in narrative structures. *Journal of Reading Behavior, 14,* 1–18.

Fuchs, D., & Fuchs, L. (1991). Framing the REI debate: Abolitionists versus conservationists. In J. Lloyd, N. Singh, & A. Repp (Eds.), *The regular education initiative: Alternative perspectives on concepts, issues, and models* (pp. 242–255). Sycamore, IL: Sycamore Publishing.

Gerard, H., & Miller, N. (1975). *School desegregation: A long-term study.* New York: Plenum.

Glass, G., McGaw, B., & Smith, M. L. (1981). *Meta-analysis in social research.* Beverly Hills, CA: Sage Publications.

Graves, D. (1978). *Balance the basics: Let them write.* New York: Ford Foundation.

Graves, D. (1983). *Writing: Teachers and children at work*. Exeter, NH: Heinemann.

Grossack, M. (1954). Some effects of cooperation and competition on small group behavior. *Journal of Abnormal and Social Psychology, 49,* 341–348.

Hansell, S., & Slavin, R. (1981). Cooperative learning and the structure of interracial friendships. *Sociology of Education, 54,* 98–106.

Hillocks, G., Jr. (1984). What works in teaching composition: A meta-analysis of experimental treatment studies. *American Journal of Education, 93,* 133–170.

Jacobs, J., & Paris, S. (1987). Children's metacognition about reading: Issues in definition, measurement, and instruction. *Educational Psychologist, 22,* 255–278.

Johnson, D., & Johnson, R. (1981). Effects of cooperative and individual learning experiences on interethnic interaction. *Journal of Educational Psychology, 73,* 444–449.

Johnson, D., Johnson, R., & Holubec, E. (1991). *Cooperation in the classroom*. Edina, MN: Interaction Books.

Johnson, R., & Johnson, D. (1981). Building friendships between handicapped and nonhandicapped students: Effects of cooperative and individualistic instruction. *American Educational Research Journal, 18,* 415–424.

Laberge, D., & Samuels, J. (1974). Toward a theory of automatic information processing in reading. *Cognitive Psychology, 6,* 293–323.

Marston, D. (1987). The effectiveness of special education: A time series analysis of reading performance in regular and special education settings. *Journal of Special Education, 21,* 13–26.

Meyer, B., Brandt, D., & Bluth, G. (1980). Use of top-level structure in text: Keys for reading comprehension of ninth grade students. *Reading Research Quarterly, 16,* 72–103.

Mezynski, K. (1983). Issues concerning the acquisition of knowledge: Effects of vocabulary training on reading comprehension. *Review of Educational Research, 53,* 252–279.

Palincsar, A., & Brown, A. (1984). Reciprocal teaching of comprehension monitoring activities. *Cognition and Instruction, 2,* 117–175.

Paris, S., Cross, D., & Lipson, M. (1984). Informed strategy for learning: A program to improve children's reading awareness and comprehension. *Journal of Educational Psychology, 76,* 1239–1252.

Paris, S., & Jacobs, J. (1984). The benefits of informed instruction for children's reading awareness and comprehension skills. *Child Development, 55,* 2083–2093.

Paris, S., Lindauer, B., & Cox, G. (1977). The development of inferential comprehension. *Child Development, 48,* 1728–1733.

Paris, S., Wasik, B., & Turner, J. (1991). The development of strategic readers. In R. Barr, M. Kamil, P. Mosenthal, & P. D. Pearson (Eds.), *Handbook of reading research* (Vol. 2, pp. 609–640). New York: Longman.

Perfetti, C. (1985). *Reading ability*. New York: Oxford University Press.

Raphael, T. (1980). *The effects of metacognitive strategy awareness training on students' question-answering behavior*. Unpublished doctoral dissertation, University of Illinois, Urbana-Champaign, IL.

Raudenbush, S., & Bryk, A. (1988). Methodological advances in analyzing the effects of schools and classrooms on student learning. In E. Rothkopf (Ed.), *Review of research in education* (Vol. 15, pp. 423–476). Washington, DC: American Educational Research Association.

Samuels, S. J. (1979). The method of repeated readings. *The Reading Teacher, 32,* 403–408.

Shany, M. (1992, April). *Increasing reading practice: Effects on reading processes and individual differences as predictors of outcomes*. Paper presented at the annual meeting of the American Educational Research Association, San Francisco.

Sharan, S. (1980). Cooperative learning in small groups: Recent methods and effects on achievement, attitudes, and ethnic relations. *Review of Educational Research, 50,* 241–271.

Short, E., & Ryan, E. (1982, April). *Remediating poor readers' comprehension failures with a story grammar strategy.* Paper presented at the annual meeting of the American Educational Research Association, New York.

Slavin, R. (1979). Effects of biracial learning teams on cross-racial friendships. *Journal of Educational Psychology, 71,* 381–387.

Slavin, R. (1983). When does cooperative learning increase student achievement? *Psychological Bulletin, 94,* 429–445.

Slavin, R. (1984). Team assisted individualized instruction: Cooperative learning and individualized instruction in the mainstreamed classroom. *Remedial and Special Education, 5,* 33–42.

Slavin, R. (1990). *Cooperative learning: Theory, research, and practice.* Englewood Cliffs, NJ: Prentice-Hall.

Slavin, R. (1991). Are cooperative learning and "untracking" harmful to the gifted? A response to Allan. *Educational Leadership, 48*(6), 68–71.

St. John, N. (1975). *School desegregation: Outcomes for children.* New York: Wiley.

Stainback, W., & Stainback, S. (1984). A rationale for the merger of special and regular education. *Exceptional Children, 51,* 102–111.

Stainback, W., & Stainback, S. (1991). A rationale for integration and restructuring: A synopsis. In J. Lloyd, N. Singh, & A. Repp (Eds.), *The regular education initiative: Alternative perspectives on concepts, issues, and models* (pp. 225–241). Sycamore, IL: Sycamore Publishing.

Stevens, R. (1988). Effects of strategy training on the identification of the main idea of expository passages. *Journal of Educational Psychology, 80,* 21–26.

Stevens, R., Madden, N., Slavin, R., & Farnish, A. (1987). Cooperative integrated and composition: Two field experiments. *Reading Research Quarterly, 22,* 433–454.

Stevens, R., & Slavin, R. (1991a, April). *A cooperative learning approach to accommodating student diversity in reading and writing: Effects on handicapped and nonhandicapped students.* Paper presented at the annual meeting of the American Educational Research Association, Chicago.

Stevens, R., & Slavin, R. (1991b). When cooperative learning improves achievement of students with mild disabilities: A response to Tateyama-Sniezek. *Exceptional Children, 57,* 276–280.

Stevens, R., & Slavin, R. (1992, April). *The cooperative elementary school: Effects on students' achievement, attitudes, and social relations.* Paper presented at the annual meeting of the American Educational Research Association, San Francisco.

Stevens, R., Slavin, R., & Farnish, A. (1991). The effects of cooperative learning and direct instruction in reading comprehension strategies on main idea information. *Journal of Educational Psychology, 83,* 8–16.

Thurlow, M., Groden, J., Ysseldyke, J., & Algozzine, R. (1984). Student reading during reading class: The lost activity in reading instruction. *Journal of Educational Research, 77,* 267–272.

Vygotsky, L. (1978). *The mind in society: The development of higher psychological processes.* Cambridge, MA: Harvard University Press.

Webb, N., & Kenderski, C. (1984). Student interaction and learning in small-group and whole-class settings. In P. Peterson, L. Wilkinson, & M. Hallinan (Eds.), *The social context of instruction: Group organization and group processes* (pp. 153–170). San Diego, CA: Academic Press.

Webb, N. (1985). Student interaction and learning in small groups: A research summary. In R. Slavin, S. Sharan, R. Hertz-Lazarowitz, C. Webb, & R. Schmuck (Eds.), *Learning to cooperate, cooperating to learn* (pp. 147–172). New York: Plenum.

Wilkinson, I., Wardrop, J., & Anderson, R. (1988). Silent reading reconsidered: Reinterpreting reading instruction and its effects. *American Educational Research Journal, 25,* 127–144.

Will, M. (1986). Educating children with learning problems: A shared responsibility. *Exceptional Children, 52,* 411–416.

Willis, S. (1990). Cooperative learning fallout? *ASCD Update, 32,* 6–8.

Wittrock, M. (1986). Students' thought processes. In M. Wittrock (Ed.), *Handbook of research on teaching* (pp. 297–314). New York: Macmillan.

10

Linking Cultures Through Literacy: A Perspective for the Future

Clement B. G. London
Fordham University

The child, the community and the nation are at risk when children do not receive the kinds of experiences that will permit them to go to school and succeed in school . . . and come out of school and succeed as family members, workers, and citizens of the greater society.
— James Comer (1980)

THE DREAM

In a very insightful discourse on salient issues of ambiguity and the persistence of rage, Greene (1983), about a decade ago, defined the American dream as "a dream about beginnings, continually new beginnings," and then further commented that "equality had to do (for some at least) with having the right to begin" (pp. 179–193). Greene went on to suggest that such was part of the creed, of the American promise: the view that each living human being, from whatever origin, was equal to every other.

A cursory glance at historical watersheds would reveal that in almost all cases at least until the mid-20th century, that person was White and male; and for many Blacks and many women, "equality" was a name for an unkept promise, or for freedom, or for the rights of which they were deprived. The very idea, however, that people were entitled to equality was a dramatic break with tradition in a world when most people were somewhat frozen in place by determinants of class differences, poverty, confining traditions, as well as resignation. It was visualized many times as

159

a kind of description of the way human beings were supposed to be in relation to one another. The fact that it denied moral equality or the equal right to opportunity was often overlooked.

Of course, U.S. imaginative and progressive writers have been aware of this and duly communicated what it signified, even as they celebrated new beginnings that philosophically seemed to define the New World. They were far more likely than were reformers or polemicists to suggest the ambiguities of equality, the constraints that limited or deflected it, the mystifications that obscured it. Action, it would seem, had to await a kind of maturity, a kind of sensitivity, a kind of agitation, if you will.

OF PROMISES TO KEEP

It is rational to conclude that more than anything else, social, political, educational, and in particular school movements at least at the level of theory within the recent past, have been about fulfilling the long-standing dream of universal education within the United States. The dialogue about this necessity owes its origin to an earlier age when, over time, the nation transcended the ideational level and gained some semblance of expression throughout much of the century by theorists, philosophers, educationists, presidents, Congress, and the courts. Basically, the theme of these efforts was the ideal that all children have a right to all education, consistent with their capability. Whatever the progress, the truth remains abundantly clear that the struggle to actualize this intent, that promise, still continues.

The fact of the matter is that the phrase "all children" has not in actuality meant *ALL* children; and therefore, for a long time, the closed school door pushed firmly by laws and cogent court rulings opened reluctantly, slowly to so-called minorities, the poor, handicapped, and non-English speakers. In essence, the rationale expressed or implied for limiting opportunities, particularly for the discriminated, came as a contradiction to ethical ideas about education for all. At any rate, although there is a sense that the stride to universal education has gained tremendous ground, that there are measures of success in bringing all children into schools (although not necessarily keeping them until graduation), it is this very success that serves to focus attention on how far the goal of the journey remains in yet fulfilling the education part, the other half of the promise (Horne, 1986; London, 1991).

However, despite their tenuous nature in some sectors of the national educational landscape, there has evolved a central concept. It is the perception that almost all children have the capability to learn at a high level, and that they thus deserve a chance to do so. This is progress. It is part of the contemporary reform movement, and included in this repertoire of students are those who are defined as difficult to teach: They are the abused, hungry, homeless, frightened, angry, the alienated from the U.S. mainstream; they are those who find themselves victims of continuing education neglect or assault on their young lives; those who are caught between the dichotomous landscape of promise and condemnation; those who have been designated as being at risk and thus, are assigned to classrooms that indeed place them at risk for eventual consignment to crime, unemployment, homelessness, vagrancy, prisons, as well as unattended illnesses. They are the entourage of neglect, the disenchanted.

Against the backdrop of large percentages of students who now opt out of schools and who belong to the entourage of neglect, many stop-gap measures of compensatory educational programs have become the norm of the larger ecological environment as serious challenges emerge and beg the will of the nation to acquiesce to these compelling needs and urgencies. One overriding challenge is against the long-held assumption that the student must "fit" the classroom. A prudent suggestion may be that of making the classroom fit the child, that is, every child. This requirement goes deeper than mere pedagogy may be willing to address. It goes to the heart of the sociocultural issues raised earlier in this discourse by Greene (1983). It implicitly calls for an acknowledgment, then the deliberate removal of the impediments, which hurt not just segments of the populace but altogether render the cultural chain as strong as the weakest link.

This great chain of being is anchored in a past. It is a past that entails an exciting history with missing chunks. It remains an unfinished, incompletely told history. Yet the U.S. quantum leap into the 21st century has had its genesis, its anchor, in its historical determinism that is undergirded by the philosophy of Manifest Destiny. The urge to conquer lands from "sea to shining sea" is an idea alive and well, and is reflected in its leadership in the race for space, a magnificent obsession with literacy, and the attainment of cultural maturity that facilitates ascendancy to the point of being in the forefront of international information processing. This is indeed a status derived from both implicit and explicit intentions; it is reflected in educational philosophy and economic determinism that served the nation as it transcends its parochialism and moves to a postindustrial, high-technology, and information-processing status of culture.

In the wake of this fantastic movement in time and place, the telling effects have been pervasive. Among other things, the nation has assumed the name of the entire continent, America, and the polity, Americans. This move implies that others of the same continent, including the people across the Rio Grande, who trespass into what not so long ago was a part of their own country, are now considered aliens. Within the country, Native Americans have been relegated to reservations very much like the Bantustans of South Africa, with limited resources of schooling, essential services, or the freedom to generate these themselves. The list may be lengthened to include other social, geographical, historical, political, economic, anthropological, and psychological factors. But suffice it to be so.

The point of concern here is that there is a plethora of cultural factors wrapped in the idea of history that is necessary for an informed populace; not in isolated, piecemeal orientation, but in structured, organized, and substantive curricular offerings for the common weal or good. The magnificent obsession with literacy and, to a lesser degree, numeracy, should become a logical benchmark for the nation in its progressive stride, not only to deal with local issues, but to overcome and transcend these with such facility as to win the unquestioned moral world leadership (Noddings, 1992).

THE DEMOGRAPHICS OF THE IDEAL AND REAL

In point of fact it is necessary to examine the dichotomous relationship between the ideal and real: what one would essentially prefer, but what in reality exists, and often jars the conscience. One such overriding issue is that of the population and the changing demographics, clearly inciting the question of preference between what some perceive one would wish to have as against what is available, rightly or wrongly. Ponterotto and Casas (1991) wrote that "we are quickly becoming a multicultural, multiracial, and multilingual society. Already 75 percent of those now entering the United States' labor force are composed of women and minorities" (pp. vii–ix).

In addition, they noted with much concern that the U.S. minority marketplace now equals the GNP of Canada, and the demographers predict that by the time the so-called baby boomers retire, the majority of these persons contributing to the social security and pension plans of primarily White workers will be racial/ethnic minorities. Moreover, several states (e.g., California) already have greater than 50% racial/ethnic minority students in the public school systems. And because the fertility rate of White citizens of the United States is declining and the population of racial/ethnic minorities continues to grow (in part because of higher relative birthrates and immigration factors), racial/ethnic minorities will become the numerical majority some time in the next 30 years. These factors portend major changes in our educational, economic, social, and political systems (Ponterotto & Casas, 1991).

In essence, according to Ponterotto and Cassas (1991), the demographic face of the United States is changing rapidly and some time during the 21st century, racial/ethnic minority groups will become the nation's numerical majority. Considering that education is the cornerstone, the most democratic as well as liberating in U.S. culture, it stands to cogent reason that culturally grounded theory, research, and practice should serve to inform curricular efforts, which attempt to address such compelling circumstances. Such efforts will require educators—as theorists, researchers, and practitioners—to be prepared to service an increasingly diverse constituency of students at schools throughout, in terms of race, ethnicity, language, and cultural values; and to incorporate these educational efforts, needs, and foci in a planned substantive, coherent, and holistic perspective (Lankshear, 1987).

As technology renders the world a global village of sorts, and as the United States settles in as the dominant national leader among states, the function of schooling here must accommodate itself to larger dimensions. Such dimensions must assume global scope and sequence, and must of necessity begin with a dynamic adjustment of what is now available, both in terms of content and process. Already the preferred place of entry for all kinds of political, social, and economic reasons, despite impediments, schooling and schools within the United States will assume far greater importance as the place where one will choose to be educated. Educational goods and services, ideology, theory, practice, and all of the accompanying circumstances—including schools and schooling—will have to adjust to larger, albeit international demands and needs as the nation grapples with international competition and the need to cope.

INTERNATIONAL COMPETITION AND THE DEMAND TO COPE AND SUCCEED

In aligning the cruciality of global production and competition for educational change, Hedley, Feldman, and Antonacci (1992) spoke of the need to alter management structures, knowledge structures, and behaviors. But the efficaciousness of these modifications, they argued, must be undertaken in the context of the new, technical era, which seriously calls attention to the need to understand aspects of other cultures, including languages. By attempting to get credence to their position, they wittingly draw sustenance from the data derived from Jones, Tinzmann, and Pierce (1992), which suggested that populations defining/constituting the work force will increasingly become non-White, urban, largely impoverished, and limited in English proficiency; that of these populations, 83% of the new workers will be a combination of women, so-called minorities, and immigrants. Therefore, at a point in educational history when change itself seems to be the only constant, schools and schooling must change altogether, if only to meet these realities (Altbach, 1988; Apple, 1992a, 1992b).

More specifically, quality classroom work and counseling services must take place in environments that affirm the dignity of all in a school community. The cultivation of such environments must become an essential factor in all decisions of the teaching–learning transaction. Literacy is perceived as being at the heart of the matter. It must come, not merely to mean, but become a reality. It must be viewed in its most comprehensive sense as defining thinking, talking, reading, and writing.

Literacy, it is perceived, must mean more than reading scores. It must mean helping students to have an informed voice in the society; it must mean being able to read, write, work, being responsible for/to one's family and to vote: basic functions of citizenship. A school's expectations should include all students becoming literate. Experience and research already confirm that this is a reasonable expectation. In addition, respect, motivation, self-esteem, and other attendant virtues come from real, empowering skills and the successful experiences that build them.

Implications of advancing such positions suggest that as educators, teachers — call us whatever you will — we should include in our repertoire of curricular and instructional constructs, initial entry to those skills for our students, based on profound pedagogical procedures, so as to lay the groundwork for other steps in lifelong educational experiences. But literacy must also derive its meaningfulness from considerate text structures that provide cultural and sociolinguistic relevance (Hedley et al., 1992). As such, it is prudent to examine literacy in the context of educational/cultural constructs.

LITERACY DEFINED

According to Chew (1992), literacy is competence in language arts: listening, speaking, reading, and writing. Chew saw language as being central to all learning and, indeed, all creative art. For him, "language is a temple in which the soul of those who speak it is enshrined. . . . The memory of the human race . . . [is] a thread or nerve of life running through all ages, connecting them into one common, prolonged, and advancing existence" (p. 7). Chew pushed his view to suggest that educators must guarantee the comfort of students with the medium of expression, their language, just as the artist must feel comfortable and knowledgeable about colors, perspective, and the like.

Among the plethora of positions defining literacy, there are those who discuss higher level thinking, critical thinking, creative thinking, as well as reflective decision making. F. Smith (1990), for example, took the position that the elements of thinking critically and creatively are in everyone's behavioral and cognitive repertoire. People may not appear to be thinking critically or creatively because the situation does not permit or call for critical or creative behavior. This does not mean that some individuals are totally incapable of thinking critically or creatively, or that they lack the training. It is just that they are not thinking in those ways, for one reason or another. (pp. 101–102)

It is clear from this position that perceptions differ. Brause (1992) spoke of literacy as one way of learning, and suggested that learning is both process and outcome. As a complex process, learning helps the individual to enhance the understanding of self and the world, through constantly evaluating tasks and procedures (p. 16). As such, literacy activities accompany our personal quest for increasing understanding, and reading and writing are among the activities that promote learning. In this sense, Brause echoed the sentiments of Chew, that we must enter into an engagement with learning, a conversation if you will, and model what is professed and believed (Batsleer, Davis, O'Rourke, & Weedon, 1985).

Thus, a difference can happen if there is a willingness to do, to take a different course, to choose alternative action, to forge a different policy for literacy. Evolving national and international circumstances would suggest the basis for creating this difference. Such a difference would require due consideration be given to the realities accompanying the new demographics based on data, the product outcomes of longitudinal studies of educators, sociologists, and demographers (Benavides, 1988; Ellsworth, 1989; Harrington, 1987; Jordan, 1989; Larson & Gerber, 1987; Schumaker, Deshler, & Ellis, 1986).

LITERACY: PERSONAL NEEDS AND
UNIVERSAL FUNCTIONS

But literacy provides for personal needs and functions. Whereas individuals use different strategies for learning and consequently develop a rich repertoire of experiences that comprise their personal knowledge, common to us all is the evolving sense of self, the ecological environment of the world around us and our roles in it. A goal of integrating all this knowledge into a more simplified, cohesive model motivates many of us to connect events in our society and across history, seeking to determine themes, commonalities, and universal patterns. Thus, as literate individuals seeking to share our understanding of the world, we use literacy activities to enhance opportunities for learning (Carver, 1977–1978; Darnton, 1982; Geyer, 1972; Goldstein, 1940).

Ellsworth (1989), in discussing some of the tensions and other conflicts derived from a lack of understanding of ethnic and cultural groups and their heritage within the mainstream United States, strongly suggested that all children should share in all aspects of the nation's legacy. This means, on one level, making available to all children all aspects of the cultural legacy. She also drew on the work of Palinscar and Brown (1988) to support her position. Citing reading as a viable means for gaining insights into themselves and the wider world, the author created children's characters, James and Marian, considered as prime candidates for participation in the richer sharing of curriculum that employs the infusion of materials. Implicit in this consideration are materials and experiences derived from various literatures of all participants and subscribers of this fascinating cultural legacy, through a variety of procedures, including interactive teaching (Apple, 1989, 1990).

In a dramatic search for literary experiences that may serve the larger, universal function of human understanding, of linking the young with the old, one culture with another, and individuals to ideas, challenges, problems, and solutions, much attention has been given to the single subject of reading. Reading theorists such as Anderson and Pearson (1984) have reasoned that schema is a structure that facilitates planful retrieval of information from memory and permits reconstruction of elements that were not learned or may have been forgotten.

Witherell and Noddings (1991) described the same process of schema as the interaction of old processes with the new, a comprehension, a mental organization. Thus the experiences in the repertoire are activated by schema in reference to a text, a picture, an object, or an action. Decades ago Goodman (1967) took the position that reading is a psycholinguistic guessing game, that it involves an interaction between thought and language. Goodman's effort is part of a long, structured, and substantive effort to find through research and practice, some of most feasible procedures for teaching reading.

Efficient reading, it is argued, does not result from precise perception and identification of elements such as letters and sounds, but rather, from skill in selecting the fewest, most productive cues necessary to produce guesses that are right the first time. The ability to anticipate what has not been seen in reading is as vital as the ability to predict what has not yet been heard in listening (Goodman, 1967). A more recent position is that taken by Chew (1992). It is part of the continuing conversation about looking at the dynamics of change within context and productive outcome. It is part of a continuing, diligent search for progress. But more importantly, it is a position that challenges us teachers to know our clientele, our students who must be served; that we must note compelling needs that continue to emerge all around us and effect everyone.

LITERACY APPLIED: COMPREHENSIVENESS AND UNIVERSAL FUNCTION

But the legitimacy of reading draws criticisms from theorists who seriously question, for example, just how many students know how to drive a car and demonstrate through other skills that they have more than a modicum of intelligence, but still cannot read. A salient issue here is competence. There is little question that many systems and schools have accommodated themselves to the idea of minimum levels of reading competence, sufficient to allow the individual to function in society (Apple, 1992b; Hawkins, 1993a).

Sticht (1978) challenged this procedure and suggested that the conceptualization of theoretical models should transcend the mere understanding of microprocesses that are involved in independent skills, such as pre-reading perceptual skills, decoding, vocabulary, grammar, literal comprehension, and inferential comprehension. The truth of the matter is that while research, teaching, and learning efforts help the understanding of cognitive psychology of reading, there is, indeed, need for additional research and practice as well as model building at the macrolevel in order to address the broader problems. Such problems include the different types and levels of literacy skills that are needed to function in society and require the pursuit of more inclusively affective and efficient programs that accommodate large-scale human resources development.

The basic issues that have been raised imply the urgency for the expansion of the concept and availability of literacy, not as a privilege, but as a fundamental given for the viability of a literate society; a postindustrial, as well as a highly competitive society, functioning in a world, rendered smaller by the incidence of high technology. In the same context, literacy must include not only language and reading, but also writing. It means also that literacy must include additionally the ability to perform tasks that combine written language with figures, graphs, tables, maps, and other cogent symbolic representations. Furthermore, content knowledge, vocabulary, and comprehension skills must be so crafted and taught in order to foster the coordination of ear, eye, and mind.

All of these suggestions imply going beyond the assumption that "virtually all children can understand most of what is said to them before they begin to read" (Calfee & Drum, 1978, p. 222), and instead, make provisions for those students who, because of adverse socioeconomic circumstances, have oral language skills that may not be well developed and thus, even though they could do well by eye as they do by ear, would still lack the vocabulary and language skills required to perform well on tasks requiring sophisticated reading comprehension.

This position is crucial because, as Laban's (1964) research data showed, students whose oral language was low at kindergarten became students low in reading skills in the fourth grade and beyond. Conversely, students who were high in preschool oral language skills became more able readers. In fact, the groups grew further apart over the school years. In other words, comprehension requires considerable practice over several years in order to develop the preferred status of automaticity of reading, in the case in which automaticity is viewed as having parity in the efficiency of language processing by ear, eye, and mind (Wynn, 1992).

In fact, many students will perform poorly on written comprehension tests because of their limitations in the languaging capabilities that underlie the use of reading. At a minimum, children ought to develop reading skills and comprehend the written language as efficiently and as effectively as they can the spoken language. Acquiring such success with the inclusion of multicultural curricula would necessitate the conceptualization and infusion of cogent theory and pedagogy, such that even though they may not necessarily provide truth per se, they may help to simplify by providing a segment of stable ground from which to operate as we seek to extend our knowledge base further. In such context, it becomes prudent that reading be viewed in the larger sense of literacy.

READING COMPREHENSION

According to Jeremiah (1993), reading comprehension is a central feature of reading productivity, where reading comprehension implies the ability to reconstruct a writer's message from a textbook or other written sources. Out of the continuing debates among theorists, some have argued that reading comprehension should be taught by way of a skill-by-skill approach, whereas others have advocated a holistic method in which the overall message of a literary piece is determined by the reader.

A reader, in an attempt to obtain meaning, may combine skills and holistic methodology. In the particular case of African Americans, reading comprehension may be fashioned within the oral tradition and cultural framework of African-American life. From the point of view of presentation, the teaching of African Americans should move beyond the concept of silence (which television viewing seems to foster), and to create an atmosphere in which talk can be used as a vehicle for improving reading comprehension. These suggestions derive credence from the fact that it has been well documented, that the oral tradition is an integral feature of African-American life. The oral tradition is African in essence. Talk and talking, in the best sense, are heard in varied settings and for various purposes. From serious to informal settings, including the speaker, the message, the audience, and the purpose of discourse comes naturally everyday to African-American life. In fact, it seems logical to conclude that the oral tradition, as one aspect of African-American life, could be incorporated into a classroom setting, because many of our students are oriented to the oral tradition. Speechifying and rap, which are now fully recognized in the business of music, are not in any way an accident of culture.

But in truth, these discussed, specific issues are not peculiar only to African Americans, although history will indicate they have their roots in African culture. Thus, although African Americans have a powerful claim to these oralities, both on the continent and in the African diaspora, as vital communication media of interaction, it is also true to say that oral language is primary and pervasive; it is alive and well although, according to Yarborough (1993), it receives low attention.

Whether expressed as dramatic play, reading aloud, writing, and use of manipulatives or the acts of speaking and listening, it is safe to accept that language is truly oral. It is, for example, what the child uses initially in order to establish communication with immediacy. Reading and writing are technically second-hand procedures. Therefore, in linking listening with speaking, it may be concluded, noted Yarborough (1993), that we listen to the equivalent of a book a week, read a book a month, and write about as much as a book a year when we include such things as postcards, letters, checks, and other professional, domestic, or job-related activities.

Therefore, oral language is crucial and its function enables sounds to assume the dynamics of personalization: a critical feature in the serious business of teaching and learning; in establishing interaction, comprehension; and those classical activities of cognition that are expressed as a consequence of internal reconstruction through analysis, synthesis, and assessment.

Because children talk before they read and write, and they express or talk about what they "know" or think they know, their oral language should be respected. The whole language philosophy seems particularly logical here for undergirding curricula that are designed to promulgate language and thus foster literacy. So, too, should cogent methodologies that are used to enhance the teaching–learning transaction.

By adding ethnic studies perspectives that are rooted in gender, age, religion, ideology, sex, class, economics, and internationalism — such as multicultural, multiethnic, multidimensional, and multipurpose curricula of integrated philosophy and methodology — we can improve disciplines and content areas and facilitate teaching and learning. A much better job may be accomplished over traditional or mainstream curricula in presenting more comprehensive and closer-to-accurate pictures of the reality of this nation and the world. These inclusions should improve current unidimensional models/modes. Therefore, well-chosen and organized methodological practices that attempt to interface with curricular offerings in the broadest of conceptualization would enhance this crucial process of education.

LINKING CULTURES WITH LITERACY

Because the heart of cultural literacy is the essence of the self—the heart itself must not be substituted—cultural inclusion assumes paramount teaching–learning importance, especially among children. Whether offered as establishing familiarity with the conventions of an author's use of language, the symbolic use of language and hints that underscore an author's intention, or the fostering of reading and interpreting, which together are accorded comparable meaning as the possession of information, cultural literacy can offer needed access to the soul and understanding of the self in the pursuit of the deepest of interests.

People who know their origins, their culture, and their history are nearer to understanding themselves. Those who understand can experience and share their knowledge and joy. Hawkins (1993b) quoted Van Sertima as opining that one is not a complete person unless one is aware of one's phase of time, especially if that phase of time is a destructive or a humiliating phase. Moreover, whatever the history, it should be studied and understood, precisely because it affects our own dislikes, our assumptions, our reflexes, our behavior(s), our emotional capacity, as well as the manner in which people think about others. Truth is.

There is a legitimacy implied about establishing the use of literature as a force of discourse. Hodge (1990) argued for an interdisciplinary understanding of the discourse of modern culture, including social semantics, a synthesis of methods and concepts from a range of disciplines, including semiotics, linguistics, psychology, sociology, and others. Hodge believed that the act of interpretation cannot be restricted to the traditional understanding of the isolated text. Social factors, agents, and processes all exist outside the text, yet are decisive components of its social meaning and rectitude.

In these times of tension and global disequilibrium between and among ethnic, religious, and racial groups the world over, educators have an important responsibility and opportunity to share in reconstruction. For example, within a single school or classroom, teachers witness opposing factions, microcosms of the groups seen on the nightly news, in which rage has, in some cases, brought down powerful governments. However, so far, the experiment that is the United States has been that of attempting to merge countless diverse pieces into a manageable whole: a whole that may construct itself as becoming larger than the sum of its parts. The polity, all of us, are the parts with our compound labels: Asian American, African American, European American, Latin American, and Native Americans. And so on down the line there are designations identifying both the proud individual histories and hopeful united futures.

However, it is in the classroom that children of all groups are most likely to encounter one another, whether face to face or through textbooks and literature. If educators, teachers, researchers, theorists, and state decision makers were to capture the moment, that is, seize the time, and explore the possibilities of linking their similarities and differences, a real and significant effort can surely emerge. There can be in a real sense an attempt to harness their interests in the development of appreciation for both human universals as well as for the individual qualities that make us all unique (Cohl, 1993).

There is both a sense of pragmatism and urgency here. It would not be unrealistic to relate the implications to the total quality management (TQM) factor (Bastingl, 1992). Here the author brings to the consciousness a magnificent strategy that in the past lacked full acceptance in the United States (the nation of its origin), but that found fertile soil in Japan, where its development has become phenomenal. The implicit factor about that strategy thrives on the conviction that "sharing a personal constancy of purpose and a dedication to continuation together, allow meaningful change to take root" (p. v).

And this reflective procedure has the potency for making substantive curricular efforts not piecemeal, erstwhile disjointed celebrations, but efforts that derive their underpinnings from shared moral, ethical, philosophical, and academic concerns. Such efforts when sequentially crafted and logically, equitably, and totally dispensed through respected pedagogy, should enable the culture to derive shared respect for ourselves and one another, as the populace moves forward as individuals, as groups, and as a nation. Although there are obviously several influences and influencers involved in this dynamic drama of educating for the common weal or good, it remains true that teachers above everyone else in this regard hold the key to opening the gate to a rich, challenging, and highly competitive future.

MULTICULTURAL EDUCATION:
PHILOSOPHY AND PEDAGOGY

Diversity of people and the purposes for public schools and public education have been strengths of the United States, but also sources of conflict. The word "multicultural" has become one of the most debated in recent educational literature. Multicultural education is one of the most recent manifestations of conflict over education and values, emerging among other issues of race, religion, and ethnicity that have traditionally dominated discourse surrounding the role of schools in addressing them. This issue has almost replaced race as a major concern, despite the fact that race-related issues are still unresolved even with the 1954 Supreme Court decision. This shift in emphasis, although it recognizes the nation's diversity, still remains a burning problem, particularly because it is related to African Americans as well as their unique history as an involuntary immigrant group.

As a consequence, the most misunderstood construct in multiculturality is the "multicultural curriculum." In many ways the concept is mired in much rhetoric and abuse, precisely because it has come to be associated with what Schlesinger (1992) called "the curse of racism, the great failure of the American experiment, the glaring contradiction of American ideals . . . and the still crippling disease of American life (p. 14). Far too many persons tend to see the efficaciousness of what multicultural education purports as being about African Americans. So, on the other hand, whereas the New York State Department of Education endorses a "Curriculum of Inclusion," New York City remains opposed to this idea. The matter has become so volatile that the political fallout is incredible.

Following the thrust of the civil rights movement of the 1960s, many groups, led by African Americans, have shifted gears and are no longer willing to protest silently and work patiently to change laws that have so far not changed behaviors and attitudes. In large measure, voices are now more persistent, and actions more visible in the face of growing repressive measures, to make the United States become in truth and in fact the multicultural, multiracial, and multicultural country that it is, in actuality, demographically structured.

In some ways, many decision makers and people of great influence hide behind the excuse of the African-American assertion, legitimate as it is, to show their opposition to a legitimate school curricular change that is very likely to be missed, as was the case of the total quality management model that gave Japan a tremendous economic fillip in the industrial world. But there is yet time for adjustment to be made; for the nation to be duly oriented to the notion that multicultural education purely and simply means the integration or inclusion of diversity across the curriculum. In essence, allowing the "voices" of the nations to be included in substantive ways that inform all and are reflective of an inclusive and respectful multicultural perspective that the nation's population indicates, all have made the nation.

MULTICULTURAL EDUCATION: A PHILOSOPHY

According to Banks (1988), culture consists of behavior patterns, symbols, institutions, values, and other human-made components of society. It is the unique achievement of a human group or constellation that distinguishes it from other human groups. Although cultures are in many ways similar, a particular culture constitutes a unique whole. Thus, culture is a generic concept with wide boundaries. As a consequence, one can describe the U.S. macroculture, as well as the microcultures within it, to include the culture of poverty, popular culture, youth culture, the Southern culture, the Appalachian culture, and the culture of the intellectual community. Values are culture based.

Because culture is the root of multicultural and multiethnic studies, education suggests a type of structure that is related in some way to a range of cultural groups. The concept itself implies more than education related to many cultures. In fact, a major aim of multicultural education should be one of educating students so that they will acquire knowledge about a range of cultural groups while they develop attitudes, skills, and abilities that are needed to function at some level of competency within different cultural environments, locally, nationally, and internationally. These cultures may be social class cultures, regional cultures, religious cultures, and national cultures (e.g., the national culture of Korea). Another appropriate goal of multicultural education is to reform the total school environment so that students from the diverse cultural groups will be able to experience equal educational opportunities.

Multiethnic education implies a kind of education that is related in some ways to a range of ethnic groups. It is also a form of multicultural education, because an ethnic group is one kind of cultural group. Multiethnic education should help students develop knowledge, skills, attitudes, and abilities that are needed in order to relate to a range of ethnic groups and to function in ethnic group cultures at some level of competency. Another appropriate goal of multiethnic education is to change the total educational environment so that it will respond to ethnic students more positively and, therefore, enable them to experience educational equality. As such, multiethnic education is essential, although not a total part of the more global concept of multicultural education. Multicultural education programs, in the United States, for example, should include a strong emphasis on ethnic and racial minorities. It should not be relegated to the simplistic idea of feeling good.

MULTICULTURAL EDUCATION: A PEDAGOGY

Consistent with a caution that some values may be irreconcilable, Nieto (1992) posited four levels of pedagogical considerations that a system or culture may accommodate in a movement toward a fair and honest multicultural curriculum. First, there is the concern for tolerance, which means that others may endure the differences but not necessarily embrace them. The next level of consideration deals with the issue of acceptance. This implies that languages and other aspects of culture should be visible in schools. The third level, the one of understanding and knowledge of different culture and groups, would require schools to use values and experiences of the students and their communities as bases for their literacy development. Here, at this level, different perspectives become common-place in learning.

To achieve this third level requires more than a change in attitude. It necessarily involves textbook publishers, curriculum developers, teachers, researchers, decision makers, and administrators of educational programs, as well as policy makers in schools. The fourth and final level is perceived as the most difficult to achieve. It is here that the most fundamental challenges to cherished and deeply held values and lifestyles get confronted. This level requires much more than accepting different cultures, because it also

> means understanding that culture is not fixed or unchangeable, and thus one is able to critique its manifestation and outcomes. Because multicultural education is concerned with equity and social justice for all people, and because basic values of different groups are often diametrically opposed, conflict is inevitable. Passively accepting the status quo of any culture is inconsistent with multicultural education. (Nieto, 1992, p. 227)

But multicultural education seeks legitimacy across the curriculum in order to undergird and inform all disciplines in substantive ways.

VALUES AND MULTICULTURAL LITERATURE

Well-written multicultural literature, like other quality literature, provides enjoyment for the reader or the listener. But in addition to the enjoyment of reading and sharing good books, there are other values for children, as members of an ethnic minority. But caution is needed here. Teachers must be careful about the selection of materials for presentation so that they do not convey wrong images. Already many U.S. citizens are filled with distorted images of society and are not prepared to value its multicultural character, especially when they are surrounded with literature that either presents minorities stereotypically or as invisible by omitting them entirely.

On another level, because of the pervasive Eurocentric monopoly and the small number of books written positively about minorities, librarians, teachers, and other adults are likely to accept all books with a picture of a minority child without carefully evaluating the stories and the stereotypes they might be fostering. It is believed that adults who work with children and literature should reeducate themselves to the social values that books pass on to children. To do this, such persons of influence must learn to evaluate and assess books written about children from all ethnic backgrounds.

It is really only recently that influencers have come to understand that certain books, because of their illustrations, themes, characterizations, and language, can perpetuate stereotypes or result in psychological damage or discomfort to children. Unfortunately, this idea was not advanced publicly until very recent times because of the growing objections to the use of certain illustrations and stereotypes in literature. Thanks to such vigilance, some measure of change has begun to take place. Literary honesty is a crucial issue here, and it ought to continue to ramify all educational goods and services. In this sense, whatever is offered as classroom text assumes special importance because of the messages sent. As a service to this compelling need for some measure of objectivity and positiveness in the selection of literature reflecting values of multicultural literature, A. Smith (1993) posited the following suggestions to serve as guidelines:

1. Through multicultural literature, minority children realize that they have roots in the past through a cultural heritage of which they can be proud; that their own culture has made important contributions to the United States and to the world.

2. By developing pride in their heritage, children improve their self-concept and develop a sense of identity.

3. Learning about other cultures allows all children to understand that people who belong to ethnic groups other than their own are real people with feelings, emotions, and needs similar to their own.

4. Reading about other cultures, including their poetry, philosophies, and products of the imagination and creativity, helps children to expand their own understanding and realization that all cultural groups have made contributions in these areas.

5. Children discover that although all people may not share their personal beliefs, and other cultures may respect different value systems, individuals can and must learn to live in harmony.

6. Through multicultural literature, children of the majority culture can learn to respect the contributions and values of the minority; they learn about historical contributions that are made by people in both the United States and the world.

7. By enjoying the traditional folk literature of ethnic minorities, children can identify with the people who created and passed down the stories through centuries of oral tradition.

8. Through the multicultural stories, children broaden their understanding of geography and natural history as they read about cultural groups living in various areas.

9. The wide range of multicultural themes helps children develop an understanding of sociological change.

10. Reading about minority members who have achieved or successfully solved their own problems helps raise the aspiration level of children who belong to a minority.

11. Reading books about ethnic minorities helps children develop a sense of social sensitivity; all people are human beings who should be considered as individuals, not stereotypes.

However, despite good intentions, the choice of text, whether for reading or other disciplines is fraught with the vagaries of complex dichotomies.

THE USE OF TEXTS AND THE PERVASIVENESS OF CULTURAL POLITICS

According to Apple (1992b), the school curriculum is not neutral knowledge. Instead, what counts as legitimate knowledge is really the result of complex power relations, struggles, and compromises among identifiable class, race, gender, and religious groups. In essence the choice about text in schools is socially constructed. The fact of the matter is that there is a great degree of conflict and confusion surrounding the business of schooling, which ideally, is supposed to drive the vast engine of democracy. Still, there is the popular view that unlike the position of the democratic modality of school opening up horizons and ensuring mobility, schooling may be seen as a form of social control, the embodiment of cultural dangers, institutions whose curricula and teaching practices threaten the moral stature of children who attend. Such are perceptions of contradiction.

Luke (1988) talked of school texts as the simultaneous results of political, economic, and cultural activities, battles, and compromises; they are designed and authored by real people with real interests; they are published within the political and economic constraints of markets, resources, and power. The meaning of texts, then, and how they are used are conditions of differing community commitments, including teachers and students.

Thus, within the context of these struggles and contradictions, what has been counted as legitimate knowledge is the result of complex power relations and struggles among identifiable class, race, gender, and religious groups. This relationship becomes exacerbated during times of social upheaval and are made manifest in the struggles by women, people of color, and others who have had to battle systems to get their history and knowledge included in the curriculum. Within recent times, the problem has become more well defined (Apple & Christian-Smith, 1991).

Conflicts over texts are often perceived as proxies for wider questions of power relations. They involve what people hold most dear. Texts are, according to Inglis (1985), messages about the future, and as part of the curriculum, they participate in creating what a society has recognized as legitimate and truthful. In a way, they help to create a major reference point for what knowledge, culture, belief, and morality are supposed to be. They are in some ways the creation of specific groups of people with vested interests.

Currently issues about texts, particularly their ideology, are attracting much attention because, for better or worse, they dominate what students learn. Therefore, although teachers end up using books in classrooms, the world of books is not really cut off from the world of commerce. Vested interests still extend a long arm in the industry. Books are not just cultural artifacts; they are also economic commodities, the products of the volatile business or dynamics of the publishing industry. They are caught up in a complicated set of political and economic battles that are highly competitive.

As such, the vicissitudes of a capitalist market get driven by the seemingly invisible hand of textbook adoption policies. Therefore, cultural domination is a fact of life for millions of students, partly because the economic control is undergirded by ideologies and systems of politics in which cultural determinants predominate. And texts have become centers of ideological and educational conflict. On the one hand they may be considered as not being conservative enough, whereas on the other hand, they may be considered too liberal or progressive and a source of contention in the cross-fire of opposing fusilage.

Today, although cries may be heard about the absence of cultural expressions, of issues such as labor, women, people of color, and others who are considered less powerful or important, other issues emerge involving different definitions of the common good. One such issue is what Raskin (1986) referred to as reference to society and where it should be heading with regard to cultural values. Both the negative and positive senses of power become essential class struggles within the context of what the curriculum is supposed to be. They thus involve the very nature of the connections between cultural visions and differential power.

Aside from cultural politics, even though it is suggested that change in materials and pedagogical processes are advanced and in which some literary inputs could bring social transformation, the dual sense of the power of curriculum and texts emerges quite clearly. The curriculum and texts become part of ideological regulation and get subjected to determinants of morality, cultural, and political correctness. Clearly, the struggle gets linked to broader concerns about who should control the curriculum in schools. And thus political and sometimes religious intervention become the critical factors with the most powerful say in a matter also truly directed to the students for whom efforts are designed to meet and answer the age-old question (Bennett, 1986).

With all the ramifications of class, politics, and power at work when new, progressive forms of curricular change are contemplated, it is little wonder that some of the best intentions get stuck in the diatribe of political and economic vested interests. A *common culture* finds it extremely difficult if not impossible to become an extension to everyone of what a minority effort may mean and believe. Rather, and quite crucially so, it requires not the stipulation and incorporation within textbooks of lists and concepts that make us all culturally literate, but the creation of the conditions necessary for all people to participate in a creation and recreation of meanings and values. Moreover, it requires a democratic process in which all people, not simply those who see themselves as the intellectual guardians of the Western tradition or the Eurocentric emphasis, can be involved in the deliberation of what is important (Apple, 1990). It goes without saying that such necessitates the removal of the real obstacles such as unequal power, wealth, and time for reflection that often stand in the way of participation (Roman & Christian-Smith, 1988).

A PERSPECTIVE FOR THE FUTURE

Walcott, in his (1992) Nobel Laureate acceptance speech, urged: "Stand close to a waterfall, and you will stop hearing its roar." This call from the prestigious statement of such a great scholar has the potential for allaying the fears or anxiety of those who would rather remain with what has traditionally been on the books because of the unknown. It requires a refreshing look at the charting of new dimensions to fit the culture within the context of preparing for the new conversations of the global universe. It should of necessity transcend those of the national spirit.

In many ways the linking of cultural issues to the dynamics of literacy within futuristic constructs is very much like a fundamental attempt to include a vital missing link in an awesome chain of being. In a way, it is like suggesting that it is never too late to be what one might have been. Moreover, when one attempts an answer to Herbert Spencer's questions about "what knowledge is of most worth?" one is indeed attempting to examine a very fundamental set of issues regarding the nature of society, the legacy of its civilization. It is not unlike the act of emplacing, shoring up, revising, or revitalizing the foundation for building an enduring educational edifice; the reformulation of a structure that must supersede the sum of its parts must require a figure and ground that, while deriving its sustenance from traditional values, nonetheless must give serious credence to contemporary and futuristic circumstances (London, 1991).

Wiley (1992) expressed his personal point of view, suggesting that it is necessary to note that,

it's not just a matter of parents not caring enough, teachers not making enough of an effort, and the kids not being motivated. It's more complicated than that. It's a combination of changing the nature of the economy that created the instability of family and community, and also raising the level of development necessary to help more people in the economy. (pp. 14–15, 16)

These comments are all reasonable, logical, and doable; they are also achievable challenges, yet they are left unattended. And the question is why? The answer may be viewed as a calculated attitude, or what Wiley defined as the nation's eternal cancer that consumes and eats at its soul, racism. The fact of the matter is that values cannot be legislated, but instead are transmitted primarily by the basic social institutions, the home, church, and school. He argued further that values learned by precepts and examples are important in building bridges of understanding and unity in our pluralistic, multicultural, local, and world community. In essence, values are influenced by religion, family, culture, education, friends, and associates.

Therefore, communication processes in our heterogeneous culture are of vital importance. When we communicate, we must be careful to disseminate a value orientation that is understandable. This makes the procedure for literacy very crucial. And it is especially essential in attaining a higher quality of life in communities where citizens come from diverse geographical, ethnic, racial, religious, and educational backgrounds. In this setting, the tenets of our value system—commitment, cooperation, and compromise—are far more productive for the country as a common denominator for human interest than a shallow display of status and acquisition or platitudinous rhetoric.

People from all walks of life have values that help to set the standards for the ordering of primary behavior in our society. The input of each is important in achieving an appropriate community quality of life. The social interaction of a small local group that is multicultural in its makeup, with an integrity of purpose that is based on commonly accepted values, can be helpful and even successful in accommodating and compromising different views.

The nation, according to Wynn (1993), needs a new moral compass to guide us through the ravages of drugs, sleazy politicians, brokers ripping off their clients, savings and loan executives driving their institutions into the ground and leaving the taxpayers to foot the bill, greedy preachers, lying presidents, teen-agers cheating on examinations and millions of others self-destructing because they simply have no hope for a better quality of life. When do we mend?

Despite it all, there is the feeling of eternal hope that harmony and inner peace can be found in following a moral compass that points in the direction of moral values. A proactive environment that nurtures and integrates our families, religious institutions, centers of education, and varied community cultures will bring about an excellence in our quality of life that is sorely needed. But this cannot happen at all if iniquitous sharing continues, because a chain is as strong as the weakest link. Dewey (1897) warned us long ago:

> I believe that the individual who is to be educated is a social individual, and that society is an organic union of individuals. If we eliminate the social factor from the child, we are left only with an abstraction; if we eliminate the individual factor from society, we are left only with an inert and lifeless mass. Education therefore, must begin with a psychological insight into the child's capacities, interests, and habits. It must be controlled at every point by reference to these same considerations. These powers, interests, and habits must be continually interpreted — we must know what they mean. They must be translated into terms of their social equivalents — into terms of what they are capable of in the way of social service. (p. 68)

But here we are at a point in U.S. history that Maya Angelou (1993) called, "the pulse of the morning," still vacillating about the obvious.

CONCLUSION

Culture inevitably buttresses a nation's determinism. Yet how it will be done in the future and the nature of its form and function are truly determined by the process of evolution. Of course, there are always factors that may hasten the process; but the use of such requires a will of enormous proportion. Culture always drives a curriculum. When a nation, for example, attempts to respond to the civilizing question, "What knowledge is of most worth?", such a nation must confront a very awesome responsibility. Often this responsibility calls into consideration dynamic, philosophical views, grounded in values that are perceived as being necessary for the promulgation of its cultural legacy.

Indeed, such legacy must be seen as being critical to the cultivation of the young progenitors who must take into the future this magnanimous bequest presented through educational orientation. Here in the United States, as elsewhere in the world, culture, regardless of its various forms and functions, has performed this undergirding responsibility. It has provided the impetus, the underpinnings, of the education process, using schools and schooling as the instrument and process for achieving such undertaking.

But so far these essential criteria have been basically unidimensional; they have reflected essentially one regional perspective—a Eurocentric perspective. And, it has done so and continues to do so with occasional inputs of snippets or reference to other cultures, including the ones it has displaced through conquest, domination, suppression, or treaty violations. In the meantime, compelling circumstances point the way for change.

Should these indicators be heeded, change processes should include such obvious ones as: the reality of a plural society, which has long emerged as an alternative replacement to the melting pot theory. The demography of the nation has changed more radically over time to reflect a more multinational conglomeration of peoples. Therefore, the growing demand for leadership and orientation must transcend distortion of universal configuration and, instead, address issues in their logical, honest, objective, rational, and pragmatic contexts.

In essence, there is a call for such efforts that must supersede shallow, biased perspectives that are epitomized by such persons as Hymowitz (1993), who, through acts of omission or commission, often reflect the mood and views of significant others: influencers and decision makers. Takaki (1993) singled out Schlesinger (1992) as distorting history in his book, *The Age of Jackson*. Takaki noted that the book ignored slavery as well as the subject of the Indian removal, all of which took place during the age of Jackson.

In taking the issue still further, Takaki noted also that Handlin (1951), whose book *The Uprooted* purported to tell the "epic story of the great migration that made the American people" implies that all the migrations came from Europe. In point of fact, Takaki called attention to the notion that the mere idea of excluding people of color makes the Schlesingers and Handlins responsible for the "disunity" of the United States. Instead, it is prudent that all who are engaged in the serious business of educating the nation's children should read the faces of their charges, who now number upward of 60% non-White in many largely urban environments. There is need for new conceptualization, organization, and presentation of educational goods and services; need too for improved curriculum, which gives due credence to literacy.

Language is the handmaiden of literacy. In the context of cultural discourse, language is the memory of power. The abuse of power is pain. Writing that aims at transforming or establishing awareness can become an act about searching for the margins that stretch the limits of accomplishments. But the politics and economics of education often move down the center, going from the idea of compromise to collusion to corruption, to vacillation and postponement.

Although the concept of progress toward understanding and awareness of the efficaciousness of culture in the dynamics of literacy continues to be futile and redundant, the struggle for decency and inclusion of relevant materials continues. It is part of a seminal human proclivity, for there will always be history, largely because there will always be dreaming and therefore conflict. Knowing or understanding and therefore becoming aware are all good strategies for preparing the unknowing. To present information, to tell a story, for example, is to activate dreams. It is to raise the consciousness, especially in this case about the obvious and inevitable, which in the context of filibuster merely prolongs the agony of deletion and miseducation born of exclusivity of the real, the truth.

The use of language reflecting multiculturism augurs well for shoring up the communication process in our heterogeneous culture. This is of vital importance. It can provide support for values transmitted and learned by both precept and example. It can become a crucial link in building bridges of understanding and unity in our pluralistic, multicultural, local and world communities.

Improving the communication process is essential, even more so now and during the ensuing years. It is especially essential in attaining a higher quality of life in communities to which citizens came from geographical, ethnic, racial, religious, and educational backgrounds that are different. Basic tenets of the nation's value system can derive greater impetus and richness that may enhance commitment, cooperation, and compromise. These altogether ascribe to ethical values, not only as they impact on the quality of life, but in the long run can become far more productive for the nation as common denominators for human interaction, harmony, and inner peace. These can supersede shallow displays of status and acquisitions, and speak instead to the import of the human condition.

This chapter, although singular in its appeal in this volume, finds hope in the import of its message. To be sure, the individual who travels alone is said to travel fastest, but nonetheless, in the company of colleagues and friends, it is also said that one may travel farther.

REFERENCES

Altbach, P. (1988). *The knowledge context*. Albany: State University of New York Press.

Angelou, M. (1993). *On the pulse of morning* [Poem read by the poet at the Inauguration of William Jefferson Clinton, President of the United States]. New York: Random House.

Anderson, R. C., & Pearson, P. D. (1984). A schema-theoretic new basic process in reading comprehension. In P. D. Pearson (Ed.), *Handbook of reading research* (pp. 255–291). New York: Longman.

Apple, M. W. (1989). Regulating the text: The social-historical roots of state control. *Educational Policy, 3,* 107–123.

Apple, M. W. (1990). *Ideology and curriculum* (2nd ed.). New York: Routledge.

Apple, M. W. (1992a). *The politics of official knowledge*. New York: Routledge.

Apple, M. W. (1992b, October). The text and cultural politics. *Educational Researcher*, 4-11, 19.

Apple, M. W., & Christian-Smith, L. (Eds.). (1991). *The politics of the textbook*. New York: Routledge.

Banks, J. A. (1988). *Multiethnic education: Theory and practice* (2nd ed.). Boston: Allyn & Bacon.

Bastingl, J. J. (1992). *Schools of quality: An introduction to total management*. Alexandria, VA: Association for Supervision and Curriculum Development.

Batsleer, J., Davis, T., O'Rourke, R., & Weedon, C. (1985). *Rewriting English: Cultural politics of gender and class*. New York: Methuen.

Bennett, T. (1986). The politics of the 'popular' and popular culture. In T. Bennett, C. Mercer, & J. Woollacott (Eds.), *Popular culture and social relations* (pp. 6-21). Philadelphia: Open University Press.

Benavides, A. (1988). High risk predictors and preferral screening for language minority students. In A. A. Ortiz & B. A. Ramirez (Eds.), *Schools and the culturally diverse exceptional student: Promising practices and future directions* (pp. 19-31). Reston, VA: Council for Exceptional Children.

Brause, R. (1992). Learning considered a model for literacy. In C. Hedley, D. Feldman, & P. Antonacci (Eds.), *Literacy across the curriculum* (pp. 286-300). Norwood, NJ: Ablex.

Calfee, R., & Drum, P. A. (1978). Learning to read: Theory, research, and practice. *Curriculum Inquiry, 3(3),* 183-250.

Carver, R. (1977-1978). Toward a theory of reading comprehension and auding. *Reading Research Quarterly, 13*(11), 8-63.

Comer, J. (1980). *School power*. New York: The Free Press.

Chew, C. R. (1992). Policies for literacy. In C. Hedley, D. Feldman, & P. Antonacci (Eds.), *Literacy across the curriculum* (pp. 3-14). Norwood, NJ: Ablex.

Cohl, C. (1993). African American: A past and future. *Instructor, 102*(6), 4.

Darnton, R. (1982). *The literary underground of the old regime*. Cambridge, MA: Harvard University Press.

Dewey, J. (1897). *My pedagogic creed*. New York: Macmillan.

Ellsworth, N. J. (1989). *Using a cognitive schema to teach problem-solving skills to urban learning-disabled adolescents*. Unpublished doctoral dissertation, Columbia University, Teachers College, New York.

Geyer, J. A. (1972). Comprehensive and partial models related to the reading process. *Reading Quarterly, 7*(4), 541-587.

Goldstein, H. (1940). *Reading and listening comprehension at various controlled rates*. Unpublished doctoral dissertation, Teachers College, Columbia University.

Goodman, K. S. (1967, February). *Reading: A psychological linguistic guessing game*. Paper presented at American Educational Research Association Conference, New York.

Greene, M. (1983). On the American dream: Ambiguity and the persistence of rage. *Curriculum Inquiry, 13*(2), 179-193.

Handlin, O. (1951). *The uprooted*. Boston, MA: Little, Brown

Harrington, D. (1987). *Beyond the four walls: Teacher professionalism in action*. New York: United Federation of Teachers.

Hawkins, D. B. (1993a). Contemporary writers/scholars discuss their craft. *Black Issues in Higher Education, 9*(26), 20.

Hawkins, D. B. (1993b). Van Sertima makes an accurate account of history. *Black Issues in Higher Education, 9*(26), 25.

Hedley, C., Feldman, D., & Antonacci, P. (Eds.). (1992). *Literacy across the curriculum*. Norwood, NJ: Ablex.

Hodge, R. (1990). *Literature as discourse: Textual strategies in English and history*. Baltimore, MD: Johns Hopkins Press.

Horne, D. (1986). *The public culture.* Dover, MA: Pluto Press.

Hymowitz, K. S. (1993, March 25). Multiculturalism is anti-culture. *New York Times,* p. A15.

Inglis, F. (1985). *The management of ignorance: A political theory of curriculum.* New York: Basil Blackwell.

Jeremiah, M. A. (1993). Improving reading comprehension of Black students. *Black Issues in Higher Education, 9*(26), 31.

Jones, B. F., Tinzmann, M. B., & Pierce, J. (1992). How thoughts are made. In C. Collins & J. Mangieri (Eds.), *Building the quality of thinking in and out of school in the twenty-first century* (pp. 185-220). Hillsdale, NJ: Lawrence Erlbaum Associates.

Jordan, J. B. (Ed.). (1989). *1988 special education yearbook.* Reston, VA: Council for Exceptional Children.

Laban, W. (1964). *Language ability: Grades seven, eight, and nine* (Project Number 1131, Monographed). Berkeley, CA: University of California Press.

Lankshear, C., with Lawle, M. (1987). Literacy, schooling and revolution. Philadelphia: Falmer Press.

Larson, K. A., & Gerber, M. M. (1987). Effects of social metacognition training for enhancing overt behavior in learning disabled and low achieving delinquents. *Exceptional Children, 54*(3), 201-211.

London, C. B. G. (1990). A Piagetian constructivist perspective on curriculum development. *Reading Improvement, 27*(2), 82-95.

London, C. B. G. (1991). Some thoughts on the consideration of a Fordham University School of Education mission statement. *Education Notes, 18*(1), 2.

Luke, A. (1988). *Literary textbooks, ideology.* Philadelphia: Falmer Press.

Nieto, S. (1992). *Affirming diversity.* White Plains, NY: Longman.

Noddings, N. (1992). *The challenge to care in schools.* New York: Teachers College Press.

Palinscar, A. S., & Brown, A. L. (1988). Teaching and practicing thinking skills to promote comprehension in the context of group problem solving. *Remedial and Special Education* (RASE), *9*(1), 53, 59.

Ponterotto, J. B., & Casas, J. M. (1991). *Handbook of racial/ethnic minority counseling research.* Springfield, IL: Charles C Thomas.

Raskin, M. (1986). *The common good.* New York: Routledge & Kegan Paul.

Roman, L., & Christian-Smith, with Ellsworth, L. (Eds.). (1988). *Becoming feminine: The politics of popular culture.* Philadelphia: Falmer Press.

Schlesinger, A. M., Jr. (1992). *The disuniting of America.* New York: Norton.

Schumaker, J. B., Deshler, D. D., & Ellis, E. S. (1986). Intervention issues related to the education of LD adolescents. In J. K. Torgesen & B. Y. L. Wong (Eds.), *Psychological and educational perspectives on learning disabilities* (pp. 329-365). New York: Academic Press.

Smith, A. (1993, January 8). *Understanding cultural diversity through literature.* Paper presented at Manhattan Council, Parents and Reading Conference.

Smith, F. (1990). *To think.* New York: Teachers College Press.

Sticht, T. G. (1978). The development of literacy. *Curriculum Literacy, 8*(4), 341-351.

Takaki, R. (1993). Race in America: The search for common ground. *Black Issues in Higher Education, 10*(2), 4, 5.

Walcott, D. (1992). *The Antilles: Fragments of epic memory.* Speech delivered at the conferring of the 1992 Nobel Prize for Literature at the Swedish Academy's 18th century headquarters, Stockholm, Sweden.

Wiley, E., III. (1992). Educators hope Clinton's stated commitment to inner-city education goes farther than that of his predecessor. *Black Issues in Higher Education, 9*(22), 14-15, 16.

Witherell, C., & Noddings, N. (Eds.). (1991). *Stories lives tell: Narrative and dialogue in education.* New York: Columbia University Press.

Wynn, C. (1993). Our moral compass points in the wrong direction. *Black Issues in Higher Education, 9*(22), 84.

Yarborough, B. H. (1993, January 8). *Oral language in literature-based activities.* Paper presented at the Winter Fordham Reading Conference, Fordham University, Graduate School of Education, Lincoln Center Campus, New York.

11

Biology of Specific (Developmental) Learning Disabilities

Archie A. Silver
University of South Florida College of Medicine

This chapter reviews some of the known and some of the speculative data relating to learning disabilities that the neuroscientist can offer to the educator and to suggest ways in which that information can contribute to education for the future. From the biologic point of view, the academic difficulties seen in children with specific learning disabilities represent only the tip of the proverbial iceberg, the visual peak emerging from a series of underlying hierarchal dysfunctions. The base of the iceberg may be specific genetic influence as yet unknown. There are, however, suggestive morphological and physiological differences in the dyslexic brain, which in their turn influence the way the brain deals with information. The way the brain deals with information may be the abnormality in central nervous processing that makes the acquisition of reading, spelling, writing, mathematics, even speaking and listening difficult. This chapter retraces the hierarchal steps proposed, reviewing evidence for each and showing how each step leads to better understanding of the syndrome we call specific learning disability.

The first step, immediately underlying the academic disability, is a defect in the way the brain deals with information impinging on it. By definition, specific learning disability is not only characterized by a discrepancy between academic achievement and intelligence but also by "a disorder in one or more of the basic psychological processes involved in understanding or in using language, spoken or written" (National Advisory Committee on Handicapped Children, 1991 Education for All Handicapped Children Act [PL-94142], 1977). The search for these "basic psychological processes" has occupied researchers for over two decades.

The subjects of these studies came from varied sources: special and mainstream school classrooms, reading clinics, pediatric, neurological, and psychiatric clinics, speech, learning, and language centers. The investigators came from diverse disciplines each with its own special orientation. In many research studies the definition of "learning disability" is not clear; boundaries of disability are not established, demographic characteristics of subjects not included, and methodology varied from search for a critical, univariate underlying neuropsychological process to sophisticated multivariate analysis. Variations in findings from these heterogeneous studies have emphasized the heterogeneity encompassed by the federal definition of learning disabilities. On the positive side, the very heterogeneity has demanded that research studies formulate a clear delineation of children included in samples and have thus encouraged the development of a clinical classification (see Table 11.1). Such a classification restricts the term *specific* learning disability to persons whose academic achievement is significantly below that expected from the individuals' age, intelligence, and educational opportunity *and* who have specific central nervous system processing deficits relating to language in any of its dimensions—in the perception, association, retention (storage), understanding, and retrieval of symbols. It does not include in that term individuals who have academic difficulty but who do *not* have the spectrum of specific processing defects relating to aspects of language. Thus, organic defect of the central nervous system, attention deficit disorders, inappropriate education, and poverty *may* each contribute to learning difficulty, But, if the specific neuropsychological deficits are not present, these individuals by definition are not considered "specific learning disabilities."

TABLE 11.1
Disorders of Learning: Clinical Classification Based on Possible Causative Factors

Group I: Extrinsic Factors	Group II: Intrinsic Factors	Group III: Combinations

a. Social and economic deprivation
b. Language differences
c. Inappropriate or inadequate prior education
d. Emotional barriers to learning
	a. Maturational lags
	  1. Specific language disabilities
	  2. Attention deficit hyperactivity disorder
	b. Organic defect of the central nervous system
	c. Tourette's syndrome
	d. Autism
	e. Generalized cognitive immaturity, cause unknown
		Categories in Group I and Group II

Note: Table 2-1 from *Disorders of Learning in Childhood* (p. 26) by A. A. Silver and R. A. Hagin, 1990, New York: Wiley. Copyright 1990 by John Wiley & Sons. Reprinted by permission.

This clinical classification has value not only because with its use, the *cause* of the learning problems of some children may be identified, but more important because each etiological group differs in terms of clinical manifestations, natural history, prognosis, treatment, and prevention. For example, longitudinal studies of children with neurological signs (the "organic" group) find that as adults, these people were most impaired in terms of academic performance and in resistance of their processing deficits to maturation (Silver & Hagin, 1964; Spreen, 1988). The management of these children must, therefore, consider the resistance of their defects to training, their predisposition to anxiety, and their tendency to impulsivity. Thus, it becomes important for educators to insist on a comprehensive evaluation of their children who have significant learning problems, an evaluation in terms of neurological and psychiatric examination, neuropsychological processing, cognitive examination, educational opportunities, and environmental status. Unfortunately, such an evaluation is an expensive undertaking and the skills needed for such a diagnosis may not be available. It is suggested, however, that a stepwise diagnostic decision tree can be planned so that the most costly and least available skills are needed for only the most puzzling child (see Figure 11.1). Educators in the future will, hopefully, become more aware than they are now of the different needs of each group in this taxonomy and may not try to impose a rigid educational placement on all.

This clinical classification also does not mean the children designated as specific learning disabilities are a homogeneous group. They are homogeneous in that *no* etiological factors may clinically be detected and they have a spectrum of specific language-related processing problems. The term *specific* is used here in two senses: In the medical sense meaning that the cause is unknown, and in the behavioral sense it implies circumscribed areas of dysfunction. The latter group is the major subject of this chapter.

THE SPECTRUM OF NEUROPSYCHOLOGICAL PROCESSING DEFECT

The processing defects of the specific learning disordered group, however, although all relating to language, may be distributed over a wide spectrum. Early studies have attempted to relate reading failure to single variables: letter matching, auditory discrimination of sounds, visual-auditory and auditory-visual integration, symbolic mediation (Barrett, 1965a, 1965b, 1965c; Birch & Belmont, 1964; Blank & Bridges, 1967; Dykstra, 1968; Hammill et al., 1987). More recent work has emphasized verbal medication difficulties (Vellutino & Scanlon, 1985) and "linguistic awareness" (Liberman, Rubin, Duques, & Carlisle, 1985). Vellutino and his group (Vellutino

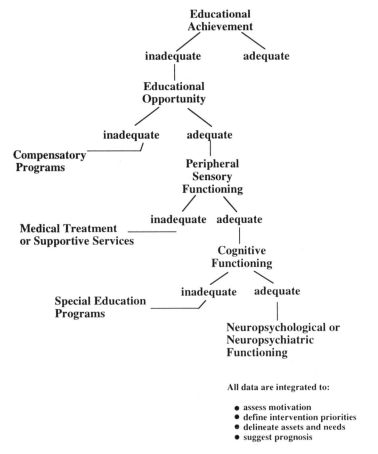

Fig. 11.1. Decision tree: Decision making in the diagnosis of learning disorders. From *Disorders of Learning in Childhood* (p. 39) by A. A. Silver and R. A. Hagin, New York: Wiley. Copyright 1990 by John Wiley & Sons. Reprinted by permission.

& Scanlon, 1985) at the Child Study Center in Albany, New York, present convincing evidence that difficulty in learning to read, as measured by word identification, "may be caused primarily by limitation in coding structural or purely linguistic attributes of spoken and printed words" (Vellutino & Scanlon, 1985, p. 210). Liberman (Lieberman, Rubin, Duques, & Carlisle, 1985), at the Haskins laboratory, found her subjects to be deficient in "lexical access and representation in short-term memory" (p. 163) a symbol–sound association deficit in modern note.

There has been increasing criticism of the single symptom paradigm, however, and increasing recognition of the heterogeneity of neuropsychological patterns in specific learning disabilities (Mattis, 1978). Multivariate statistical methods (Q technique and cluster analysis) on a broad range of cognitive and linguistic variables (Rourke, 1985) have tended to uncover a spectrum of subtypes, which, not surprisingly, may be classified into three types: a generalized language subtype, a visual-processing deficit subtype, and a mixed type containing elements of each. There are some variations of this generalization. For example, Satz and Morris (1981) found a specific language naming group and an "unexpected group" with no impairment on any of the neuropsychological tests; Petrauskas and Rourke (1979) found body image problems in their sample with finger gnosis immaturities in both hands. In general, however, in spite of the diversity in samples of children studied—their source, their ages, intelligence, demographic patterns—there is a consensus in the range of subgroup patterns. The "verbal deficit group" has lower verbal scores than performance scores in the Wechsler Intelligence Scale for Children-Revised (WISC-R), poor performance on the Peabody Picture Vocabulary Test (PPVT), disorders of naming, problems with auditory comprehension, imitative speech, difficulty in putting sounds together to make words and problems with sequential processing; the deficient visual-spatial graphomotor group has intact auditory-sequential processing but has difficulty in the orientation of the body in space as seen in finger gnosis, right–left orientation and in constructive finger praxis and in visual-motor function; the mixed verbal and spatial deficit group has characteristics of each. Different patterns of academic achievement may correlate with different patterns of neuropsychological processing (Fletcher, 1985). For example, children with phonological sequencing problems may have most of their academic difficulty in reading; those with visual-spatial problems may be the poor handwriters and have difficulty in mathematics. Pennington (1991) agreed that each neuropsychological pattern is clinically reflected to specific areas of academic difficulty.

NEUROPSYCHOLOGICAL DEFECT AND REMEDIAL EDUCATION

The importance of understanding the pattern of neuropsychological processing in children with specific learning disabilities is both theoretical and practical: theoretical to determine whether the subgroups differ in their neural substrates and perhaps ultimately in etiology; practical in the use of neuropsychological patterns to guide treatment, to predict diagnosis, and to develop programs for prevention. In treatment, for example, as the neuropsychological deficits and assets are profiled, what is the most effective way of treating the educational problem? Should the emphasis of remediation be to utilize the intact areas or to strengthen the weak ones? For example, if children with a reading disability have inadequate skills in temporal sequencing of auditory stimuli and intact visual-spatial ones, should they be trained with techniques to enhance their verbal skills (deficit training) or should we utilize their intact visual-spatial skills (compensatory training)? This is a question with practical importance in education.

There is abundant evidence that the nervous system is not static but retains a capacity to change even in adult life. Learning is defined as the process of acquiring new information, memory as the persistence of learning in a state that can be retrieved. Learning and memory require changes in existing neural circuits, which may involve multiple cellular mechanisms within single neurons. Learning induces changes in the properties of membrane channels, resulting in an increase in release of neurotransmitters. Memory involves a persistent change in the relationship among neurons, with the terminals of neurons undergoing striking morphological change, increasing in number and length of dendritic branches and dendritic spines. In addition, there is an increase in numbers and sensitivity of sites on the axon terminals from which neurotransmitters are released. Conversely, where there is a deprivation of stimulation there is a decrease in complexity and number of dendrites and dendritic spines (Rosensweig & Bennett, 1976). There is convincing evidence that stimulation is necessary for function and that stimulation can change the morphology of the neuron, the number and complexity of dendritic spines, the number of sites for neurotransmitter release, and the sensitivity of receptor sites.

Undifferentiated stimulus, however, is not the critical factor for induction of morphological change. There may be a need for stimuli to be *specific* in permitting a *specific* function to emerge. The stimulus must match the function it is intended to induce. In short, the neural networks subsuming a specific function may need stimulation specific to that function.

Applying these considerations to the problem of learning disabilities, a deficit visual-motor function may be improved by direct training of that function, by exercises to stimulate visual-motor function and body image orientation, and that training in temporal auditory sequencing can enhance the ability to place sounds and even meaning in correct temporal sequence. There is some clinical evidence that this is so. Basing their intervention on the principle of training of deficit areas of neuropsychological function, Hagin, Silver, and Kreeger (1976) devised a series of developmentally sequenced exercises to train deficits in aspects of spatial orientation and temporal organization found to be deficient in 8- to 10-year-old children with specific reading disability. Significant improvement in deficit function was achieved with such training, and with that improvement, there occurred a significant improvement in word identification and in reading comprehension (Silver & Hagin, 1974).

The same principle was utilized in a program for the prevention of learning disabilities (Silver & Hagin, 1976, 1981; Silver, Hagin, & Beecher, 1981). As we reviewed the spectrum of neuropsychological immaturities in children with specific learning disabilities, we suggested that they might be understood as a defect in spatial orientation and auditory temporal sequencing. A test battery to profile the distribution of skills in these neuropsychological functions in 5- and 6-year-old children for whom learning disability was predicted, was introduced into kindergarten and first grade. A 3-year controlled study revealed the success of this program in terms of reading achievement, word identification, comprehension, and social and emotional adjustment. The improvement was sustained in a 6-year follow-up.

In contrast to the deficit training model, Lyon (1985a, 1985b) suggested teaching methods to utilize the *strengths* in neuropsychological patterns found in children with specific learning disabilities. Five learning-disabled children selected from each of four empirically derived subtypes (language, global, visual-perceptual, no processing defect) were all given a *phonetics* program of remediation for 1 hour each week for 26 weeks. The visual perceptual type and the no processing defect type showed significant gain in word recognition and in reading comprehension. Satz (Satz, Morris, & Fletcher, 1985) suggested that the auditory memory, auditory comprehension, and sound blending defects found in the language deficit subtypes impeded their response to phonics and that remedial efforts be directed at the *intact* functions. It may well be that in the classroom, children with specific learning disabilities should be *taught* via their intact processing channels, that is, the children in the Lyons study who had intact auditory processing were taught with auditory inputs. However, at the same time if we ever hope to remediate the learning problems resulting from deficit functions, we had better provide exercises to improve those deficit functions. When that is done the child can learn through all channels.

The identification and grouping of neuropsychological types in children with learning disabilities gives promise of the development of more specific methods of remediation than the multisensory approach so frequently in use now. Equally important, the detection in kindergarten or even before kindergarten of the neuropsychological processing immaturities underlying reading, spelling, writing, and mathematics offers hope of preventing these learning disabilities from ever developing. As of this writing, systematic evaluation of intervention methods for children with specific learning disabilities, however, is still limited. Proposals to study treatment methods have been requested by the National Institute for Child Health and Human Development.

READING AND CEREBRAL LATERALIZATION

Why should children and adults with specific learning disabilities have these defects in the way their brain deals with the reception, storage, comprehension, and retrieval of symbols? A relationship between language and cerebral lateralization for language was documented by the early neurologists almost 150 years ago (Broca, 1861; Dax, 1878) and in 1917 Hinshelwood, a Glasgow eye surgeon, related what he called congenital word blindness to a focal agenesis of the left angular-gyrus. To Orton (1937/1989), too, the problem of hemisphere specialization for language was central in understanding the spectrum of developmental language problems in which he included reading, spelling, and writing.

The adequacy of hemisphere specialization for language has been a focus of research, particularly since the initiation and clinical application of dichotic listening techniques by Broadbent (1954) and Kimura (1973) at the Montreal Neurological Institute. The principles of dichotic listening have also been applied to the visual and to the tactile modalities. Two different perceptual stimuli within the same modality are simultaneously presented to the left and right sensory fields. Stimuli from the right sensory field are processed predominantly in the left hemisphere; those from the left in the right hemisphere. "Any asymmetry in hemisphere processing of particular stimuli may be reflected in response asymmetry to left vs. right stimulation as measured in accuracy and in reaction time" (Witelson, 1976, p. 235).

The original dichotic listening tests in the early Broadbent–Kimura studies used strings of different digits presented simultaneously in groups of three pairs via earphones to the right and to the left ears. The task was to recall in order as many of the digits the subject heard in each ear. Kimura observed that normal adults have a mean right-ear advantage (presumably a left hemisphere dominance for language) on this dichotic digit task. The magnitude of right-ear advantage, however, is generally small (5% to 10%) and the test–retest reliability very low. The right ear advantage for normal adults has been found with words, nonsense syllables, pairs of consonant-vocal syllables formed with stop consonants (*b, g, p, t*), Morse code, and processing and ordering temporal information. On the other hand, when musical cords and melodies are used instead of digits or words, there is a left-ear advantage (i.e., right hemisphere processes these stimuli more accurately than the left). In children with specific learning disabilities, Satz (1976) summarized the research of dichotic listening studies, as revealing "a lag in the development of ear asymmetry with no significant right ear advantage at any age level" (p. 282). In other words, in the child with a specific learning disability there may be lack of clear-cut hemisphere specialization for processing auditory information.

Studies in visual half-field presentation are summarized by Zaidel (1985): "It is by now commonly agreed that letters, words or digits are better recognized in the right visual field than in the left visual field" and the "left visual field (is superior) for recognition of complex forms, recognition of dot figures, face recognition and line orientation" (pp. 147–148). However, unlike consistent right visual field superiority for recognizing verbal material (letters, words), left visual field superiority for recognizing nonverbal stimuli is smaller and less consistent. A review of 14 hemivisual field studies (Bryden, 1988) in children with learning disabilities found eight of them to confirm the conclusion of less lateralization in poor readers than in adequate readers. Four of the studies found equal lateralization, and two found poor readers more adequately localized. Witelson (1976) found, however, that not only is there poor lateralization for language in learning disabilities, but in reviewing her study of 85 right-handed boys aged 6 to 14 with reading disability on dichotomous tactile stimulation tests, there is also a lack of right hemisphere specialization for spatial processing.

The general conclusion of dichotic listening, visual half-field studies, and dichotic tactile and haptic stimulation tests is that the normal asymmetry in hemisphere function is not attained in children with specific learning disabilities, that in these children hemisphere specialization for the processing of information is not well established.

The conclusions from the dichotomous sensory presentations—that left hemisphere specialization for language and right hemisphere specialization for spatial processing are not well established in children with specific learning disabilities—received some confirmation from morphological and physiological studies. Coffey, Bryden, Schroering, Wilson, and Mathew (1989) measured the flow of blood to frontal, temporal, and parietal areas in 14 strongly right-handed medical students undergoing tests during a resting base line condition and during performance of a two-tone pitch discrimination dichotic listening test. The data suggest that

"perceptual asymmetry observed with nonverbal dichotic stimuli is associated with increased regional cerebral blood flow (RCBF) to the contralateral posterior temporal cortex. These observations are the first to provide direct validation for the use of dichotic listening tasks as a tool to investigate brain functional asymmetries." (p. 51)

Rumsey et al. (1987) studied regional cerebral blood flow in 14 men with severe developmental dyslexia and in control subjects under three different conditions involving tasks of increasing cognitive difficulty. With reading and comprehension of words, the dyslexic group showed more activity in the left hemisphere, suggesting that dyslexics do not process information as efficiently as do control subjects.

Morphologically there are also differences in the direction of decreased hemisphere specialization in "dyslexics." Examination of the brain in eight people (six males and two females) diagnosed with "dyslexia," whose ages ranged from 12 to 88 years at the time of death, revealed a difference in the pattern of gross asymmetry found in normal brains (Galaburda, 1989).

Normally in autopsies of unselected brains, in 65% to 70% of them the left temporal language area is larger than the right, the posterior third of Broca's area contains greater surface area on the left side than on the right, and the areas of the angular gyrus relating to language are larger on the left than on the right. In 10% of routine autopsies these anatomical differences were larger on the right side than on the left and in 20% to 25% there was no size difference. In all of Galaburda's cases of dyslexia, however, the brain was symmetrical in each of these areas. Galaburda concluded that this is a strong statistical association and that symmetry, a variation from the expected structure, is significant in the dyslexic brain.

Suggestive confirmation of this gross anatomic anomaly is seen in computerized tomography (CT) scans. In a study of 24 young adults and adults diagnosed as having "developmental dyslexia," 10 showed a "reversal" of the usual asymmetry seen in the nondyslexic right-handed population (Hier, LeMay, Rosenberger, & Perio, 1978). Instead of asymmetry in which the left superior temporal area was the larger, in the 10 patients described by Hier et al. (1978) it was the right side that appeared larger. A later study (Rosenberger & Hier, 1979) found that in 53 children/young adults who were two grade equivalents below grade level in reading at some point in their school careers, 42% showed a wider right than left pariatooccipital region. "Reversed cerebral asymmetry" measured by the CT scan correlated with the prevalence and, to some extent, the degree of relative verbal intellectual defect as measured by the Wechsler scale.

The weight of evidence from simultaneous presentation of stimuli to the right and to the left sensory fields, from investigation of regional cerebral blood flow and even from gross anatomical studies, suggests that in the individual with specific learning disabilities, clear-cut hemisphere specialization for language has not been established.

We have so far described some of the difficulties individuals with specific learning disabilities have on processing information and we have suggested that in these individuals somehow the asymmetric functioning of the normal brain and the establishment of hemisphere specialization is not clearly evolved. Will electrophysiological data help us understand these differences more fully?

THE STANDARD ELECTROENCEPHALOGRAM

In spite of the fact that a review of 12 studies encompassing 664 children with reading disabilities revealed 47% of them to have abnormal electroencephalograms (EEGs) (Hughes, 1985), Benton and Pearl (1978) stated that "few conclusions about the nature of the relationships between electroencephalographic abnormality and specific reading retardation can be drawn from the large body of data which includes a number of suggestive findings, but at the same time so many conflicting results" (p. 465). The standard EEG, recording electrical potential from the scalp under conditions of "passive record," with the subjects' eyes closed and the brain supposedly at rest, has yielded controversial data. Hughes stated that the overall average of 45% abnormal EEG in children with reading disabilities is significantly higher than that for controls (7%–29%). Four general patterns of abnormality have been described: positive spikes, excessive occipital, sometimes temporal, slow waves, diffuse slow waves or abnormally slow background rhythm in the waking state and epileptiform activity. These studies are plagued with problems relating to imprecise boundaries of samples, failure to recognize the heterogeneity of the samples, different etiology, natural history, symptoms and prognosis of their subjects. The positive spike pattern in the frequency range of 6-7 per second and 14 per second are viewed by a majority of electroencephalographers as a "normal variant"; the occipital slow waves also are difficult to distinguish from the occipital slow waves found in the posterior regions of children under age 15; diffuse slow waves have been reported in from 3% to 50% of the subjects and epileptiform activity only occasionally appears. The presence of these four types of waves in the standard EEG may also appear in a variety of neurological and psychiatric disorders and thus are not considered as specific for specific learning disorders but may give clues as to the underlying pathology in the *nonspecific* disorders of learning. An observation that may be of interest is the beginning use of carbamazepine, an anticonvulsant, in children with language problems (not specific) who have temporal lobe EEG abnormality with high voltage show (delta and theta) wave or temporal spikes. Hughes also reported an old study (W. L. Smith, Phillippus, & Guard, 1968), which found improvement in verbal and full-scale IQ using ethosuximide (an anticonvulsant) in children with positive spike EEG. Hughes (1985) stated, "Too many significant correlations have been found to disregard this test (i.e., standard EEG) although in the awake and sleep EEG we can hope to find significant abnormality in less than one half of these patients" (p. 74).

THE QUANTIFIED ELECTROENCEPHALOGRAM

The advances in computer technology of the last decade or so, the development in solid-state analog amplifiers has now made quantified electroencephalography possible. Rather than the visual reading of the standard EEG, dynamic changes in the EEG may be recorded and analyzed by computer under conditions in which the brain is responding to sensory inputs (evoked potentials) or challenged by task requiring active processing of information (event related potentials). The techniques pioneered by Frank Duffy of the Children's Hospital in Boston (Duffy, Denckla, Bartels, & Sandini, 1980; Duffy, Denckla, Bartels, Sandini, & Kiessling, 1980) and by E. Roy John (John, Prichep, Fridman, & Easton, 1988) at New York University Medical Center are increasing in use as more experience is gained with these techniques and as the declining cost of the computer hardware has made the machines more accessible.

The waveforms recorded by the EEG from electrodes over the scalp range in frequency between 0 to 25 cycles per second, with four main groups identified: delta (0.5–3.5 Hz), theta (4.0–7.5 Hz), alpha (8–13 Hz), and beta (13.5–25 Hz). The Duffy technique reduces the complex waveforms obtained in response to different testing conditions into their wavelengths (called spectra) and the quantity of the forms with that frequency (power). The result is a power spectrum plot for each frequency at each electrode. This reduces the complex data of the EEG into a set of four single numbers (a power for each of the four spectral bands) at each electrode, much as a weather map records the temperature and barometric pressure at various cities throughout the nation. With these data as a base, contour lines for the power of each spectral band may be drawn and the resulting topographical map may be displayed on a computer driven video screen with colors to indicate the power of each band as it is distributed over the surface of the scalp. This technique is called brain electrical area mapping (BEAM). The topographical map is not static but may be studied over time as the brain responds to stimuli and challenges. One can observe the changes in the brain waves as stimuli are presented, actually observing the brain activity in electrical motion. Still photographs may be taken at any point in the sequential display. These records not only are a map of the power spectrum but may also identify the relationship of waves between electrodes (coherence) and between homologous parts of the brain so that hemisphere difference may be observed. Duffy developed statistical methods (statistical probability mapping) to delineate regions of the brain in which brain electrical activity from an individual subject differs from that of a referenced (norm) population.

Two papers have reported BEAM studies for "dyslexic" boys (Duffy et al., 1980; Duffy, Kiessling, et al., 1980); the subjects of the first consisted of 8 dyslexic boys and 10 non-dyslexics, presumably normal, age 9 to 11. The 8 dyslexic boys filled the criteria for "pure" or specific reading disability; two were left-handed, 2 ambidextrous, and 4 right-handed. The controls were similar to the dyslexic group in socioeconomic status and IQ; two were left-handed, 1 ambidextrous, and 7 right-handed. The EEG was recorded during 12 different tasks: 2 "simply resting brain activity," 10 designed to activate either the left hemisphere (speech and reading), right hemisphere (music and geometric figures), and both (paired visual-verbal associations), visual and auditory evoked potential, and tasks requiring difficult phonological discrimination. Significant differences from controls were found in four regions: bilateral medial frontal (supplemental motor), left anteriolateral frontal (Broca's area), left midtemporal (auditory associative), and left posterolateral quadrant (Weinicke's area, parietal associative, and visual associative areas). The authors concluded that "dyslexia-pure may represent a dysfunction within a complex and widely distributed brain system, not a discrete brain lesion" (p. 417).

The data of BEAM may not only be recorded in topographical form but also in plots of positive and negative waveforms that appear in time-locked sequence in response to the evoking stimuli and to events designed to challenge the brain in specific ways. In evoked potential challenges, for example, *positive* waves at 282 ms after visual stimuli (flashes from a strobe light) were found in dyslexic boys but in controls *negative* waves were found at the same interval. For auditory evoked potentials, *positive* waves appeared in dyslexic subjects, *negative* in controls. In attempting to obtain rules for diagnosis of dyslexia from the data obtained in the study of 18 boys, the Duffy group was able to identify correctly 80% of their 24 subjects (the original 18 plus 3 normal and 3 dyslexic boys). The identifying features appeared to be the auditory evoked potential tasks that involved phonological discrimination and auditory evoked potential task involving clicks. These features probed left brain and right brain activity.

The group in New York (John, Prichep, Fridman, & Easton, 1988) took an approach slightly different from that of Duffy, although the ultimate goal in detecting significant differences between "normal" and various clinical entities was the same. John and his associates approached the problem mathematically, deriving a set of questions that transforms data from resting EEG or from waveforms resulting from 58 tasks that challenge sensory, perceptual, and cognitive functions into standardized form (Z statistics) so that they may be compared with data obtained from a normative group. This technique is called *neurometrics*. The normative data were derived from subjects age 6 to 90 years, and include descriptions of absolute power (as in BEAM); relative power (power for each frequency band, divided by total power across the frequency bands); mean frequency and coherence; and asymmetry between homologous leads for all delta, theta, alpha, and beta bands. Evoked potentials and event related potentials are received in 10 ms latency intervals for a duration of 500 ms after stimulus onset. The Z transform is the number of standard deviations by which an individual observation differs from the mean of a reference set. The neurometric technique was able to identify abnormality in approximately one half of the patients in three diagnostic groups: those at risk for "neurological disorder," general learning disorders, and specific learning disorders. John et al. (1988) found children with different patterns of achievement to have different neurometric profiles. When different neurometric patterns were examined, the theta excess group had poor performance on tasks requiring sustained attention, the delta excess deficits in digit span and trail making tests, the auditory evoked potential asymmetry had more errors on color naming and trail making and longer delays on digit span. These data must be interpreted with caution because John's learning-disordered children were a heterogeneous group, coming from a special education facility, and not meeting the criteria for specific learning disability. Although John's conclusions may be questioned on the basis of questionable normative data and heterogeneity in his test samples, and Duffy may be criticized for his small numbers of subjects, the vista they opened is broad in potential application. Their studies yielded information concerning electrical correlates of cognitive activity, spatial location of the generators of electrical activity, and when correlated with behavioral, neurological, and neuropsychological measures, they have the potential of becoming useful instruments for meaningful subgrouping of children with disorders of learning. Furthermore, the fact that event-related potentials may be obtained from young children and infants may lead to early electrophysiological detection of specific learning disability (SLD) perhaps by 3 years and form a basis for early identification and prevention.

However, although there have been many other studies describing the evoked and event-related potentials in response to specific stimuli, most of these studies have been *explorative,* attempting to establish the consistency of the waveforms and then attempting to interpret *meaning* of the brain potentials thus evoked. Few have addressed the problem of children with a specific learning disability. For a start, norms for children of different ages are not yet available, the discrete boundaries of subjects are not clearly stated, and methodologies have not been uniform across studies, which prompted Hughes (1985) to state that "nearly all permutations and combinations of results have been reported in the visual evoked potential of the dyslexic" (p. 76). Findings with auditory evoked potentials, however, suggest that "it was as though these individuals (dyslexics) had no left cortex but instead offered two right hemispheres" (Fried, Tanguay, Boder, Doubleday, & Greenside, 1981, summarized by Hughes, 1985, p. 87). A more recent review of electrophysiological studies of the brain may be found in Zapulla, LeFever, Jaeger, and Bider (1991).

CYTOLOGY OF DYSLEXIA

By now we have presented evidence that there is a difference between the workings of the brain of children with specific learning disability and those who do not have such a problem. Not only in terms of the way the brain processes information, but also in the gross morphology of the brain where, if preliminary findings are to be confirmed, the normal gross brain asymmetry is not found in dyslexic individuals. Can this difference be found in the microscopic structure of the dyslexic brain? Here, too, comparison with the normal brain is possible. The anatomical finding in unselected brains of asymmetry in areas related to language is reflected in cytological difference as well. In the normal brain there is a greater number of cells in the left posterior portion of the superior temporal gyrus (Wernicke's area) and in the left angular gyrus (the visual-auditory association area) than in the right (Eidelberg & Galaburda, 1982, 1984; Galaburda, Sanides, & Geschwind, 1978). Many of the gross and microscopic anatomic asymmetries described in the brain of adults and children are also present in the human fetal brain (Witelson & Pallie, 1973), suggesting that the asymmetry is not the result of experience but that the child is born that way. Another interesting finding of Witelson (Witelson & Kigar, 1988) is that the midsagittal area of the human corpus collosum varied with hand preference, consistently larger in left-handed and ambidextrous people than in right-handers.

Applying these findings to the microscopic studies of the brains of dyslexics he examined, Galaburda (1989) found evidence of (a) ectopias, collections of neurons appearing outside the expected locations and associated with distortion of the architecture of the brain; (b) microdysgenesis (abnormal appearing neurons), focal and multiple, variable in number and distribution, but in all having a common location in the anterior language area. In addition, two of the male brains and both female brains contained scars, first thought to be minor strokes, but because they contained myelin, the scars must have occurred early in development. These scars have been found in a strain of autoimmune laboratory mice, giving cause to speculate on the role of autoimmune disorders in learning disabilities.

Galaburda speculated on the meaning of the anatomical and morphological findings in the brains he examined. In unselected brains, there is a normal regressive decrease in number of neurons in the right hemisphere without decrease in number of the left. This is not so in the dyslexic brain. As a result, the dyslexic brain may be excessively connected between the two hemispheres and not enough connections within each hemisphere.

MAGNETIC RESONANCE IMAGING AND POSITRON EMISSION SCANNING

The anatomic studies of Galaburda have been done with small numbers of specimens. Techniques for morphological and physiological studies of the brain, more applicable to larger numbers of living subjects, are now available. We have mentioned studies using computerized axial tomography (CT) in which the brain may be imaged in successive layers and in successive orientations. Other techniques—magnetic resonance imaging (MRI), positron emission tomography, and single photon emission tomography—are now available. These newer methods, just as are the quantified electrophysiological techniques, are still engaged in developing their basic data, the development of norms at various ages, and in their application to intracranial disease such as strokes, injury, and tumors. The problem of specific learning disabilities has not yet attracted major attention. An example of a pertinent CT study related to anatomical areas of the brain involved in memory was seen in Dennis et al. (1991) and by Durara et al. (1991), who correlated CT abnormality with memory defects in 46 children and adolescents with brain tumors, finding that defects in short-term memory for serial order of pictures corresponding to heard words, were found when medial temporal structures were impaired, but that semantic associations were not affected. Presumably, different areas of the brain are involved in processing each type of language function.

In contrast to the static pictures obtained with CT (x-ray) and magnetic resonance images, a positron emission tomography (PET) scan reveals a dynamic picture of brain function, able to trace biochemical pathways, the distribution of neurotransmitter receptors and enzymes, and the distribution of cerebral blood flow as the brain is at work. It has already been useful in detecting abnormality of glucose metabolism and cerebral blood flow (CBF) in schizophrenia, affective disorders, obsessive compulsive disorders, alcoholism, cocaine abuse, and panic attacks. The PET scan is based on the principle of detecting the results of emission of positrons from the nuclei of various elements; those most commonly used are carbon-11, oxygen-15, fluorine-18, and nitrogen-13. These elements may be used to label almost any physiologic or pharmaceutic compound without altering the chemical properties of that compound. Thus F-18 deoxyglucose (the positron-emitting label of deoxyglucose) may be injected into the blood stream of the patient and as the glucose is metabolized, its concentration may be measured by the concentration of the emitted positrons. Actually, what is measured is the effect of the positron as in the process of emission, it strikes an electron to yield two photons or gamma rays. The photons are detected by crystals that fluoresce when exposed to ionizing radiation. This only begins to suggest the technical difficulty in this procedure. Practically, the positron emitting labels have only a short half-life; C-11, for example, has a half-life of 20.4 min; F-18 has a longer half-life of 110 min. This means the radioactive substance must be manufactured, attached to the substance under study, injected into the patient, and the scan recorded, all in that time frame. PET scan studies must be done close to a cyclotron, which manufactures the labeled substance. The cost to set up such a program is high—in the millions of dollars; the corresponding cost to the patient must also be high, ranging at this writing from $3,000 to $7,000 per scan. Equally important, although PET advocates assure that the injected radioactivity poses no undue radioactive risk to the patient, this too must be considered. In our own city of Tampa, Florida, a cyclotron unit and scanning instrument has been built in one of our local hospitals, but as yet has not been used for the study of learning disorders. Normative data for children are scant.

In the University of Miami, cerebral metabolic activity was studied in right-handed adult dyslexic males and in nondyslexic males (Gross-Glen et al., 1991). Significant group differences in regional metabolic rates were found in the prefrontal cortex and in the inferior region of the occipital lobe, with higher rate of flow noted in the inferior occipital lobe for dyslexics. Also, in contrast to the asymmetry observed in prefrontal and inferior occipital area of nondyslexics, the dyslexic pattern was more symmetric. The authors concluded that individuals who suffer from familial developmental dyslexia as children activate different brain regions during reading as adults, when they are compared to adults without such childhood history. In attempting to detect areas in the brain important for storage of motor skills, Seitz, Roland, Bohm, Greitz, and Stone-Elander (1990) observed regional cerebral blood flow in normal adults as they learned a complicated sequence of finger movements. Cerebellar circuits and circuits in the corpus stratum were identified as the areas involved in learning these praxic skills. The Seitz paper is cited here because spatial orientation of the body image as found in right–left discrimination, finger gnosis, and finger praxis is part of the spectrum of neuropsychological defects found in children with learning disabilities. Regional cerebral blood flow in 11 volunteers mapped the anatomical structures activated in storage, recall, and recognition of a visual pattern (Roland, Guly, Seitz, Bohm, & Stone-Elander, 1990). Learning changed the blood flow in the primary visual cortex, visual association areas, temporal pole, and medial temporal striatum. Recall, however, activated parieto-occipital visual areas that are presumably storage sites. The processing of single words and auditory patterns was traced in RCBF studies in six normal volunteers from the cyclotron unit of Hammersmith Hospital in London (Wisc et al., 1991). During verb generation, there was activation in left premotor and prefrontal cortex although the subjects did not vocalize during the task. It appears that the act of retrieving words from semantic memory activates networks concerned with the production of speech sounds.

The PET scans of normal volunteers are supplemented by studies of individuals with known pathology (acquired aphasias, dementias), but the literature is as yet scant with respect to learning disabilities. Rumsey et al. (1992), using water labeled with positron emitting oxygen, found a difference between dyslexic men and controls when given a phonological rhyme detection task (subjects are presented with paired words, asked to identify those that rhyme). Control subjects increased blood flow in the left temperoparietal cortex near the cingular gyrus; dyslexic men activated a more anterior temporal region.

Up to now we have attempted to retrace the hierarchial steps that ultimately may be expressed as a specific learning disability: the neuropsychological processes that reveal defects in the way the brain of the child with specific learning disability deals with information in the perception, association, storage, and retrieval of symbols; how these processing defects may be distributed along a spectrum with all combinations of visual-spatial problems and auditory temporal sequencing problems; that underlying all of these problems with language may be a defect in the development of a clear-cut hemisphere specialization for various language functions. It appears that both hemispheres are caught up in this ill-defined specialization. Much work has been done in unraveling the electrophysiological parameters of learning disability with new technology quantifying our older visual analysis of the resting electroencephalogram and studying the brain's response to stimuli and to paradigms where the brain is actively engaged in work. Morphological and physiological data tend to support the clinical findings.

FAMILIAL AND HERITABLE BASIS OF SPECIFIC LEARNING DISABILITY

Having said all this we still do not know the cause of specific learning disability (SLD). There is evidence to believe that specific reading disability, the most researched and possibly the most prevalent of learning disorders, may have an inherited basis and the inherited basis may be due to an abnormality in gene or genes, the exact location and nature of which is unknown. The evidence springs from family and twin studies and from more recent attempts to identify the chromosome on which the hypothesized gene or genes for specific learning disability is located.

The familial nature of specific reading disability was noted as early as 1905 when, in a journal called *Opthalmoscope,* Thomas described "congenital word blindness" in two brothers and in the sister and mother of another child with what we now would call reading disability. A stream of observations from Hallgren in 1950 through Owen's studies in the 1970s (Owen, 1978), and the data from the Colorado Reading Project in the 1980s (Pennington, 1990), all substantiate the conclusion that there is a high prevalence of specific reading disability within families. Owen compared children in a special remedial program for educational handicapped (EH) in the Palo Alto, California, Unified School District who were 1½ to 2 years below grade level in spelling and/or reading with their same-sex siblings. A control group of academically successful children (SA) and their siblings was also tested. Results indicate that (a) the EH siblings were slightly below grade level expectancy in reading whereas the siblings of successful students were almost a year above grade level; (b) the WISC subtest scores of both EH children and their siblings were highly correlated on tests of comprehension and similarities; the correlation was not significant for SA children and their siblings; and (c) the parents of EH children had academic problems in the language area in their school career. The same general findings characterized the Colorado Reading Project data. One hundred twenty-five children with reading disability (96 boys, 29 girls) and their families were matched with 125 control children and their families and each was given a battery of neuropsychological tests. Their findings may be summarized: (a) comparing brothers of probands with brothers of controls, reading was 1 standard deviation lower; (c) comparing sisters of probands with sisters of controls, reading was about .4 sigma lower; (c) comparing parents of probands with parents of controls, scores were lower .8 sigma on reading, symbol processing, and spatial reasoning for fathers and .5 sigma for mothers of probands.

DeFries (DeFries, Fulker, & La Buda, 1987) estimated that in families of children with reading disability, over 60% of the longitudinal stability would be attributed to family influence compared to 1% in the controls. He further estimated that sons of fathers who have reported reading problems have a 40% risk of developing a reading disability (seven times the risk); sons of mothers with reading problems have a 35% risk (five times normal). For daughters of a reading-disabled parent, the risk is 17% to 18% but still 10 to 12 times the risk of daughters of parents without reading problems. In general, results demonstrate the familial nature of reading disability.

Twin studies also suggest that "genetic factors are an important source of individual differences within the reading disability group, whereas environmental influence shared by members of twin pairs are not an important source of variation" (DeFries, Olson, Pennington, & S. D. Smith, 1991). Based on the literature to 1988, 47 monozygotic twins (Mz) and 64 dizygotic twins (Dz) were reported. The coincidence rate for Mz twins was 85%, for Dz twins 29% to 55%, a significant difference ($p > .05$). The Colorado Group (Pennington, 1991) studied 101 total pairs of Mz twins, 73 pairs of same-sex Dz twins, and 41 pairs of opposite sex Dz twins. The concordance rates are 70% for Mz, 48% for Dz twins, which is still a significant difference. Parenthetically, the current twin sample of the Colorado Reading Project includes 149 males with reading disability and 156 females, a 1 to 1 ratio.

An alternative test of genetic etiology is the use of multiple regression analysis of twin data (LaBuda, DeFries, & Fulker, 1986). When probands have been selected because of deviant scores on a continuous measure, the scores of Mz and Dz twins would be expected to regress toward the mean of an unselected population. If there is a genetic etiology to the reading scores, then the regression toward the mean should be greater for Dz twins than for Mz twins, assuming their initial scores are similar. In testing this hypothesis, the scores of Mz co-twins regressed .22 standard deviation units, whereas that of Dz twins regressed .86 standard deviation units. Estimates of heredity from these scores are about 30% to 50%.

Although there is evidence for hereditability of SLD, the mode of trans- mission is yet unknown and the location of the gene or genes responsible is still obscure. Early studies by S. D. Smith, Kimberling, Pennington, and Lubs (1983) identified 9 families with 84 family members in which a history of reading disability occurred in three successive generations in an apparently autosonomal dominant mode of transmission. In this sample, there was a heteromorphism in the A and C bands of the centromere and short arm of chromosome 15, suggesting that there may be a gene (or genes) on chro- mosome 15 that influences reading ability. The probability that the co- transmission of the chromosome identified with reading disability was statistically a high one, but there were wide variations in statistical proba- bility among families. Then S. D. Smith, Pennington, Kimberling, and Ing (1990) increased their sample to include 250 individuals in 21 families. Also, methods for study of DNA fragments became available. Using these tech- niques, wide variations in probability of co-transmission were found, sug- gesting that only 20% of the families of children with reading disability manifest apparent linkage to chromosome 15 (Pennington, 1991). However, the linkage analysis component of the Colorado Reading Project is increas- ing the number of families for study and searching chromosome 6 for other possible genetic linkage. Heterogeneity is likely to be found in complex disorder where the ultimate phenotype may be influenced by a variety of genetic and nongenetic pathways. The detection of specific gene or genes means that the tendency, the genetic makeup associated with SLD, can be detected early, at birth or even before birth.

If and when the gene and/or genes are located, the next step is to determine what protein that gene encodes, and then what that protein does. Then we might better answer what causes the cells in the brain to follow unusual pathways so that brain asymmetry is not established, so that the brain cannot process information in an efficient manner so a specific learning disability results.

SUMMARY

This chapter has outlined the patterns of neuropsychological processing defects found in children with specific learning disability and has presented some evidence to suggest that hemisphere specialization is not as well established in this child as in the normal learner. Educational techniques for effective remediation of children with SLD may depend on their unique pattern of disabilities and abilities. There is evidence that with specific training of defects, the maturation of the defective function may be enhanced and in the process word identification and reading comprehension improves. In children in whom this training is successful, there is evidence that hemisphere specialization is also enhanced. Successful programs of early identification and remediation have been developed utilizing these principles. Can these principles be utilized in the preschool children—in 3-year-olds?

Newer electrophysiological techniques, utilizing probes that detect brain electrical activity while the brain is at work have identified areas of the brain that generate abnormality in electrical activity in children with SLD as they attempt to deal with cognitive tasks. Physiologically, the blood flow in these areas also appears different from that found in the non-learning-disabled child as the brain is at work. There is also suggestive difference in brain morphology as seen in CT scan, MRI, and even in gross and microscopic examination of the dyslexic brain. PET scans give promise of detecting further difference, in the way the brain utilizes glucose, for example, in the brain of those with learning disabilities. These biological differences indicate that children with specific learning disabilities are more than academic underachievers; the indication is that SLD has a long biological antecedent, different at birth and perhaps genetically even before birth.

The future should bring greater understanding of the biological nature of SLDs, which will aid in the identification, management, and ultimately the prevention of specific learning disabilities.

ACKNOWLEDGMENTS

This chapter is based on material from Silver and Hagin (1990) brought up to date by review of the literature since 1990.

REFERENCES

Barrett, T. C. (1965a). Predicting reading achievement through readiness tests. In *Reading and inquiry* (pp. 26–28). Newark, DE: International Reading Association.

Barrett, T. C. (1965b). Relationship between measures of pre-reading visual discrimination and first grade reading achievement. *Reading Research Quarterly, 1*, 51–76.

Barrett, T. C. (1965c). Visual discrimination tasks as predictors of first grade reading achievement. *Reading Teacher, 18,* 276–282.

Benton, A., & Pearl, D. (Eds.). (1978). *Dyslexia: An appraisal of current knowledge.* New York: Oxford University Press.

Birch, H. G., & Belmont, L. (1964). Auditory-visual integration in normal and retarded readers. *American Journal of Orthopsychiatry, 34,* 852–861.

Blank, M., & Bridges, M. W. (1967). Perceptual abilities and conceptual differences in retarded readers. In J. Zubin & G. A. Jarvis (Eds.), *Psychopathology of mental development* (pp. 401–412). New York: Grune & Stratton.

Broca, P. (1861). Nouvelle observation d'aphemia produite par une lesion de le moitie posterieure des deuxieme et troisieme circonvolutions frontales. *Bulletin de la Societe Anatomie, 6,* 398–407.

Broadbent, D. E. (1954). The role of auditory localization in attention and memory span. *Journal of Experimental Psychology, 47,* 191–196.

Bryden, M. P. (1988). Does laterality make any difference? Thoughts on the relation between cerebral asymmetry and reading. In D. L. Molfese & S. J. Segalowitz (Eds.), *Brain lateralization in children* (pp. 509–526). New York: Guilford Press.

Coffey, C. E., Bryden, M., Schroering, E. S., Wilson, W. H., & Mathew, R. J. (1989). Regional cerebral blood flow correlates of a dichotic listening task. *Journal of Neuropsychiatry, 1,* 46–52.

Dax, M. (1878). *L'Aphasie.* Paris: Delahaye.

DeFries, J. C., Fulker, D. W., & LaBuda, M. C. (1987). Reading disabilities in twins: Evidence for a genetic etiology. *Nature, 329,* 537–539.

DeFries, J. C., Olson, R. K., Pennington, B. F., & Smith, S. D. (1987). Colorado Reading Project: An update. In D. D. Duane & D. B. Gray (Eds.), *The reading brain* (pp. 53–87). Parkton, MD: York Press.

Dennis, M., Spiegler, B. J., Fritz, C. R., Hoffman, H. J., Hendrick, E. G., Humphreys, R. P., & Chuang, S. (1991). Brain tumors in children and adolescents II: The neuroanatomy of deficits in working, associative and serial order memory. *Neuropsychologia, 29,* 829–847.

Duara, R., Kushah, H., Gross-Glenn, K., Barker, W., Jallad, B., & Pascal, S. (1991). Neuroanatomic differences between dyslexic and normal readers on magnetic resonance imaging scans. *Archives of Neurology, 48,* 410–416.

Duffy, F. H., Denckla, M. B., Bartels, P. H., & Sandini, G. (1980). Dyslexia: Regional differences in brain electrical activity by topographic mapping. *Annals of Neurology, 7,* 412–420.

Duffy, F. H., Denckla, M. B., Bartels, P. H., Sandini, G., & Kiessling, L. S. (1980). Dyslexia: Automated diagnosis by computerized classification of brain electrical activity. *Annals of Neurology, 7,* 421–428.

Dykstra, R. (1968). Summary of the second grade phase of the cooperative research program in primary reading instruction. *Reading Research Quarterly, 2,* 49–70.

Eidelberg, D., & Galaburda, A. M. (1982). Symmetry and asymmetry in the human thalamus. Cytoarchitectonic analysis in normal persons. *Archives of Neurology, 39,* 325–332.

Eidelberg, D., & Galaburda, A. M. (1984). Inferior parietal lobule: Divergent architectonic asymmetries in the human brain. *Archives of Neurology, 41,* 843–852.

Fletcher, J. M. (1985). External validation of learning disability typologies. In B. P. Rourke (Ed.), *Neuropsychology of learning disabilities* (pp. 184–211). New York: Guilford Press.

Fried, I., Tanguay, P. E., Boder, E., Doubleday, C., & Greenside, M. (1981). Development of dyslexia: Electrophysiological evidence of clinical subgroups. *Brain and Language, 12,* 14–22.

Galaburda, A. M. (1989). Ordinary and extraordinary brain development: Anatomical variation in developmental dyslexia. *Annals of Dyslexia, 39,* 67–80.

Galaburda, A. M. Sanides, F., & Geschwind, N. (1978). Human brain. Cytoarchitectonic left-right asymmetries in the temporal speech region. *Archives of Neurology, 35,* 812–817.

Gross-Glen, K., Duara, R., Barker, W. W., Lowenstein, D., Chang, J. Y., Yoshii, F., Apicella, A. M., Pascal, S., Boothe, T., Sevush, S., et al. (1991). Positron emission tomographic studies during serial word reading by normal and dyslexic adults. *Journal of Clinical and Experimental Neuropsychology, 13,* 531–544.

Hagin, R. A., Silver, A. A., & Kreeger, H. (1976). *TEACH—Learning tasks for the prevention of learning disabilties.* New York: Walker Educational Books.

Hallgren, B. (1950). Specific dyslexia ("congenital word blindness"). A clinical and genetic study. *Acta Psychiatrica et Neurologica Scandinavia* (Suppl. 65), 1–287.

Hammill, D. D., Leigh, J., McNutt, G., & Larsen, S. (1987). A new definition of learning disabilities. *Journal of Learning Disabilities, 21,* 109-113.

Hier, D. B., LeMay, M., Rosenberger, P., & Perio, V. P. (1978). Developmental dyslexia. *Archives of Neurology, 35,* 90-92.

Hinshelwood, J. (1917). *Congenital word blindness.* London: Lewis.

Hughes, J. R. (1985). Evaluation of electrophysiological studies on dyslexia. In D. B. Gray & J. F. Kavenaugh (Eds.), *Behavioral measures of dyslexia* (pp. 71-86). Parton, MD: York Press.

John, E. R., Prichep, L. S., Fridman, J., & Easton, P. (1988). Neuromatrics: Computer-assisted differential diagnosis of brain dysfunctions. *Science, 23,* 162-169.

Kimura, D. (1973). The asymmetry of the human brain. *Scientific American, 228,* 70-80.

LaBuda, M. C., DeFries, J. C., & Fulker, D. W. (1986). Multiple regression analysis of twin data obtained from selected samples. *Genetic Epidemiology, 3,* 425-433.

Liberman, I. Y., Rubin, H., Duques, S., & Carlisle, J. (1985). Linguistic abilities and spelling proficiency in kindergartners and adult poor spellers. In D. Grey & J. F. Kavanaugh (Eds.), *Behavioral measures of dyslexia* (pp. 163-176). Parton, MD: York Press.

Lyon, G. R. (1985a). Educational validation of learning disability subtypes: Preliminary findings. In B. P. Rourke (Ed.), *Neuropsychology of learning disabilities: Essentials of subtype analysis* (pp. 228-256). New York: Guilford Press.

Lyon, G. R. (1985b). Identification and remediation of learning disability subtypes: Preliminary findings. *Learning Disabilities Focus, 1,* 21-35.

Mattis, S. (1978). Dyslexia syndromes: A working hypothesis that works. In A. L. Benton & D. Pearl (Eds.), *Dyslexia: An appraisal of current knowledge* (pp. 43-58). New York: Oxford University Press.

National Joint Committee for Learning Disabilities. (1991). *Learning disabilities: Issues in definition.* Unpublished manuscript. (Available from Drake Duane, c/o The Orton Society, 724 York Road, Baltimore, MD 21204)

Orton, S. T. (1989). *Reading, writing and speech problems in children.* Austin, TX: Pro-Ed. (Original work published 1937)

Owen, F. W. (1978). Dyslexia — genetic aspects. In A. L. Benton & D. Pearl (Eds.), *Dyslexia: An appraisal of current knowledge* (pp. 265-285). New York: Oxford University Press.

Pennington, B. F. (1990). Annotation: The genetics of dyslexia. *Journal of Child Psychology and Psychiatry, 31,* 193-201.

Pennington, B. F. (1991). *Diagnosing learning disorders.* New York: Guilford Press.

Petrauskas, R., & Rourke, B. P. (1979). Identification of subgroups of retarded readers: A neuropsychological multivariate approach. *Journal of Clinical Neuropsychology, 1,* 17-37.

Roland, E., Guly, B., Seitz, R. J., Bohm, C., & Stone-Elander, S. (1990). Functional anatomy of storage, recall and recognition of a visual pattern in man. *Neuroreport, 1,* 53-56.

Rosenberger, P. B., and Hier, D. B. (1979). Cerebral asymmetry and verbal intellectual deficits. *Annals of Neurology, 8,* 300-304.

Rosensweig, M. R., & Bennett, E. L. (Eds.). (1976). *Neural mechanisms of learning and memory.* Cambridge, MA: MIT Press.

Rourke, B. P. (Ed.). (1985). *Neuropsychology of learning disabilities: Essentials of subtype analysis.* New York: Guilford Press.

Rumsey, M. M., Andreason, P., Zametkin, A., Aquino, T., King, A. C., Hamberger, S. D., Pikus, A., Rapoport, J., Cohen, R. M. (1992). Failure to activate left temporoparietal cortex in dyslexia: An ^{15}O PET study. *Archives of Neurology, 49,* 527-534.

Rumsey, J. M., Berman, K. F., Denckla, M. B., Hamberger, S. D., Kruesi, M. J., & Weinberger, D. D. (1987). Regional cerebral blood flow in severe developmental dyslexia. *Archives of Neurology, 44,* 1144-1150.

Satz, P. (1976). Cerebral dominance and reading disability: An old problem revisited. In R. M. Knights & D. S. Bakker (Eds.), *Neuropsychology of learning disorders: Therapeutic approaches* (pp. 273–294). Baltimore, MD: University Park Press.

Satz, P., & Morris, R. (1981). Learning disability subtypes: A review. In F. J. Pirozzolo & M. C. Wittrock (Eds.), *Neuropsychological and cognitive processes in reading* (pp. 109–141). New York: Academic Press.

Satz, P., Morris, R., and Fletcher, J. (1985). Hypotheses, subtypes and individual differences in dyslexia: Some reflexions. In J. B. Grey & J. F. Kavanagh (Eds.), *Behavioral Measures of Dyslexia*. Parkton, MD: York Press.

Seitz, R. J., Roland, E., Bohm, C., Greitz, T., & Stone-Elander, S. (1990). Motor learning in man: A positron emission tomographic study. *Neuroreport, 1,* 57–60.

Silver, A. A., & Hagin, R. A. (1964). Specific reading disability: Follow-up studies. *American Journal of Orthopsychiatry, 34,* 95–102.

Silver, A. A., & Hagin, R. A. (1974). *Effects of perceptual stimulation on perception, on reading, and on the establishment of cerebral dominance for language.* Report to the Carnegie Corporation, New York. (available from the Carnegie Corporation)

Silver, A. A., & Hagin, R. A. (1976, 1981). *SEARCH: A scanning instrument for the prevention of learning disability* (2nd ed.). New York: Walker Educational Books.

Silver, A. A., & Hagin, R. A. (1990). *Disorders of learning in childhood.* New York: Wiley.

Silver, A. A., Hagin, R. A., & Beecher, R. (1981). A program for secondary prevention of learning disabilities: Results in academic achievement and in emotional adjustment. *Journal of Preventive Psychiatry, 1,* 77–87.

Smith, S. D., Kimberling, W. J., Pennington, B. F., & Lubs, H. A. (1983). Specific reading disability: Identification of an inherited form through linkage and analysis. *Science, 219,* 1345–1347.

Smith, S. D., Pennington, B. F., Kimberling, W. J., & Ing, P. S. (1990). Familial dyslexia: Use of genetic linkage data to define subtypes. *Journal of American Academy of Child and Adolescent Psychiatry, 29,* 204–213.

Smith, W. L., Philippus, M. J., & Guard, H. L. (1968). Psychometric study of children with learning problems and 14-6 positive spike EEG patterns, treated with ethosuximide (Zerontin) and placebo. *Archives of Disorders in Childhood, 43,* 616–619.

Spreen, O. (1988). Prognosis of learning disability. *Journal Consulting and Clinical Psychology, 56,* 836–841.

Thomas, C. J. (1905). Congenital "word-blindness" and its treatment. *Ophalmoscope, 3,* 380–385.

Vellutino, F. R., & Scanlon, D. (1985). Verbal memory in poor and normal readers: Developmental differences in use of linguistic codes. In D. Gray & J. Kavenaugh (Eds.), *Behavioral measures of dyslexia* (pp. 177–214). Parton, MD: York Press.

Wise, R., Chollet, F., Hadar, U., Friston, K., Hoffner, E., & Frakowak, R. (1991). Distribution of cortical neural networks involved in word comprehension and word retrieval. *Brain, 114,* 1803–1817.

Witelson, S. F. (1976). Abnormal right hemisphere specialization in developmental dyslexia. In R. M. Knights and D. S. Bakker (Eds.), *Neuropsychology of learning disorders* (pp. 233–255). Baltimore, MD: University Park Press.

Witelson, S. F., & Kigar, D. L. (1988). Anatomical development of the corpus callosum in humans: A review with reference to sex and cognition. In D. L. Molfese & S. J. Sagalowitz (Eds.), *Brain lateralization in children* (pp. 35–57). New York: Guilford Press.

Witelson, S. F., & Pallie, W. (1973). Left hemisphere specialization for language in the newborn: Neuroanatomical evidence of asymmetry. *Brain, 96,* 641–646.

Zaidel, D. W. (1985). Hemifield tachistoscopic presentations and hemispheric specialization in normal subjects. In D. F. Benson & E. Zaidel (Eds.), *The dual brain* (pp. 143–155). New York: Guilford Press.

Zapulla, R. A., LeFever, F., Jaeger, J., & Bider, R. (Eds.). (1991). Windows on the brain: Neuropsychology's technological frontiers. *Annals of the New York Academy of Science* (monograph series), p. 620.

III

CONTEXTS FOR LITERACY

12

A Literacy Context for the 21st Century Child

Patricia A. Antonacci
James M. Colasacco
Fordham University and Yonkers Public Schools, New York

It is a typical day in September: The day begins to shorten, and most evenings are sharpened by their cool breezes. To the teacher, these are clear indicators of the new beginnings of another school year. To the young child, they represent the emergence of a new world, founded in the beginnings of school.

Both the teacher and the child pass through the classroom door on their first day with hearts filled with hope, while their minds spiral with expectations for success. To launch the school year, the teacher bestows the basal readers, the symbol of the grade-level curriculum to be mastered by the children who accept and embrace their new tools for shaping a successful life. Routines are quickly established: Children know their reading groups; they understand the importance of completing their assigned pages in the workbook; and they eagerly await their turn for instruction in the small reading group, a chance to read aloud and yield the correct answer to the teacher's question.

Shortly, the evidence surfaces that the first days of school have evaporated: Workbooks are scarred with red marks, pages have been ripped and torn from notebooks, and the new crayons and pencils have been lost or broken. This splintering of school supplies is symbolic of the children's and teachers' shattered dreams for success and their depressed expectations for learning. Now the September promises begin to disintegrate: Members of the slowest reading group just don't hear the sounds; they can't complete their workbook pages independently; they fail to recognize words from their preprimers. Finally, the large group of students reading below grade level confirmed by their scores on the standardized reading achievement

213

test are the teacher's affirmation of failure. These are the rituals to which we have become accustomed; they are the passages of the school year that we endure year after year.

One purpose of this chapter is to seek an answer to the question: Why does the current literacy context continuously fail our students? A second purpose is to suggest a design for a new literacy context for the 21st-century student that we believe will breathe a lasting promise into each literacy event undertaken by the child and the teacher.

TRADITIONAL CONTEXTS OF LITERACY LEARNING

The basal reading program defines a traditional literacy context. To understand the transmutation of the *children of promise* (defined by teachers' initial perceptions of students on the first days of school) to *children at risk* (defined by teachers' altered perceptions of students when literacy instruction begins), we need to enter a traditional school context where formal reading instruction takes place. It is here where children begin to have their first experiences in learning to read and write.

Most U.S. elementary classrooms are entrenched in the basal reading program (Goodman, Shannon, Freeman, & Murphy, 1988; Shannon, 1983, 1989). This wide use of the basal reader is critical to understanding the traditional context of literacy instruction, because these published materials are the tools that literally control how reading is taught (Artley, 1980; Duffy, 1982). That is, for most elementary school teachers, reading instruction is the *application of commercial materials* (Shannon, 1983, 1989). Reading is the interaction of the child with these published materials (Shannon, 1989); therefore, all the experiences the young student encounters during this part of the day flow from the basal reading program. These are the events that define the traditional literacy context. Thus within the traditional literacy context, good reading instruction is equated with the effective use of the basal reader, the student workbooks, and the teacher's manual. Because the basal reading program is fundamental to reading instruction, its description and its application will provide insights into traditional literacy contexts.

The basal reading program is treated by teachers and administrators as "the technological solution to the problems of teaching students to read" (Shannon, 1989, p. 54). This entrenchment in published programs by school districts across the United States derives from a belief system of both administrators and teachers who employ the basal reader for instruction. Shannon (1983) explained their conviction that effective reading instruction is using the basal reading program as it is prescribed by the publishers. Both teachers and administrators look to these publishers as the experts, whose construction of materials provides the technology that delivers the most effective method of instructing young children in learning how to read. The format and the directions embodied in these materials are perceived by administrators and teachers as scientific reading instruction (Shannon, 1989).

Efficiency is at the heart of the basal reading program, a feature inherent in its design. The publishers have fashioned an effective management system: A set of well-defined literacy lessons are constructed for each grade level. Both the stories in the basal reader and the skills that are taught and practiced are graded and sequenced. To achieve the major goal of beginning reading instruction, which is the decoding of words, stories are constructed on a readability formula and a graded controlled vocabulary. The results are contrived stories that lack the elements of good narrative as well as rich language.

A distinctive feature of the program is the teacher's manual that has become its foundation. Each lesson is accompanied by a set of detailed directions enabling the teacher to deliver the reading instruction with the least amount of thought and effort.

Another feature that clearly defines the basal reading program is the scope and sequence of skills after which instruction is designed. The major assumption in utilizing this hierarchal sequence of discrete skills is that the sum of the parts is equal to its whole: If students master each skill within the scope and sequence, they will be able to read. Therefore, skill lessons are arranged sequentially, and mastery is sought through direct instruction and sufficient practice provided by numerous exercises in the workbook and additional worksheets. To determine whether mastery has been achieved, unit tests are provided. When a child has not reached mastery, further practice on the skill is suggested, so additional worksheets are prescribed.

Another feature that marks the basal reading program is the grouping procedures. It is strongly suggested that teachers create three homogeneous groups designated by the students' reading ability. The major difference with respect to instruction is pacing. The high-ability group is paced through the materials at the quickest rate, whereas the lowest group takes the longest amount of time to complete the required materials.

This simple description of the basal reading program provides a glimpse into a traditional context for literacy instruction. Indeed, it deserves the descriptive notation of "systematic approach to teaching reading," but what about its effects on instruction? Teachers and administrators truly believe that applying the basal reader as directed by the publisher will result in the most effective reading instruction because their belief is tied to the equation that a technologically designed reading program equals the science of teaching reading, thus no one will tamper with the proposed reading instruction.

The publishers make the decisions involving reading instruction. The lessons are designed by the publishers who are perceived as the experts, so the same lesson may be applied to all students with minimal or no changes by the teacher. Therefore, the teacher who uses the basal reading program effectively need not make rational judgments related to teaching and learning: The publisher's materials have predesigned the instruction so that the teacher need only deliver (Shannon, 1989).

In reality, teachers are freed from making decisions concerning instruction. "Their knowledge of reading and instruction is frozen in a single technological form" (Shannon, 1989, p. 55), so they do not need a personal philosophy of how learning occurs, nor do they need strategies to apply a theory of learning. All they need to do is to implement a basal reading program effectively, because the reading process is perceived as working through a set of materials. Even when teachers were helped to make decisions related to instruction using a basal reading program, they found it difficult to maintain this decision-making role (Duffy, Roehler, & Putnam, 1987).

We live with the perception that the basal reading program never fails to teach. But what happens for so many children who attempt to learn their first literacy lessons through these expertly designed and scientifically proofed instructional guides? Remember those children who came through those classroom doors on the first day of school, truly believing that they would learn to read and write; and remember their teachers who shared this same belief for each child. Quickly the promise for all became the promise for some and the despair of many.

Children are not gaining mastery over each skill at their designated grade level. Even with additional practice sheets, they do not achieve the objectives. The teacher religiously follows the directions set forth in the teacher's guide, but the desired results are not achieved.

Just as effective teaching has been defined by the efficiency of delivery of the published program, student success has been defined in terms of "maximization of students' gains in test scores" (Shannon, 1989, p. 55). It is now inevitable that these children will not be "on grade level" when the standardized tests are administered. Thus the teachers' initial expectations for these children are quickly revised, while the final proclamation of the young child's success or failure is made by the standardized test scores. At a very early age, when children do not read at grade level, the socially constructed *at-risk* level is bestowed on them. The blame for failure is not attributed to teachers or to the instructional program they have used to create the literacy context. After all, it is the child who has failed to learn to read when an expert program has been applied. The joyful voices that once supported the *"children of promise"* have changed to the angry cries of despair:

Every child is just not a learner.
They just don't have the prerequisite skills.
Their language is deficient.
They lack the "experiences," because they are culturally deprived, and
this places them at a disadvantage to comprehend text.
They are unable to attend and to stay on task.

The list of excuses to explain the children's failure increases with time and with the diversity of student populations.

It has been too long that we have misdirected the blame for failure: We have neglected to evaluate the published programs that have been the mainstay of the traditional literacy context; nor have we questioned why administrators and teachers select and apply the basals in the light of such a high rate of failure. It is time to uproot the traditional context of literacy. It is time to design a context that meets the demand for the multiple literacies for the 21st-century student.

The traditional literacy context must be abandoned for several reasons. First, if more and more children meet failure as early as the first grade, it is clear that such instruction just does not work. Second, a view of the child as an active learner who is continuously engaged in the construction of meaning has been seriously neglected by basal reading programs. Third, the responsibility for learning is assumed by a published program that directs instruction. Placing the responsibility for learning back into the hands of the educational partners will reaffirm the importance of literacy learning and will change the very nature of literacy instruction. Finally, the narrow view of literacy—perceived as a discrete set of isolated skills—that is defined in the daily reading lessons is inadequate for the demands of the multiple literacies required in the 21st century. Goodman (1986) stated emphatically that such literacy settings ignore and are incompatible with what children already know when they enter school; indeed "no published instructional program has ever provided the generalizations and concepts that people must develop to learn to read and write" (p. 109).

CONTEXTS THAT PROVIDE THE FRAMEWORK FOR THE CONSTRUCTION OF MEANING

In considering a design for a context that would meet the challenges of the literacies demanded by the 21st-century child, let us first establish the relationship between context and the construction of meaning.

We live within a network of contexts: our family, church, community, work, or school. Each of these contexts engages us in activities by the very nature of our membership within the group. Many of these activities become memorable experiences that provide the conceptual knowledge or schemata we call upon to construct meaning.

The children seated before us in the public school classroom bring a unique set of experiences from their unique network of social contexts; woven together, they form the fabric of their lives. These children represent *diversity*.

Contemplate the context of family alone; such reflection will support the nature of diversity with its implications for meaning construction. Children may be part of a family structure that is defined by a single male parent. The dominant language spoken by the adult member is a language other than English, and his religious affiliation is not considered an institutionalized mainstream religion. Because this head of the family works at night, the children spend much of their time during the day with a caregiver who is not of the same ethnic background and does not share the same religious affiliation as the children or their parent. In their family context, the children will experience up to three different languages and enjoy a variety of foods, celebrations, folktales, music, and so forth, from at least two different ethnic backgrounds. They will also observe different religious holidays than those that may be imposed on them in school. So before entering school, their family will have provided them with many experiences which, together with the network of contexts, determine their conceptual knowledge. They do not leave it at the doorstep as they enter school; it is their web of significance that they call on as they actively construct meaning.

Having viewed only one of these children's network of contexts, we begin to understand the levels of diversity that children bring to our classroom. It is this diversity that must be considered for our new literacy context. We will no longer view diversity as "something" to deal with, addressing the issue through "add on's" in the curriculum. We will bear witness to diversity; diversity is a strength, and so we will let it happen. We will hold a continuous celebration in honor of diversity, for it provides us with the essence of meaning. We will learn from each other, because we collaborate as we construct meaning together.

DESIGNING A LITERACY CONTEXT FOR THE
21ST-CENTURY CHILD

The challenge for the creation of a new literacy context for the 21st-century child, therefore, lies ahead. To insure the promise of literacy for each student there are essential components that are the foundation of the new literacy context.

The following are the components that provide the blueprints for a new literacy context.

Central to the new literacy context is the *child as learner* who actively constructs meaning. In the foreground is the "child mind [who] asks questions, seeks order, and corrects its own learning" (Bissex, 1984, p. 99). The second component of the blueprint includes a broad view of literacy. Literacy for the 21st century presents a serious challenge to schools; demands for *multi-dimensional literacies* create the need to design a context where students are actively engaged in literacy events that incorporate varied discourses, use a wide variety of symbol systems and technology, and provide authentic purposes for uses of all forms of language. *Collaboration* is the third essential component of the new literacy context. In most of our experiences, both on the job and at home, we naturally engage our talents and efforts to the completion of a task. Language learning through collaboration, not isolation, is encouraged in the new literacy context. The *classroom environment* is the fourth component that is the heart of the new context. Children come to our kindergarten classrooms with a command of language, which speaks of the rich language provided in their homes. What we learn from language experiences within the home provides us with insights for creating effective classroom environments to support literacy growth and development. *Assessment* is the component that insures the dynamic and interactive nature of the learning process. Its position at the end of this chapter does not downplay its importance; as an ongoing process, it yields the essential data for the creation and the revision of the curriculum. Figure 12.1 provides a further description of each component of the new literacy contexts for the 21st-century child.

The Child as a Learner

Within these new literacy contexts, instruction and literacy events are determined by how children learn. The following are the significant behaviors demonstrated by the child as a learner.

Adults Play a Significant Role in Helping Children Construct Meaning. The way language is used in the home demonstrates its rapid growth and development at the early stages in the child's life: Parents, caregivers, and members of the community provide the *scaffolds* the child needs, encourage talk on a topic of interest, listen and talk to the child. Vygotsky (1978) suggested that learning is a social process and children learn through social interaction, that is, through the assistance of knowledgeable others. According to Vygotsky (1978), a child confronted by a task that is "just beyond his reach," is engaged in learning that is known as the child's *zone of proximal development.* The task is too difficult for the child. With the

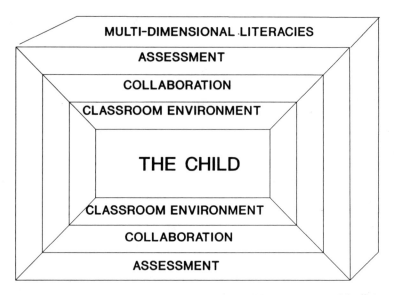

Fig. 12.1. A literacy context for thee 21st-century child. Components of the literacy context.

guidance of an adult, however, the child will learn to complete the task independently. The event is scaffolded by an adult who provides this assistance until the child no longer needs it, because the child has come to know. In other words, Wells (1986) clearly stated that the role of the adult in helping the child construct meaning through language is a collaborative one: "to build up a shared structure of meaning about the topic that is the focus of their intersubjective attention" (p. 45). Thus through these social interactions adults provide children with the specific help they need to acquire higher mental development.

Just as learning to speak and learning to mean are social processes, so is learning about the print conventions of language. Very early children begin to understand the social contexts of literacy through their earliest experiences with the writing forms of language in their homes. For example, they see adults reading and writing for different purposes: writing down telephone messages and notes to a family member or friend, making a list for marketing; reading the directions to operate the VCR, reading a recipe, a street sign, or a menu in a restaurant. Within the family context, "children learn to organize their environment through the use of print" (Taylor, 1983, p. 54). The print world is all around them!

The Child Is the Active Participant in Constructing Meaning Through Language. Lindfors (1985) emphasized that it is through these "real communication events" as an active participant that the child learns how language is used. Thus language acquisition is not a passive event whereby knowledge is transmitted to the learner, nor is literacy acquired by going "through" a set of grade-level materials. Rather, all forms of language growth are "an active process of creative construction" (Lindfors, 1985, p. 55); and it is through this use of their language that children come to learn as well as learn language. We see language and learning intricately entwined.

Let us consider how children who are actively engaged in text construct meaning. There is no meaning inherent in the text alone; rather, meaning can only be constructed as the reader transacts with text. The set of meanings that a reader derives is dependent on an interaction between the reader and the text. The reader's schema, or conceptual knowledge, plays a significant role in constructing meaning during the process of reading (Spiro, Bruce, & Brewer, 1980). The text becomes the blueprint that the reader uses in this new act of meaning construction. Thus this process "requires readers—real live readers with ideas and attitudes of their own—to interpret what the author is saying" (Langer, 1982, p. 41). Rosenblatt (1991) further expressed the dynamic, personal, and complex relationship between reader and text as a transactive process:

> Transaction especially seems to be needed for a description of the act of reading. Reading is always a particular event, involving a particular reader, a particular item of the environment—a text—at a particular time, under particular circumstances. A person becomes a reader by virtue of a relationship with a text. A text is merely ink on paper, until some reader (if only the author) evokes meaning from it. . . . Reader and text are mutually essential to the transaction; meaning happens during the transaction between the reader and the text. (p. 116)

It is critical therefore to understand and to accept that the diversity among children who actively construct meaning will produce a variety of interpretations from a single text. Thus if we acknowledge that reading is an interactive and transactive process, we begin to appreciate multiple interpretations of a text rather than a single correct answer.

The fact that children are active participants in constructing meaning who do not deny their language or their social experiences in knowledge construction is critical to the design of the new literacy context. Geertz (1973) refered to Max Weber's description of man's culture as his "webs of significance he himself has spun" (p. 5); and in searching for meaning, he used these very webs of significance. Therefore, to help a child, an adult must acknowledge the child's culture, his "webs of significance" that are used to construct meaning.

Multidimensional Literacies

There is a demand for a multidimensional literacy context for the 21st-century student. What will no longer suffice is the application of the assembly-line technology to literacy instruction: "Assembly-line technology divides the process of production into simple unskilled elementary tasks" (Blauner, 1964, p. 97) much the same way as the basal-reader program's delivery of reading instruction. Wolf (1990) deprecated these text materials for their barren language and lack of authenticity. Literacy contexts must take into account technology, multimedia, a variety of symbol systems including graphics, the diversity of authentic readings that utilize different types of discourse, and finally a variety of purposes and functions for uses of literacy provided for young readers and writers. What we are calling for has been expressed as a *literacy of thoughtfulness* by policy analyst Brown. Our multidimensional literacy can be achieved in an educational setting described by Perkins (1992), where there is "thinking centered learning, where students learn by thinking through what they are learning about" (p. 7).

Collaboration

Peer Collaboration.   Peer collaboration must become the prominent social structure within the new literacy context if learning is to occur. The major foundation supporting collaboration is the issue of the social milieu in learning.

Vygotsky (1978) argued that "every function of the child's cultural development appears twice: on the social level, and later, on the individual level; first, between people (interpsychological), and then inside the child (intrapsychological)" (p. 57). For any learning to take place, students first help each other through collaboration, that is, classroom talk. The knowledge gained through social interaction is then internalized by individual students. Learning has its origins in collaboration because it is a social process. The development of knowledge is mediated through "the use of language, [which empowers] . . . the growth of concepts and the developing structure of the mind" (Bruner, 1987, p. 8).

Within the classroom, collaboration takes place in small groups. These groups are created not on the ability of students, but on the basis of socially constructed tasks. That is, students may elect to join a group because of a joint interest. Diversity is the mainstay of the group; it is enriching, and it is encouraged. Using their backgrounds and experiences, children construct meaning; a greater diversity within the group permits a wide range of information. Further, it fosters cognitive advancement when children attempt to incorporate others' viewpoints into their own (Mead, 1934).

Without social interaction and an elaborate range of viewpoints and thinking, there would be no intellectual development (Parker & Goodkin, 1987).

In these collaborative efforts toward intellectual growth, it is not always the teacher who provides the scaffold to the child who needs assistance. It may be another child. Through collaboration and negotiation in constructing meaning, through simple talk, through deliberate efforts in joint problem solving, the result is simple but very profound to the learner: Its outcome is the reorganization of schema, the restructuring of knowledge. Collaboration advocates the joint construction of meaning through talk and invites risk taking, an element that is present in all learning, and without which there can be no movement beyond the status quo (Wertsch, 1985).

Teacher Collaboration.   The role of the teacher has changed; the teacher is no longer the person in front of the classroom doing all the talking, the transmitter of knowledge. The teacher with the students collaborate to construct meaning together. They actively engage in seeking answers to honest questions where there are no correct answers.

The teacher is the researcher within the classroom. Studying, watching, and observing the child's mind engaged in tasks, hypothesizing, gathering evidence, and solving problems. The teacher is the *kid-watcher* who is studying the child to provide optimal learning: to provide a scaffold for the child who needs assistance in all areas of language learning; to begin instruction within the child's conceptual framework; to build collaboratively on the child's knowledge base; and to use literacy as a tool for the child's learning.

Teachers no longer feel the sting of professional isolation, for their collaboration goes beyond the classroom walls. They move out of the classroom joining forces with all educational partners in designing the new literacy context. Teachers and parents are mutually concerned about framing the most effective design for the child's achievement. Their discussions focus on aspects of the student's success and ways to foster it. The teachers' collaborative efforts reach out to the community, engaging its resources in fashioning authentic literacy events for the students. Teachers, administrators, and other staff together join forces planning, assessing, and revising blueprints for an appropriate literacy context where each child will meet with success. Their dialogue is ongoing and collegial; and the outcome of their discussions is joint decision making to the solution of any problem that may occur.

Classroom Environments That Support Literacy

Essential in designing a rich literacy environment for our young readers and writers is the acknowledgment that all components of the literacy context are interdependent. Therefore, principles regarding the nature of language, the child as a learner, the elements of collaborative learning as well as assessment, will be outlined so that environments to promote growth in language learning may be tailored for students' specific needs.

Classroom Talk Is Not Only Encouraged Because It Is Essential to Learning. Talk promotes learning through concept development (Vygotsky, 1978); it develops language (Wells, 1986); it generates and develops topics for writing (Dyson & Freedman, 1992); it promotes story understanding (Doake, 1986). For "it is in talk, that tasks are defined, negotiated, and evaluated, and by means of which the students' participation is monitored and assisted, that students and teachers engage in the dialogic co-construction of meaning, which is the essence of education" (Wells & Chang-Wells, 1992, p. 33). Educators must get used to noisier, productive learning environments.

Practice and Use of Language Is Encouraged. If students are to become experts in the use of all forms of language, they need to be engaged in authentic literacy tasks. Such tasks represent language use for a wide variety of functions (Halliday, 1975). Failure to promote the full range of language runs the risk of inhibiting growth in all aspects of language.

Students Are Encouraged to Take Risks Becoming Actively Engaged in a Wide Variety of Literacy Ventures. Without taking risks, children's learning will experience gridlock at the very least. Students need to receive support of all educational partners when taking risks while engaged in learning activities; mutual respect among the members of the community of learners is the key in encouraging and promoting risk taking that supplies the implicit sustenance in the learning process. Learners will not fear making mistakes, because mistakes will be viewed as approximations that lead to success.

The nature of the literacy events designed for students affects their willingness to take risks. For example, filling in the blanks on a worksheet and reading grade-level texts that are followed by predictable questions to answer, demand little, if any, engagement or risk taking by the student; and such tasks produce inert knowledge that cannot be used or applied for problem solving or other activities (Perkins, 1992). Learning activities that require reflective and critical thinking, however, charge learners to engage in the construction of meaning and in problem solving, which at their very heart is risk taking. The rationale is simple: "Learning is a consequence of thinking" (Perkins, 1992, p. 8).

Because There Is an Expectation of "Success for All," Children Perceive Themselves as Learners. Teachers are "kidwatchers" who monitor the child's language, and the literacy tasks are specifically designed to facilitate the student's growth that will result in success. Success is not measured through the comparison of students' scores with the grade-level norm. It is not measured by a paper-and-pencil test taken by all students within a grade. Rather, success is individual; it is relative to the child's own literacy experiences and knowledge. A student's performance on a task within his range of literacy development serves as the barometer of success.

Authentic Tasks Are Embodied in Literacy Events that Restore Relevance to the Curriculum. Children learn to read from the best models of language, such as E. B. White's *Charlotte's Web;* they learn to write by creating their own stories they know will be published and placed on the display bookshelf next to Robert McCloskey's *Make Way for Ducklings.* Through these experiences, "children do breathe in and soak up the rules, the uses, and the kinds of knowledge essential for literacy" (Wolf, 1990, p. 123).

Demonstrations and Modeling Are Provided By More Experienced Learners. Within an environment that fosters respect and trust among its members, learners will be motivated to become the apprentices when necessary, or at other times, to serve as the master who demonstrates expertise in performing a literacy task. This concept is quite natural in home environments where children are learning to speak: In the parent–child relationship the parent with more expertise helps the child with less expertise in language acquisition, and older siblings or caregivers assume the role of expert in an apprenticeship process. Modeling and demonstrations are a significant part of the child's oral language development. Therefore, central to effective literacy environments are modeling and demonstrating of how print works by the experts—a teacher or classmate who has acquired the skill. Indeed it is inherently impossible to simulate the family language models within the classroom. However, Cazden (1992) is convinced that the teachers' role and an essential part of their work is to provide rich language models for children. The literacy concepts must include the full complexities of text.

Response and Reflection Are Essential Elements of Literacy Environments. Response and reflection foster the child's construction of knowledge. Children need to know how they are doing; an error or mistake may lead to cognitive growth. Because its goal is not to judge but to promote learning and expertise, the response required should "be embedded in a climate of high expectations of the learner's ability to, ultimately, 'get it all together' " (Cambourne, 1988, p. 76). Response should be coupled with the student's reflection about the given problem. Piaget (1976, 1978) called this a time for cognitive structures to emerge or to change. According to *reflective abstraction,*

> knowledge is constructed by thinking about, or reflecting upon, actions in specific situations. When children encounter obstacles to their goals, they reflect upon current courses of action and represent possibilities for alternative actions. They then integrate the representations of possible actions to achieve a more extensive system of internalized actions or thoughts. (Bidell & Fischer, 1992, p. 113)

Natural Assessment

Natural Assessment Insures the Dynamic and the Interactive Nature of the Learning Process. The traditional notions that assessment brings to mind — a process that is judgmental and a quantitative definition of reading achievement — must be discontinued. Bound to these conventional notions is evaluation as a "one-shot-deal measure," a test administered at a specific point in time. Furthermore, traditional assessment is linked to considering products; it is not at all concerned about the processes involved in arriving at a solution to a problem, or an answer to a question, or a set of concepts that have been employed to frame an answer. Finally, in assessing language growth and development, traditional instruments are constructed the same way that traditional contexts of literacy have been constructed: They test a narrow set of discrete skills. Therefore, traditional assessment tests only a narrow aspect of literacy.

The new literacy contexts for the 21st-century student abandon all beliefs that are related to the traditional concept of assessment, for its foundation is distinctly different.

Assessment Is an Ongoing Process that Occurs in a Variety of Contexts; It Is What Propels Its Dynamic Nature. One very important aspect of assessment is its purpose: One objective of authentic or natural assessment is to determine individual language growth and development. Natural assessment views the child's language behaviors to determine the most effective path to proceed in their development. Another purpose of assessment is to determine the processes that students use for the different language forms. Finally, assessment within our new literacy context seeks to determine the appropriateness of instruction, including the task used to develop the language behaviors of each child. Because these purposes are different from the traditional tools of evaluation used for assessing student achievement, the new model of assessment will be dressed in unconventional clothing.

Alternative Forms of Assessment Is the Mark of the New Literacy Context. As an ongoing process, assessment begins from the very first day a student enters the classroom until the student leaves. It operates under the watchful eyes and ears of the teacher who is always the "kidwatcher" observing the child in a variety of language contexts. To the teacher who is the ethnographer, observation is the most important tool; not taking memory for granted, the teacher records the child's language behaviors in a variety of contexts over time. Now the teacher is the observer and quickly changes to participant-observer. The teacher not only views these data as a record of the child's language achievements, but as a source to revise the child's curriculum and instruction. Assessment becomes the blueprint for designing and redesigning the literacy environments for the children's maximum growth and development.

Student Portfolios Are Created to Celebrate Achievement in Learning. Literacy products as well as anecdotal records of the child language processes are found in the portfolios. They are not used to pass judgment on the students. Rather, the portfolio is known and accepted as a celebration of the child's successes and achievements. Students select what they believe exemplifies their best efforts of work to be included in the portfolio. Representing a wide variety of language forms and behaviors, the student portfolio contains artifacts of achievement.

Elements of student portfolios might consist of the following: samples of student performances, such as taped oral readings; different genres of a student's writing; writing from different phases to demonstrate their process skills, from draft to the finished piece; reflections from the journal; responses to readings, such as story maps and graphics; poems; plays; inventions on the author's writing; collaborative writing; jokes; songs; personal communication; published and unpublished pieces; retellings of narrative and expository text that the student read or listened to; illustrations for books and other stories. Along with students' sample performances are the annotations collected by the teacher through her careful observations.

What goes into the portfolio is decided by collaboration of the student and the teacher. There is no prescription; there is no standardization of what does and does not belong in a portfolio. Students' portfolios are different, because they reflect individuals' efforts on their own continuum of growth and progress in literacy. Just as portfolios differ one from another within a class, so do the portfolios differ from one class to another, because each class has a culture of its own, determined by its members at a given time. Together their "webs of significance" collaborate in the construction of meaning; their portfolios will contain artifacts derived from their joint participation.

SUMMARY

What we have described are two distinct literacy contexts: The first is the traditional context that employs commercial materials with a cookbook approach to apply the basal readers. The second is a design for a new literacy context for the 21st-century student. Its foundation is a philosophy of how children learn and construct meaning. The major attributes of this literacy context include (a) the child as learner, (b) collaboration, (c) the classroom environment, and (d) multidimensional literacies. The placement of assessment at the end of this chapter is not intended to deemphasize its crucial role: Assessment is an ongoing process that is part of instruction and learning; it serves to tailor the curriculum to meet the needs of each child; it occurs in a variety of contexts, because of the multidimensional nature of literacy; it is not judgmental, for it is a means to celebrate and continue the growth and progress of each child.

REFLECTION

The first day back after the summer vacation, Danice entered his third-grade classroom, his head hanging low, his eyes cast down and lips pursed tightly. He no longer shared the excitement of the new school year; too many times his attempts ended in failure. Three years of school had taught Danice not to expect success: No one else expected him to succeed. Besides there was too much pain and humiliation associated with the experience of learning to warrant Danice giving it further thought.

For 3 years Danice had worked in a traditional literacy context: In first and second grades, he felt the sting of being placed in the lowest reading group, of trying to complete worksheet after worksheet that gave him practice in sounds, of trying to sound out words. Danice never felt like a reader or writer, because he wasn't engaged in real reading; he doesn't remember reading a book or the encouragement that would lead him to a desire to read. Early in the second grade, Danice was "at risk" and pulled out twice a week to attend reading lab. There he did much the same thing that he did in class but at a slower rate: He practiced his sounds, read from preprimers, and filled in workbook pages.

Discouraged by these patterns of failure, Danice sought new ways to achieve: He soon found that he could excel at being a persistent troublemaker, even surpassing most of his peers. This accomplishment gave him status, often accompanied by removal from class and suspension; and on those days, he did not have to finish those workbook pages or read those first-grade stories. This strategy had worked for him so far; for the most part, Danice was receiving a type of recognition.

Early in December, Danice walked out of the reading lab, rushed up to the principal and hugged him. This behavior was not typical for Danice, who was known by everyone as the "hardened troublemaker"; the administrator was confused. What has happened to Danice that caused a sudden expression of joy?

In that wordless and unexpected moment of surprise, the assistant principal understood what was happening to this third-grader. The new reading lab teacher brought a new philosophy, a new literacy context. Within this literacy context, Danice was perceived as a learner, a reader, and an author. He reads real books, writes real stories, asks real questions. Danice no longer worries about making mistakes, because he knows that they approximate what he knows and will eventually disappear. His practice in literacy is quite different, because it is real. Making choices on what to read and write is also a part of learning that Danice loves. Danice has found a place in school where there is no pain, no shame, and an experience of joyful learning. To a child like Danice who has experienced the effects of two divergent literacy contexts on learning, the differences are real and compelling, for it is marked by personal success or failure.

Through this explicit mapping of two divergent literacy contexts, we hope to establish the compelling need for change. If our call has not been loud enough to hear, the simple reflection on Danice caught between two literacy contexts will stand as our proclamation for deliverance.

REFERENCES

Artley, S. (1980). Reading: Skills or competencies? *Language Arts, 57,* 546–549.

Bidell, T. R., & Fischer, K. W. (1992). Beyond the stage debate: Action, structure, and variability in Piagetian theory and research. In R. J. Sternberg & C. A. Berg (Eds.), *Intellectual development* (pp. 100–140). Cambridge, MA· Cambridge University Press.

Bissex, G. L. (1984). The child as teacher. In H. Goelman, A. Osberg, & F. Smith (Eds.), *Awakening to literacy* (pp. 87–101). London: Exeter.

Blauner, R. (1964). *Alienation and freedom: The factory worker and his industry.* Chicago: Phoenix Books.

Brown, R. G. (1991). *Schools of thought: How the politics of literacy shape thinking in the classroom.* San Francisco: Jossey-Bass.

Bruner, J. (1987). *Making sense: The child's construction of the world.* New York: Methuen.

Cambourne, B. (1988). *The whole story: Natural learning and the acquisition of literacy in the classroom.* New York: Ashton.

Cazden, C. (1992). Whole language plus: Active learners and active teachers. In C. B. Cazden with P. Cordeiro, M. E. Giacobbe, & D. Hymes (Eds.), *Whole language plus: Essays on literacy in the United States and New Zealand* (pp. 5–16). New York: Teachers College, Columbia University Press.

Doake, D. B. (1986). Learning to read: It starts at home. In D. R. Tovey & J. E. Kerber (Eds.), *Roles in literacy learning: A new perspective* (pp. 2–25). Newark, DE: International Reading Association.

Duffy, G. (1982). Response to Borko, Shavelson, and Stern: There's more to instructional decision-making in reading than the "empty classroom." *Reading Research Quarterly, 17,* 295–300.

Duffy, G. G., Roehler, L. R., & Putnam, J. (1987). Putting the teacher in control: Basal reading textbooks and instructional decision making. *Elementary School Journal, 87,* 357–366.

Dyson, A. H., & Freedman, S. W. (1991). Writing. In J. Flood, J. M. Jensen, D. Lapp, and J. R. Squire (Eds.), *Handbook of research on teaching the English language arts.* New York: Macmillan.

Geertz, C. (1973). *The interpretation of cultures.* New York: Basic Books.

Goodman, K. (1986). *What's whole in whole language.* Portsmouth, NH: Heinemann.

Goodman, K., Shannon, P., Freeman, Y., & Murphy, S. (1988). *Report card on basal readers.* New York: Richard C. Owen.

Halliday, M.A.K. (1975). *Learning how to mean.* London: Edward Arnold.

Langer, J. A. (1982). The reading process. In A. Berger & H. A. Robinson (Eds.), *Secondary school reading: What research reveals for classroom practice* (pp. 39–51). Urbana, IL: National Conference on Research in English and ERIC Clearinghouse on Reading and Communication Skills.

Lindfors, J. W. (1985). Oral language learning: Understanding the development of language structure. In A. Jaggar & M. T. Smith-Burke (Eds.), *Observing the language learner* (pp. 41–56). Newark, DE: International Reading Association.

Mead, G. H. (1934). *Mind, self and society.* Chicago: University of Chicago Press.

Parker, R. P., & Goodkin, V. (1987). *The consequences of writing: Enhancing learning in the disciplines.* Montclair, NJ: Boynton/Cook.

Perkins, D. (1992). *Smart schools: From training memories to educating minds.* New York: The Free Press.

Piaget, J. (1976). *The grasp of consciousness* (S. Wedgewood, Trans.). Cambridge, MA: Harvard University Press.

Piaget, J. (1978). *Success and understanding* (A. J. Pomerans, Trans.). London: Routledge & Kegan Paul.

Rosenblatt, L. M. (1991). The reading transaction: What for? In B. M. Power & R. Hubbard (Eds.), *The Heinemann reader* (pp. 114–127). Portsmouth, NH: Heinemann.

Shannon, P. (1983). The use of commercial reading materials in American elementary schools. *Reading Research Quarterly, 19,* 68–85.

Shannon, P. (1989). *Broken promises: Reading instruction in twentieth-century America.* New York: Bergin & Garvey.

Spiro, R. J., Bruce, B. C., & Brewer, W. F. (Eds.). (1980). *Theoretical issues in reading comprehension.* Hillsdale, NJ: Lawrence Erlbaum Associates.

Taylor, D. (1983). *Family literacy: Young children learning to read and write.* Portsmouth, NH: Heinemann.

Vygotsky, L. S. (1978). *Mind in society.* Cambridge, MA: Cambridge University Press.

Wells, G. (1986). *The meaning makers: Children learning language and using language to learn.* Portsmouth, NH: Heinemann.

Wells, G., & Chang-Wells, G. L. (1992). *Constructing knowledge together: Classrooms as centers of inquiry and literacy.* Portsmouth, NH: Heinemann.

Wertsch, J. V. (1985). *Culture, communication and cognition: Vygotskian perspectives.* Cambridge, MA: Cambridge University Press.

Wolf, D. P. (1990). For literate lives: The possibilities for elementary schools. In C. Hedley, J. Houtz, & A. Baratta (Eds.), *Cognition, curriculum, and literacy* (pp. 121–136). Norwood, NJ: Ablex.

13

Early Intervention Strategies for Family Literacy

Patricia A. Chiarelli
Haverstraw–Stony Point School District
Fordham University

In many schools an increasing number of children are entering kindergarten and/or first grade with special needs. Teachers label them emotionally and socially "needy," and ask why? Why can't they pay attention? Why can't they talk and share ideas? Why can't they wonder? Why aren't they curious? Why aren't they ready to learn when they enter school? For each child there is a unique set of causal factors. Whether the reason is physical, psychological, or social, these children have failed to clear a hurdle in their cognitive, linguistic, and social development on which later success depends; failure in the early grades does guarantee failure in later schooling even if remedial programs such as Chapter 1 are provided (Slavin, Karweit, & Wasik, 1992–1993). We need to look beyond school instruction for remedies.

Society is more dependent on our schools to address the needs of at-risk children. But with changing social contexts, the school's partnership with families no longer happens naturally. The programs that have the strongest evidence of effectiveness for preventing school failure are currently available and replicable (Slavin, Karweit, & Wasik, 1992 1993). Many of these programs address the literacy needs of families while their children are in school. However, we cannot wait to address the needs of these children when they enter school. We need to examine those programs that reach out to families in their communities before their children enter school because preparation for literacy must begin before children start school. The early years are crucial for language learning and the best preparation for literacy learning is learning to talk and having many opportunities for conversation (Clay, 1992). This chapter examines early intervention strategies for family literacy and focuses on one of the most important activities for early literacy development that provides a wealth of opportunity for dialogue, the practice of adult caretakers reading to children from the earliest possible age. The following questions are be addressed:

1. Why is family storybook reading a successful strategy for early literacy?
2. What are the components of early intervention programs for literacy that include storybook reading and how are they funded?
3. What have we learned and what do we need to do now?

WHY FAMILY STORYBOOK READING IS A SUCCESSFUL STRATEGY

There is overwhelming agreement among theorists and researchers that reading to children contributes directly to their literacy development (Bruner, 1984; Clay, 1982; Mason, Peterman, & Kerr, 1988; Smith, 1975; Taylor, 1983; Teale, 1984; Wells, 1986). A shared book experience is described by Holdaway (1979) as an activity involving the initial oral reading of a story by an adult concurrent with continuous, spontaneous, and/or directed dialogue between child and adult. Rereading, initiated by either child or adult, may follow, which provides opportunity for reconsidering story events and deepening understanding. The role of the adult has been described as one that provides scaffolding upon which the child learns to understand (Bruner, 1984; Heath & Thomas, 1984; Ninio & Bruner, 1978). The adult builds one comment or question on another, each time relinquishing more control, until finally the child internalizes the strategies and can perform them independently. Wells (1986) viewed the child as an active meaning maker and the adult as the one who triggers the mechanism and influences the rate to help children reinvent language for themselves.

It is not enough to provide storybook reading when children enter school; Teale (1987) questioned whether classroom storybook reading can substitute for the more intimate one-to-one interactions at home. Edwards (1989) stated, "In institutional interactions, a child is unlikely to achieve the level of understanding or develop the participation strategies made possible by the parental tutorial" (p. 249). A growing body of research suggests parents need to play a larger role in the education of their children, and we need to help them create a "curriculum of the home" (Peterson, 1989, p. 6). When parents are committed and actively involved, children have better grades, attitudes, and long-term achievement than those of disinterested parents (Henderson, 1988; Rich, 1985). Vandegrift and Greene (1992) described involved parents as supportive, sympathetic, reassuring, understanding, and with a high level of commitment to their children and their education, but they are also active; they are doing something observable that reflects their level of commitment. According to Bempechat (1990), one of the observable behaviors that positively affects the cognitive and academic socialization of children is the provision of tutoring and scaffolding in literary events. No other literary event provides as much opportunity for tutoring and scaffolding, for promoting the value of literacy, than family storybook reading. Teale's (1984) four aspects of the cognitive and affective effects on children's development of literacy is depicted in Table 13.1.

Using the technique of retrospective analysis in a longitudinal ethnographic study, Wells (1986) found that the quantity and quality of the language interaction in the home was a more important factor in the acquisition of literacy than external factors such as poverty, overcrowding, socioeconomic class, or parents' literacy levels. Achievement in reading was the best predictor of overall achievement at age 10, and the best predictor of reading achievement at age 7 was a literacy test administered upon entrance into school. Further analysis of the language activities before school that could have affected the acquisition of literacy indicated that shared storybook reading was the most important predictor in the knowledge of literacy.

The shared book experience is an activity in which the child is socialized into a particular pattern of literacy activity that relates directly to school literacy activities, and in this way, provides a link between home and classroom literacy. According to Teale (1984), children who do not have the

TABLE 13.1
The Effects of Reading to Children on Their Literacy Development

Cognitive/Affective Effects	Specific Understandings Being Developed
1. Functions and uses of written language	Vocabulary, syntax
	Written language is different from oral language
	Transmission of the literacy heritage of a culture
2. Concepts of print	Directionality, metalinguistic awareness
Concepts of books	Book handling, book conventions
Concepts of reading	Global sense of what reading is about
3. Attitudes toward reading	Books are associated with extremely positive, secure, and enjoyable atmospheres
4. Reading strategies	Response to literature, self-monitoring techniques, life to text interactions in which one uses knowledge to make sense of text

experience of being read to before they enter school do so at a disadvantage. Further ethnographic evidence, like that of Wells (1986), indicates that sex, race, economic status, and setting are not significant correlates of literacy (Heath & Thomas, 1984; McCormick & Mason, 1986; Taylor & Dorsey-Gaines, 1988); parents with even marginal literacy skills can serve a critical role in bringing storybooks to children.

THE DESCRIPTION OF PROGRAMS

Federal Initiatives

One of the first initiatives for parent involvement came from federal Title I funding in the 1970s. Parent advisory boards were mandated, but they met infrequently and served merely as a way to communicate to parents how funds were being used. The Hawkins–Stafford School Improvement Amendment of 1988 renewed the mandate and broadened the definition of parent involvement to better identify parent interests, needs, language, cultures, and to design more appropriate programs that are responsive to those definitions (D'Angelo & Adler, 1991). In the fall of 1992, an addendum to Head Start was passed requiring the centers to link parents with community services.

The Fund for the Improvement and Reform of Schools and Teaching (FIRST), a program of the Office of Educational Research and Improvement (OERI), was established in 1988 to not only encourage creative and innovative thinking by local school districts and individual schools to design and implement new possibilities for school/family/community partnerships, but also to share information about projects and reforms that have already demonstrated success. The branch of FIRST that is responsible for parent involvement in literacy programs is the Family School Partnership Program (FSPP; Epstein, 1991). Selection of grants is made by an advisory board of the secretary of education. Fourteen out of 414 FIRST-FSPP applications received funding in 1989; 31 new programs were funded in 1990 with those programs being funded again in 1991. In 1992, 18 new programs with an emphasis on preschool programs were funded, costing a total of $2.6 million, and $1.6 million was also appropriated to continue previously established programs. Competition is usually announced in September by the Federal Register and applicants must submit an eight-page preapplication document to the FIRST office of the OERI. The department will select 50 who will then be invited to write full applications (B. Gray, personal interview, 1992). A description of some of its programs is provided in the following paragraphs (Cross, 1991).

The Parents as Partners Intergenerational Literacy Project (1989–1990), a collaboration between Boston University and the Chelsea Public Schools, sought to improve the literacy and parenting skills of parents. University staff members working out of a community center offered a "story time" program for children while their parents were taught strategies for improving their own literacy and ways to become involved in their children's education.

With a $97,000 grant, Margaret Lee, the Chapter 1 coordinator of Greensville County, Virginia, created the Mobile Parent Resource Center (1988–1992), a comfortable, colorful, customized 34-ft mobile home housing everything from pamphlets on parenting to construction paper. In the rear of the van is a small classroom filled with toys, books, and educational games. The program was structured around two assumptions: parents wanted to help their children but lacked the time, resources, and skills, and parents could not come to the schools so the schools had to come to them (Merina, 1992).

Another federal initiative is Even Start, a two-generational program linking the education of underachieving parents with the education of their children to help them understand their role and influence in the success of their children's education. It also establishes cooperative projects that build on existing community resources to create a new range of services. The Even Start program was begun by Congress as a national demonstration program in 1988 with the initial year funding of $14.8 million. Since that time funding has been increased to nearly $90 million nationally, with New York's share at $7.4 million. In the 1991–1992 school year, 225 projects were funded nationwide (Walton, 1993).

Program participants are parents eligible for adult basic education, and parents of children from birth to age 7 who reside in a federal Chapter 1 school attendance area. Minimum funding is $75,000; new grants are competitive and require application to a state educational agency. The federal share would be not more than 90% of the total cost of the program in the first year, decreasing 10% a year to a final minimum of 60% in the fourth year.

Even Start intervention outlined by the U.S. Department of Education (1991) presents a program process model that describes the design, delivery, and receipt of services by participating families. The design components include strategies that encourage collaboration with other agencies, recruitment, retention, and staff development. The services provided—parent education to enhance child development, adult basic education, and early childhood education—are supported by special inclusions for transportation, child care, health care, home visits, counseling, translators, and meals. Stipulated in the outcomes for parents are three literacy behaviors: shared literacy events with children, increased use of literacy materials, and literacy resources in the home. The outcomes for children include age-appropriate cognitive, language, and social skills.

State Initiatives

At the state level, the New York Board of Regents adopted a regulation in March 1992 that requires every public school district to develop and adopt a play by February 1994 for the participation of parents and teachers with administrators and school board members in school-based planning and shared decision making. The mandate is further described in a New York State Education Department booklet (1992): "It shall be the policy of the Board of Regents that the State Education Department will require a parent participation component in the development and implementation of relevant policy and program initiatives, and evaluate such participation as part of the monitoring and school review process" (p. 6).

The New York State Prekindergarten Program (New York State Education Department, 1990) administered and monitored by the Division of Child Development, was begun in the 1970s to service 4-year-old children from economically disadvantaged families. Program variations are considered; for example, a program for 3-year-olds would be funded if all 4-year-olds had already been serviced, and home visits by a trained staff member could be included to help provide educational activities for parents and children at home. Each program is mandated to provide the following services: education, health and nutrition, social services, parent involvement, staff development, coordination with other early childhood and community agencies, and continuity of services to the third grade. Two components, the educational curriculum and parent involvement, are described further.

The major educational goals of the program emphasize learning how to learn, the development of social competencies essential to cope successfully with the school environment and profit from learning activities, and a comfortable transition from home to school. Although mandates for the educational program include such things as provision for a variety of learning styles, sharing of cultures, a child-centered curriculum that encourages curiosity and exploration of the environment, and frequent opportunities for discussion with peers and adults, there is no specific description of literacy activities. It is stipulated that there should not be a prescribed curriculum, that the curriculum should emerge from the children's needs and interests, but the board of regents failed to provide necessary guidelines for the literacy development of both children and adults. Out of a list of 12 different suggestions for materials, there is one short listing for the inclusion of a book display in the classroom. A prekindergarten classroom should be a print-rich environment in which the language of print is identified, nurtured, and cherished. Such an educational goal would certainly consider the needs and interests of the children.

The component of parent involvement stipulates that parents must be involved in every aspect of the program. A parent advisory board must be recruited and maintained to meet at least four times a year to advise staff in the operation and planning of the program, with a staff member designated as liaison. The parent involvement component must offer a wide range of options in order to develop a true partnership: school visits, conferences with staff about individual children, home visits by personnel, parent education workshops, employment in the program, and incidental contacts such as telephone calls.

In one of the initial formal evaluations of the New York State Prekindergarten Program (Irvine, 1979), the specific component of parent involvement was researched concerning its effect on the children's cognitive development. Findings revealed a highly significant favorable effect of parent involvement on three cognitive aspects (general reasoning, school-related knowledge and skills, and knowledge of verbal concepts) regardless of the child's age, mother's education, or family income. This study provided pervasive evidence of the broad impact parents can have on their children's learning. Encouraging parents to participate in their children's education is one highly cost-effective technique for improving children's education performance.

Community Initiatives

A program that is more clearly defined around storybook reading is Motheread, Inc., of Raleigh, North Carolina. Founded in July 1987, the model was initially designed to respond to the needs of low-literate female adults wanting to improve their literacy skills in order to read to their children, and has been replicated in a variety of community-based settings. In contrast to the programs described previously, Motheread is a private nonprofit organization funded by various foundations, humanities councils, businesses, service groups, churches, and contributions from individuals. The adult program promotes literacy from the idea that mothers will do for their children what they will not do for themselves.

In seminar-style classes, parents develop their own literacy as they discuss themes and interpretations of carefully chosen children's books. They also become writers of stories themselves, create audiotapes, and complete the learning cycle by transferring their knowledge to the children in "lap learning" during story-sharing hours in child-care and educational settings in the community. In addition, Motheread conducts classes in women's correctional facilities and provides curriculum and staff development services to other programs concerned with literacy, such as Even Start, Adult Basic Education, and Chapter 1.

There are secondary outcomes to the literacy programs of Motheread as reported by the participants themselves. Class groups are often seen as support groups, as parents discuss the difficulties they are having, for example, in parenting. As reading involves relating text to personal experiences, parents grow to understand themselves and their children better through the lessons that literature offers.

Motheread has programs in at least seven counties of North Carolina and is also helping other states — such as Vermont, Florida, Mississippi, and Minnesota — to start their own programs. It has received national recognition in publications of the Barbara Bush Foundation for Family Literacy and the Laubach Literacy International. For more information, contact Carolyn Dickens, director of programs (at 919-781-2088).

University-School Initiatives

The Parents as Partners in Reading Program was an intervention project initiated by Michigan State University in the 1987–1988 school term that involved university and school-based teams developing effective strategies for parents — in this case — mothers, to learn how to read to their children. Although the number of participants was small — 25 mothers and their children — the program provides a successful model for intervention because it shifted from *telling* to *showing* parents how to read to their children. For many nonmainstream parents, reading is not a literacy event in their home and books are not a regular staple in their cupboards.

A component of the program that facilitated attendance at the sessions in the school was support from the community in the form of transportation and child care. Support came from local sources, a businessperson who worked with the Social Services Department, a priest from a Catholic church who helped with recruitment, the school librarian who provided parents with reading materials and kept a record that was shared with the children's teachers, and school administrators who helped publicize the program and create a warm, friendly welcome to parents who had never felt comfortable in a school environment before. Clearly, the collaboration among the stakeholders of the program contributed to its success.

Of particular significance to the success of the program is the design of the intervention itself, which consisted of three phases: coaching, peer modeling, and parent–child interaction. There were 23 weekly sessions, each lasting 2 hours, over a 7-month period during the 1987–1988 school year.

During *coaching,* parents met as a group with the university leader; it was felt that a group setting would be less threatening than one-to-one interaction. The leader modeled book-reading behaviors and introduced video-tapes that had been collaboratively created by the children's teachers and the university staff. The videotapes consisted of a teacher explaining specific strategies, such as body management, book handling, varying one's voice, language interactions, and a general progression of steps to follow with a story, attention getting, questioning, labeling, and providing feedback, and then a demonstration of the strategies with one of the target children. Coaching was interactive with discussion focused on promoting parents' ability to talk about the content of the books and strategies for book reading, and resulted in the parents developing an internal understanding of what it meant to share books with children.

In the second phase of the intervention, *peer modeling,* parents began to direct the book-reading sessions themselves as they took turns modeling particular strategies and received feedback from the other parents. They began to provide each other with the same instructional scaffolding the university leader had provided for them earlier.

During the final phase, *parent–child interaction,* parents had total control as they brought their children to the sessions and used the strategies directly with them. As parents finely tuned and structured their strategies, their children became more active participators, in turn internalizing the strategies now passed to them by their parents.

The data used to evaluate this intervention program were based on observations made by the university program leader, which showed that the children had increased their knowledge and ability to participate in book-reading interactions with their parents, and also by the children's teachers who reported an improvement in knowledge of story grammar and written language, directionality, and most important in the ability to participate in classroom reading interactions. Reports from parents also indicated former helplessness was replaced by confidence in their ability to help in their children's literacy development. Such observational data are valid and appropriate for the small sample used in this intervention program. The components of the program have been so specifically described that replication and further study of different varieties and sizes of populations are facilitated (Edwards, 1991).

In 1988, the Partnership for Family Reading began to operate as a joint venture between Montclair State College (New Jersey) and a group of Newark, New Jersey, public schools. The project served 26 classrooms in seven Newark schools, the majority of which were kindergarten and first-grade classrooms, and presented 80 sessions during the period of September 1988 to December 1990. As of September 1991, additional schools in the area were initiating similar projects.

The major part of the program involved workshops for adult family members that provided information about quality children's literature and strategies for discussing books with children with the emphasis on comprehension. However, the project also included joint activities for parents and children, such as a family reading festival at the college, staff development in the schools, and classroom and school libraries open for home borrowing. Although the majority of participants were mothers, sessions were also attended by grandparents, uncles, and other adult relatives.

Program evaluation seemed to have evolved from the informal reports gathered from participants. Parents remarked that they "hadn't realized" that preschoolers would be interested in books; they read more to their children, becoming role models as they became interested in reading for themselves and advancing their own education. Informal parent–teacher contact confirmed that books were being read and enjoyed at home and students reported to their teachers about home reading. Adults were invited into the school to read to the children and schools saw a general increase in all aspects of parent involvement. Librarians reported an increase in circulation as more parents took advantage of established parent-borrowing periods. Handel stated that participation varied by school, influenced by such factors as disorderly neighborhoods or unsuccessful recruitment due to the unwelcome atmosphere of some schools.

WHAT HAVE WE LEARNED AND WHAT DO WE NEED TO DO NOW

The descriptions of programs were provided to give an overview of variations in program components. With the increased pressure from government for parent involvement at both the federal and state level, many more programs will be surfacing across the nation in the near future. At the federal level, guidelines are provided, funding is ample, the program definition comes from the applicants, but the competition is considerable. At the state level, mandates for components are provided, but a strong component for literacy development is not defined; in the initial evaluation, outcomes were in broad areas of cognition not specifically concerning knowledge of literacy or strategies for understanding or discussing literature.

Community-based initiatives were more suited to individual community needs; support was elicited from several resources in the community. The workshops conducted were extremely interactive, allowing participants to share ideas and problems with each other; the program of instruction was built on the needs they expressed. The mothers' literacy was encouraged particularly with the publication of their writing. An extension of this program to include any family members, specifically fathers, would be worthwhile.

Although the State University of Michigan initiative was instituted by a large university, the number of parents serviced was small (only 25). Such a project would certainly be more manageable but perhaps more difficult to replicate with larger or more varied populations. A strong component of the project was the design of the intervention. Initial modeling by the university facilitator was followed by practice and then total control by the participants. This scaffolding served as a model to the participants as they scaffolded strategies for their children during the shared book experiences. The use of videotapes allowing the modeling to be reviewed and studied was very home based as the children in the video were part of the program. In a previous study, Edwards (1989) completed a more in-depth study of five mothers' development of successful book-reading behaviors. She provided an excellent observational checklist (p. 240) for such behaviors that can also be used to formulate instruction in workshops.

The Montclair–Newark project was a project of a larger scale than Michigan because it involved several schools in a district. The Guidelines for Replication (Handel, 1991) are clear and can be modified to suit different kinds of populations. Evaluation involved all stakeholders, however, the procedures used in the evaluation were not fully described; data were gathered from informal conversations but questionnaires or written reports might also have been used.

Except for the programs at the state level, evaluation was largely informal. These programs were reported as successful in journals and government reports and it would seem that their further funding and dissemination is proof of their success. Bearing in mind the need for more clearly defined methods of evaluation, a list of criteria that schools can use for the development of programs for early intervention strategies for family literacy can be gleaned from the programs presented.

The process of program development could include the following:

1. *A needs assessment.* Describe the demographics of the community, for example, the format and members of households, the ages of family members, whether the area is urban, rural, or suburban, and where and when possible participants work. Find out whether parents would be better served with home visits and/or sessions at school and the convenient times for contact. Question organizations in the community about family needs, social service agencies, churches, businesses, child-care providers, and preschools. Contact PTA associations and ask for help in gathering information. Solicit help in recruiting participants at the same time. Set more specific goals, for example, the number of families and or a particular geographic area.

2. *Recruitment.* Search for key families or individuals who are knowledgeable about the area. Set up a partnership with social service agencies (it

is impossible to solicit involvement from parents who are worried about their survival). Secure the services of or hire parent advocates who may be professional social workers or parents themselves. Involve all families, even those that are hard to reach. Lure families with free books, refreshments, entertainment by storytellers, free child care, and transportation; rent and show the film by Trelease (1983) on family storybook reading.

3. *Improve communication.* Have staff make home visits. Send out newsletters on school events from classrooms to home and from schools to the community. Have neighborhood small businesses put up flyers. Use technology, audio and videotapes, local cable television and radio stations. Get local newspapers to advertise events, available services, or write an article on the program. Provide translators and versions of written reports in other languages when necessary.

4. *Implementation.* Research and study the components of several programs. Two excellent published materials are: *Readers, Writers, and Parents Learning Together* (Katonah, NY: Richard C. Owen Publishers, Inc.) and *Parents as Partners in Reading* (Chicago: Children's Press). Allow interaction among participants, avoid lecturing, get feedback after every session, evaluate continually and modify according to needs. Offer a broad range of activities to encourage support and participation. Hire a coordinator (there should be at least one in every district to do inservice training) to guide school staff, to promote partnerships with other resources and agencies. Allow an extended period of time for the program to work; one year is not enough to work out problems and see results; start small and build surely.

5. *Costs.* Epstein (1991) advised the following initial funding for each level; state: $100,000; district: $50,000; school: $15,000–$30,000. Funding can be secured by application to federal or state agencies, through school budgets, from corporation grants, donations from smaller businesses and community organizations, or PTA fund raisers.

6. *Attitude.* Have high expectations for parents. In a review of the literature on parent involvement, Bempechat (1990) reported that many teachers have low expectations, especially for lower class parents, that they will follow through on commitments to help their children; however, lower class does not necessarily predict less effective parent practices. Assume that parents care about their children's academic progress but may not know how to help them. Teacher attitudes and support are crucial to successful parent involvement programs; yet there is a paucity of teacher training on the topic. Schools need to see parents as more than background support (food, clothing, etc.) and establish true partnerships.

There is a limited number of studies on parents' book-reading behaviors with their children. Such research would necessitate descriptive, longitudinal methods that are very laborious (Edwards, 1989). In the meantime, schools who have begun to reach out to parents need to extend their efforts to include parents of preschool children, and need to complete the partnership package by reaching out into the community for support. We do have a common goal, as stated by the past administration, to insure that every child is ready to continue to learn upon school entry. This common goal links schools, parents, and community in a partnership, bringing together their resources and collective imagination. If society is depending more on our schools to help at-risk children, then we need to accept that challenge and initiate that partnership. Programs, developed from thorough needs assessments, implemented with careful attention to feedback from all stakeholders, have to be successful. It might involve one individual in a school or district to create the needed spark, who realizes that one ounce of prevention is worth a pound of remedial services.

REFERENCES

Bempechat, J. (1990). *The role of parent involvement in children's academic achievement: A review of the literature*. New York: ERIC Clearing House on Urban Education. (ERIC Document Reproduction Service No. ED 322 285)

Bruner, J. (1984). Language, mind and reading. In H. Goelman, A. Oberg, & F. Smith (Eds.), *Awakening to literacy* (pp. 193–200). Portsmouth, NH: Heinemann.

Clay, M. (1982). *Observing young readers: Selected papers*. Portsmouth, NH: Heinemann.

Clay, M. (1992). Language policy and literacy learning. *Reading Today, 10*(3), 3–4.

Cross, C. (1991). The FIRST grants: Federal leadership to advance school and family partnerships. *Phi Delta Kappan, 72*(5), 383–388.

D'Angelo, D. A., & Adler, C. R. (1991). Chapter 1: A catalyst for improving parent involvement. *Phi Delta Kappan, 72*(5), 350–354.

Edwards, P. A. (1989). Supporting lower SES mothers' attempts to provide scaffolding for book reading. In J. B. Allen & J. M. Mason (Eds.), *Risk makers, risk takers, risk breakers: Reducing the risks for young literacy learners* (pp. 222–250). Portsmouth, NH: Heinemann.

Edwards, P. A. (1991). Fostering early literacy through parent coaching. In E. H. Hiebert (Ed.), *Literacy for a diverse society: Perspectives, practices, and policies* (pp. 199–213). New York: Teachers College Press.

Epstein, J. (1991). Paths to partnerships: What we can learn from federal, state, district, and school initiatives. *Phi Delta Kappan, 72*(5), 345–349.

Handel, R. D. (1991). *The partnership for family reading: A collaboration of Montclair State University and Newark public schools: Guide to replication*. New York: ERIC Clearing House. (ERIC Document Reproduction Service No. ED 341 744)

Heath, S. B., & Thomas, C. (1984). The achievement of preschool literacy for mother and child. In H. Goelman, A. Oberg, & F. Smith (Eds.), *Awakening to literacy* (pp. 51–72). Portsmouth, NH: Heinemann.

Henderson, A. T. (1988). Parents are a school's best friends. *Phi Delta Kappan, 7*(2), 148–153.

Holdaway, D. (1979). *The foundations of literacy*. Portsmouth, NH: Heinemann.

Irvine, D. J. (1979). *Parent involvement affects children's cognitive growth*. Albany, NY: The University of the State of New York, The State Education Department, Division of Research, Prekindergarten Evaluation Unit.

Mason, J. M., Peterman, C. L., & Kerr, B. M. (1988). *Fostering comprehension by reading books to kindergarten children* (Tech Rep. No. 426). Urbana, IL: University of Illinois, Center for the Study of Reading.

McCormick, C., & Mason, J. M. (1986). *Use of little books at home: A minimal intervention strategy that fosters early literacy* (Tech. Rep. No. 388). Urbana, IL: University of Illinois, Center for the Study of Reading.

Merina, A. (1992, December). School-parent team makes kids winners. *NEA Today,* pp. 12–13.

New York State Education Department. (1990). *Guidelines for the implementation of the New York State Prekindergarten Program.* Albany, NY: Division of Child Development Services.

New York State Education Department. (1992). *Parent partnerships: Linking families, communities, and schools.* Albany, NY: Office of Elementary, Middle, and Secondary Education.

Ninio, A., & Bruner, J. S. (1978). The achievement and antecedents of labelling. *Journal of Child Language, 5,* 1–15.

Peterson, D. (1989). *Parent involvement in the educational process.* Eugene, OR: ERIC Clearing House on Educational Management. (ERIC Document Reproduction Service No. ED 312 776)

Rich, D. (1985). *The forgotten factor in school success, the family: A policymaker's guide.* Washington, DC: The Home and School Institute. (ERIC Document Reproduction Service No. ED 263 264)

Slavin, R. E., Karweit, N. L., & Wasik, B. A. (1992-1993). Preventing school failure, what works? *Educational Leadership, 50*(4), 10–18.

Smith, F. (1975). *Comprehension and learning.* New York: Holt, Rinehart & Winston.

Taylor, D. (1983). *Family literacy.* Portsmouth, NH: Heinemann.

Taylor, D., & Dorsey-Gaines, C. (1988). *Growing up literate: Learning from inner city families.* Portsmouth, NH: Heinemann.

Teale, W. H. (1984). Reading to young children: Its significance for literacy development. In H. Goeman, A. Oberg, & F. Smith (Eds.), *Awakening to literacy* (pp. 110–121). Portsmouth, NH: Heinemann.

Teale, W. H. (1987). Emergent literacy: Reading and writing development in early childhood. In S. E. Readance & R. S. Baldwin (Eds.), *Research in literacy: Merging perspectives* (36th Yearbook of the National Reading Conference, pp. 45–74). Rochester, NY: National Reading Conference.

Trelease, J. (1983). *Reading aloud: Motivating children to make books into friends, not enemies.* Springfield, MA: Reading Tree Productions.

U.S. Department of Education. (1991). *Even Start Family Literacy Program* (Statute Part B of Chapter 1 of Title I of the Elementary and Secondary Act of 1965 as amended [20 USC 2741-2749]). Washington, DC: Author.

Vandegrift, J. A., & Greene, A. L. (1992). Rethinking parent involvement. *Educational Leadership, 50*(1), 57–59.

Walton, A. L. (1993, March). *State Education Department* (Bulletin). Albany: University of the State of New York.

Wells, G. (1986). *The meaning makers.* Portsmouth, NH: Heinemann.

14

Vocational Education in the 21st Century

Charles S. Benson
National Center for Research in
Vocational Education
University of California, Berkeley

In this chapter I try to present a vision of a "new" vocational education program intended to serve as a major element of reform of innercity secondary education. The objective may strike some people as startling, for the "old" vocational education appears to be withering away in major urban areas. Nevertheless, our studies at the National Center for Research in Vocational Education (NCRVE) demonstrate the pedagogical power of hands-on academic education, that is, of presenting academic concepts in a real-life context. Indeed, a combination of such practices as contextual learning, cooperative learning, teacher collegiality, and establishment of a focus, or identity, for a high school may be the educational structure that innercity youth have been waiting for.

Before I launch into a discussion of the main components of the new vocationalism, as we see them, I beg leave to draw some lines around today's subject. First of all, NCRVE's program of research is confined by our terms of reference to the study of educational and training institutions in the public sector. Although I would like to think that my arguments fit private institutions as well as public, I cannot present documentation to justify that hope. Second, my information does not allow me to deal in detail with problems and potentials in particular schools of any single city, such as New York; rather, I offer a kind of national composite view of urban secondary education.

SOME MATTERS OF DEFINITION

We start with troublesome matters of definition. The Carl D. Perkins Vocational and Applied Technology Education Act of 1990 ("Perkins II") defines vocational education as "organized educational programs offering a sequence of courses that are directly related to the preparation of individuals in paid or unpaid employment in current or emerging occupations requiring less than a baccalaureate or advanced degree." The words "less than" are often interpreted as meaning an education "not as good as," but the intellectual complexity of skills acquired in some vocational programs in our community colleges, my observation suggests, exceeds those demanded for a degree in some of our 4-year colleges and universities. In Germany, as in the United States, an identifiable number of completers of vocational programs continue to a university degree; in Germany, both the engineering and banking professions prize this kind of "double major." The federal definition also violates the language: If vocational education in common-sense terms means preparation for work, then Harvard Law and Harvard Divinity are both vocational schools!

One feels, nevertheless, a need for some distinctions within the whole broad field of learning. As a start, let's say that the world of work consists of people who create knowledge, on the one hand, and people who interpret and use knowledge, on the other. We can call programs for the first group "academic"; for the second, it might be "applied science and technology." For me, technology, including knowledge of "how things work," is a legitimate component of the liberal imagination. Dreams of glory—I would like to think Leonardo would have agreed with this perception, together with Benjamin Franklin and Thomas Jefferson. And this is the way I read Whitehead (1929).

Another way to distinguish theoretical versus applied fields is in pedagogy—the manner of presentation of instructional content. In secondary schools, academic courses are most commonly taught in 50 minute sessions in classrooms that are mainly bare, using text lecture, blackboard, chalk, and written homework. No emphasis is given ordinarily to drawing relationships between different subjects. Likewise, the secondary teacher does not commonly lead students to understand the connection between the content of a subject and its use in interpreting processes or solving problems in life and work as adults know it.

Applied learning, as practiced in its more fully developed forms, uses block scheduling, meaning that periods are of varying length, but generally include some classes of 3 hours in length or more. Teachers work as teams— English, math, and technology is one common teacher set. As work on a given topic proceeds, students, both individually and in groups, assume greater responsibility for planning instructional activities and for measuring results of student performance, while the teacher moves into the role of coach. Project and transfer-oriented training is emphasized, meaning inter alia, that interdisciplinary connections are drawn and theory is introduced "just in time" for solution of problems in close to real-life work contexts.

The school is likely to have an industrial focus, with professionals from leading firms of the industry being physically present at frequent intervals. The industry focus, when it is effective in strengthening shared interests, helps develop a collegial atmosphere among students, among faculty, and between the two groups. In summary, applied learning is, from the point of view of the typical student, more active, integrated, and innovative than traditional academic instruction. When all this comes together, one expects that students gain confidence in their ability to learn and in their ability to teach, both learning and teaching being useful capacities in the training-intensive workplace.

I mention these matters of definition not to pretend that we can change the name of vocational education, nor even to suggest that we should. Rather, I bring them up in an attempt to say that vocational education, broadly conceived, is more than the odd assortment of one-semester courses in keyboarding, auto shop, and retailing.

DIVERSITY IN OCCUPATIONAL EDUCATION

One thing to note is that even in terms of the federal definition, vocational education does not have the field of occupational preparation unto itself. Though becoming a less and less common practice, some youth acquire work skills from parents or relatives. A vast amount of occupational preparation is conducted in the workplace (on-the-job training, or OJT), but the United States is almost unique among nations in the unorganized, informal manner in which most OJT is provided and in the scant regard that most employers give to training, beyond vestibule training, of their workforces (excluding the professional and technical workforce). Turning back to the public sector, one finds that there are also occupational training programs carried forward under the Jobs Training Partnership Act, the Job Corps, the Job Opportunities and Basic Skills (JOBS) program under the Family Support Act, the military, and correctional institutions. Many community-based organizations have training programs, financed by a variety of means.

These observations about our "system" of occupational preparation, if it can be called a system, are well known. What may not be so well recognized is the wide diversity just within the field of vocational education itself. To make a point of contrast, consider college preparatory programs. In content, they are quite uniform nationwide. A family can move from Yonkers to Tulsa and not miss a beat in the academic preparation of its children. The basic design of the college preparatory program has been accepted by secondary schools across the nation. (This is not to say that standards of rigor are uniform. The program at Bronx High School of

Science is of a different standard from that of my home district, Richmond, California, now just emerging from bankruptcy.) From whence comes the uniformity of design of the college prep program? Not from federal control, of course, but from college admissions standards, textbook writers and publishers, and, especially important, the existence of a set of measures of student attainment, national in scope and generally accepted by the population, of which the most prominent is the Scholastic Aptitude Test (SAT).

The degree of diversity in vocational education is at the other end of the spectrum from college prep. (As Henry David, former director of the National Assessment of Vocational Education, loved to note: "Everything one can say about vocational education is true." [personal communication, 1978]) I do not refer to the fact that different schools or different districts may give priority to different occupations: health professions versus precision manufacturing, for example. Such would be a sensible and appropriate kind of distinction to practice. What I am alluding to are the differences in program content under a given occupational specialty. Consider the field, for example, of metal working. In one secondary school, the advanced lab or shop will be run by a highly qualified machinist. The class will be using computer-assisted drafting and design equipment along-side computer numerically controlled cutting tools. The course will be in an orderly sequence in which the students will already have progressed from hand work with vise, files, and calipers on through the use of manually controlled machines. Worker safety, management of a machine shop, metallurgy, and quality control procedures, drafting, and design will be included in the sequence, as will a lot of math taught in a contextual setting. A math instructor will be available on call to students in the metal working program. In the labs and shop, well-used math texts will be in evidence. One of the instructor's main problems will be to persuade his students to stay on to get their high school diplomas, instead of taking one of the high-paid work offers they are receiving even before graduation.

In another secondary school, the metal working program may consist of two stand alone, one-semester courses, conducted in a lab or shop with the appearance, in Sewall's (1987) words, of "industrial museums," serving as "crucibles of unemployment" (p. I-8). Both programs, the good and the deficient, carry the same title. Only by getting (or, alas, sometimes being trapped) inside can one tell the difference. How did such a diversity under a single program title come into being? Vocational education is a program that is subject to a certain amount of federal government direction, while college prep mainly is not. Since 1917, vocational education has received federal categorical funds, subject to strict auditing and control features. Yet it is the college prep curriculum that shows relative uniformity. Vocational education lacks a minimum desired standard of quality, even though it is subject to the centralizing effects of federal influence. To help explain the difference in this regard between college prep and vocational education, I think the following two points may be relevant.

1. Lack of a System of Skills Certification

There is a great deal of skills certification that goes on in the United States, but it is fragmented among a wide variety of certifying boards, industry associations, and state agencies. More seriously, there is little connection between the content of skills certification in a particular line of work and educational programs. No state has yet established guidelines to ensure that industry skills standards are used by educational authorities to set objectives for vocational programs and to guide assessment of student outcomes. Whereas most serious students in the college prep track have a pretty good idea of what they need to learn to enter the college of their choice (if not *why* they need to learn such things in any more fundamental sense), students preparing themselves to go directly to work or to attend a community college are only accidentally informed, for example, if parents or close friends have had experience in a line of work of interest to a student, or if the student is lucky enough to be in a school with a strong vocational program. Ironically, in those few fields where industry standards tend to inform the content of the curriculum—nursing, cosmetology, and residential construction—we face relatively little international competition in our labor markets.

Deficient vocational curricula can continue to exist because little effort is made to define adequacy of curricula. This is about as far as we can get in terms of policy from Germany, where enormous effort is made to specify what knowledge and skills are required in different lines of work. These specifications are published by the federal government and have the force of law.

2. Lack of Assessment of Student Outcomes in Applied Learning

In the United States, there is a vast amount of assessment of students' academic attainment. In California, for example, schools are required to present a "report card" of scores of student performance in standard subjects. These are translated into percentile rankings of each school and the results are published in the major newspapers. Nationally, test results as compiled by the Educational Testing Service (ETS) and the college board make headlines. ETS, the board, and other testing agencies create a "standard of worth" for academic performance.

Similar standards of worth are not generally available for applied learning. Indeed, few nationally recognized tests of applied learning even exist, whether or not they are based on well-developed industry skills standards. Beyond anecdotal evidence from local employers (whose own standards of excellence may be deficient), vocational educators lack benchmarks to measure the rigor and currency of their offerings.

In the absence of curricula designed relative to reasonably high standards of industrial skills and lacking measures of student attainment in applied fields that are valid over regions or the nation, good and bad vocational programs can exist side by side in a school district with little documentation of the discrepancy between the two types.

THE PLACE OF VOCATIONAL EDUCATION IN THE COMPREHENSIVE HIGH SCHOOL

I venture to say that the comprehensive high school has never been a comfortable place for vocational educators and the students they serve. The leadership of a typical secondary school—the principal and the council of department heads—is likely to reflect their academic backgrounds, not their experience in business and industry, and the same can often be said of the background and experience of counselors. The school will more probably measure its success in terms of student admissions to first-line colleges and universities, regardless of major. That is, a Harvard admit with an undefined major, reading one of the quantitatively soft fields, counts just as much as an admit to MIT of a student with a technological bias toward the applied field of materials science and a probable career in environmental restoration. Least of all is the school likely to pay a lot of attention to a graduate who goes immediately to work, even when the graduate has acquired the skills for interesting and profitable employment. The academic bias of the comprehensive high school is reinforced by the likelihood that the most vocal and influential group of adult clients of the institution will be university-educated parents. Their voices are more clearly heard by school board members and central office staff than the voices of working-class parents and employers.

There are other problems for vocational educators in the setting of the comprehensive secondary school. Vocational teachers and counselors (if there are any!) need to be in touch with employers and labor organizations. Only through close contact can they evaluate changes in labor market demand, solicit contributions of equipment and supplies for instruction, and serve as a link between students and those who control job opportunities.

The need to have contact outside the school is greater for vocational teachers than academic; yet rarely does the school budget provide telephones and local travel allowances for the vocational teachers. As compared with good academic instruction, good vocational education has resource requirements going beyond adequate teachers' salaries, small class size, and so on: There is a need for extra instructional space, expensive equipment (expensive to buy and expensive to maintain), and consumable supplies. If the school, as suggested earlier, has a natural academic bias, these extra expenses may not be well recognized in the school's budget. The federal vocational acts, with their confinement of federal vocational dollars to vocational teachers and students under strict audit controls, have served to isolate vocational teachers and students from their academic counterparts, thus defeating one of the main ideals of the comprehensive school. At the same time, the federal vocational dollars have never been substantial enough to overcome the budget shortfalls already mentioned.

These disabilities of vocational education are long-standing. However, the current educational environment poses new handicaps for the field. The K–12 educational reform movement of the 1980s had certain common features across most states, two of which were the following: to increase the number of academic courses required for high school graduation and to increase the number of academic courses required for admission to college. The school day, generally speaking, was not lengthened sufficiently to allow students to continue taking the number of vocational courses that had been their wont and to meet requirements for diplomas and college entrance. The limit on vocational enrollments is not being relieved, as districts, facing recessionary shortfalls of both state and local revenues are reducing the number of periods in the secondary school day. Also, the computerization of the U.S. workplace is making vocational education even more expensive to provide. Vocational educators need a lot of computers in their classrooms, along with computer-directed equipment, and the instructors need retraining.

Aggregating to the national level, nobody has a very good idea of what is happening to vocational enrollments in secondary schools. One problem is different definitions of "vocational student" across the states and another is double counting in some of the biggest states. Transcript analysis of 1990 National Assessment of Educational Progress (NAEP) records is our best bet for understanding changes in enrollments, but the analysis has not been completed. In the meantime, one *thinks* that the numbers of vocational students and instructors are both in decline. Here are some illustrative data. In Pennsylvania, a major industrial state, occupational vocational enrollments for grades 10–12 dropped steadily between 1979–1980 and 1989–1990, falling from 178,646 to 78,943, a decline of 66% (Pennsylvania Council on Vocational Education, 1991). All public enrollments in grades 10–12 also fell (from 493,067 in 1979–1980 to 351,755), but the proportionate drop was smaller (29%). Vocational student enrollment as a share of total enrollment in grades 10–12 went down from 36.2% in 1979–1980 to 22.4% in 1989–1990. All the while, the number of special needs students in vocational programs remained relatively constant.

A similar kind of story shows up in two reports recently completed at NCRVE. The first, by Selvin, Oakes, Hare, Ramsey, and Schoeff (1990), was based on a set of case studies in Los Angeles schools. All three were geographically close (sharing the same labor market area), but they were very different otherwise, especially in socioeconomic composition of their student bodies. Yet with respect to vocational education, the same conclusion applied to each, namely:

> The reader will quickly recognize that vocational education commands very little of our attention. Neither our descriptions of the curriculum and coursetaking decisions, nor our summaries of the curricular issues that are salient to the staffs or the students focus primarily on vocational education. Rather academic concerns dominate each of our cases. This was not our intent at the outset of the study. To the contrary, we scrutinized each piece of printed material and approached each interview with an eye to uncovering as much as we could about the schools' vocational programs and the students who participate in them. Simply put, there was little to be found. . . . Vocational education is nearly invisible in each of the three quite different high schools we examined. Few vocational courses are offered on campus, and few students take advantage of the specialized area vocational programs available to them. Consequently, issues about vocational education simply don't loom large in the minds of those who work in our schools. Perhaps even more striking (and distressing) than the lack of visibility of vocational education are the negative perceptions that so many have about it. (p. 11).

Little and Threat (1992) reported on case studies of five different California comprehensive secondary schools (different from those studied by Selvin et al., 1990), along with comparative data from a set of schools in Michigan. Here is the basic message:

> Vocational teachers are a disappearing breed in these schools. The pattern . . . shows a steady record of decline in total numbers and in full-time assignment of vocational specialists. . . . Program declines place vocational teachers in a precarious position, forcing them to accept or seek split assignments across departments or schools, or to take special out-of-classroom assignments at the school level. Such programmatic shifts also place difficult demands on schools which, bound by state credentialing and assignment laws and by locally negotiated contracts honoring tenure and seniority, may be hard-pressed to place vocational teachers in classes they are both authorized and entitled to teach. By the third year of our study, ten teachers who had been teaching vocational classes were teaching remedial classes in academic departments (e.g., basic math) or courses in other

non-academic departments (health or physical education). Others were teaching newly created electives that satisfy student interest without being visibly consistent with a departmental vocational orientation such as multiple sections of Photography I. (pp. 25-27)

THE AREA SCHOOL SOLUTION

If comprehensive schools, especially those in inner cities, are not good sites for vocational programs, what are other options to offer youth occupational preparation? For many years, the option of choice was area or regional vocational schools. Area schools provide only a vocational program typically, and they enroll students on a half-day basis, with the other half day being spent in the home high school. On the face of it, area schools have advantages over vocational programs in comprehensive institutions.

1. Their mission is exclusively occupational preparation. This means that the principal (director, head) is more likely to be a person committed to that field. Excellence of faculty in skills development is likely to be noticed and rewarded, not ignored or trivialized as in some comprehensive schools. Faculty morale and collegiality should be at a higher level than in the other setting.

2. The area schools are likely to operate in an entrepreneurial fashion, to their apparent advantage. No student is required to attend an area school or assigned to it. The area school must appeal to students to survive. One of the best "pitches" such a school can make to prospective students is this: "Study here and you will have an interesting and rewarding job. It can be a job for a career or a job to help you pay for college." To make good on that promise, administration and faculty must stay in close touch with employers and labor organizations. To sell the school to students, they must sell the graduates of the schools in the labor market. Being in touch brings currency to the program of study as well as a sense of reality, probably contagious from faculty to students. Closeness to employers also brings gifts of equipment and supplies, school visits, and so on.

3. For reasons that I cannot specify, area vocational programs draw more state money per student than programs in comprehensive schools. One reason may be that the schools establish a political base through their contacts with business, industry, and labor. In any case, the more generous financing is a boost to faculty morale and activity.

In spite of their apparent advantages, area schools have not served to solve the problem of how to provide occupational preparation services to secondary age youth. Some youth are reluctant to leave their home high schools, one reason being that they may miss out on extracurricular activities. Principals, so it is reported, are even more reluctant to see any substantial number of students leave school to attend a program at another institution, and, so it is said, they discourage study in area schools. Innercity schools fear that students who go away from the home high school will not arrive at the area school: In their eyes, travel is an invitation to truancy or worse.

These difficulties have been exacerbated by the 1980s style of education reform, as students come to feel that they do not have time for half-day area programs within their crowded school day. The upshot is that many area schools now serve primarily adults in search of retraining after job dislocation or upgrade training. Delaware recently closed its area schools in favor of full-time vocational high schools. One of the features of the new vocationalism is integration of academic and vocational studies. As was noted in Delaware, separating academic and vocational teachers in two different schools makes such integration even more difficult than it is ordinarily. My assessment, for whatever it is worth, is the following: Notwithstanding the excellence of many area vocational programs, these institutions have not succeeded in acquiring a sufficiently large and enthusiastic following among secondary age students to stand as a major component of educational reform in urban areas.

THE NEW VOCATIONALISM: WHAT IT LOOKS LIKE

From what I have reported so far, a reasonable person could conclude that vocational education should be dropped from the secondary curriculum. If one refers to costly job-specific training for dead-end occupations, conducted in isolation from the rest of the secondary program, I would probably be in favor of this proposition. On the other hand, our studies at NCRVE, along with work done elsewhere, suggest that something we call the "new vocationalism" has sufficient promise and potential to deserve a fair test — a fair test to see if it is indeed an answer, or even a partial answer, to the distressing conditions of innercity schools. To drop experimentation with vocational education in secondary schools may be a classic case of throwing the baby out with the bath water.

How, then, might one describe the new vocationalism, and what are the bases for suggesting it has promise in the urban setting? One place to start to answer these questions is to be found in the federal Carl D. Perkins Vocational and Applied Technology Education Act of 1990, popularly known as "Perkins II." For over 70 years — that is, from the Smith–Hughes Act of 1917 — Congress has supported separation of academic and applied studies. Suddenly, federal funds were to be used in such ways that students learned theory and practice in a common instructional process. The act specifies that integrated programs aim at "strong development and use of problem-solving skills and basic and advanced academic skills (including skills in the areas of mathematics, reading, writing, science, and social studies) in a technological setting."

In addition, the act proposes that teachers and their students gain "strong experience in and understanding of all aspects of the industry the students are preparing to enter (including planning, management, finances, technical and production skills, underlying principles of technology, labor and community issues, and health, safety, and environmental issues)." Lastly, in terms of substantive matters, the act proposes establishment of 4-year curricula, linking, in the typical case, the last 2 years of high school and a 2-year community college program in a seamless scheme of preparation for a defined set of occupations, such as the allied health professions, electronics, and computer science. Here I would like to discuss programs in middle and secondary schools, not community colleges, and I emphasize the first two proposals of the act: "integration" and "all aspects of the industry."

I do not propose here a detailed discussion of what Perkins II requires and what it does not require, nor do I wish to be constrained by narrow definitions of the two main concepts mentioned earlier. I would like to describe a reform package related to but expanded beyond a literal reading of the federal act. A lot of what follows is commonsensical, but I do refer to literature when applicable. There are six components in the program.

1. The Middle School

The Jefferson Junior High School of Technology in southwest Washington, DC, is closely allied with its geographic neighbor, Communications Satellite Corporation (COMSAT). Yes, the school has received a lot of money from COMSAT for computers, software, and other electronics, and not every middle school can be so lucky. Yet, being in this particular school setting helps one understand how important early information about work is to young people. The students at Jefferson know a lot about the telecommunications industry, and they are excited about being a part, later on, of such a big, socially significant enterprise, an enterprise of many kinds of different, but interrelated, occupations.

The students appear to be able to distinguish between labor and work. Labor can be hard, solitary, and intrinsically meaningless. One engages in labor, if one has to, for survival, not for human development. Work, on the other hand, is activity centered on human growth, growth in the capacity to acquire extrinsic rewards and in the capacity to make real contributions to life on this planet. To reinforce this latter idea, scientific heroes from COMSAT visit Jefferson, give talks, and mingle informally with students.

The proximity to a center of applied science helps students to understand that there is a relationship between what they are being asked to learn in their courses and labs and what they would use as engineers, and so forth, in the telecommunications industry, or in modern industry in general. The school is available to residents of its attendance zone. It is majority minority. Teachers appear to be happy to work in such an institution. The school is open from early morning until well into the evening on school days; it is also open on Saturdays.

It may be granted that I have described a school with elements that cannot be replicated very widely, but in two ways, I think, we should try to simulate the Jefferson atmosphere. First, around the ages of 13 to 15, we should try to help young people distinguish between labor and work, with work being what people like to do, oftentimes in congenial groups. Along with that we should try to help young people understand the varieties of purposeful activity in adult life. Innercity children may find it hard to grasp such understandings from observations in their neighborhoods. The next step is to help young people perceive the general connection between educational attainment (finishing school with academic skills) and getting work.

In a second simulation, middle school students would be helped to understand the idea of prerequisites. That is, the students would be helped to appreciate the fact that if one is going to get good work, one must take certain courses in junior high and do work up to a certain level in order to become prepared for senior high studies. To shift the example, M. M. Washington High School, also in DC, prepares its graduates, mainly young women, for jobs in allied health professions. The school has relationships with its feeder middle schools in order to impress on middle school students (a) the attractiveness of careers in the health fields and (b) the need to take biology and algebra I in middle school to be able to succeed in the required courses, anatomy among them, in M. M. Washington High School.

Students, except those who have a clear line of sight on the college prep program, may lack information to connect school work with what would be great fun to do with their lives. To reduce dropping out on the one hand, and failure to acquire the knowledge to succeed in rigorous high school courses on the other, I suggest a Jeffersonlike atmosphere in middle school is essential. Even a first-rate high school program cannot overcome early student attrition.

2. Integration (Transformation) of Academic and Vocational Studies in Secondary Schools

In the later years of the reform decade of the 1980s, the voice of business was added to the chorus of complaints about the educational system.

Business leaders deplored high dropout rates in a time when the ratio of working-age adults to dependents (old and young alike) was shrinking rapidly; they found the high school diploma virtually meaningless as a measure of graduates' academic prowess, and they professed to be shocked, measurement problems aside, at the low positions of U.S. students in international comparisons of students' skills and knowledge. Academic and vocational educators responded (in part) by blaming each other. The academics found vocational courses too narrow and empty of intellectual substance. Outside the college prep track, students wandered around aimlessly in incoherent sequences of low-level courses from both the general and vocational tracks. Truancy was high and homework was virtually nil.

On their side, the vocational educators saw academic teachers as failing to motivate students, because their courses were arid and boring. Teachers spent too much time talking at students. Students had too much seat time and their behavior was too passive. There was too much emphasis on individual competition and too little on collaborative efforts of students. Problems were designed to show one right answer, which is to say they were not designed to show alternative solutions with strengths and weaknesses to be compared.

Enter the cognitive scientists, such as Resnick (1984), Scribner (1986), Lave (1988), and Raizen. Raizen (1989), in her NCRVE report stated:

Cognitive science has been uncovering more and more about what makes for effective performance, how people learn, and what facilitates and impedes effective learning. Cognitive scientists have been modeling the processes going on in the individual learner's head. Sociologists and anthropologists have been observing learning in social groups and learning in context, that is, using the given physical setting and available tools as part of the structure of learning. The development of technology and cognitive science research have been intimate partners. Not only has the computer enabled the development and testing of cognitive theory and the construction of effective training programs, it may even change the questions through its influence on the nature of work and, hence, on the competencies needed by workers. Some researchers see the computer's effects as more fundamental still, forecasting that it will become a tool for reorganizing the knowledge and skills structures in people's heads. (p. 31)

In their report to NCRVE, Grubb, Davis, Lum, Plihal, and Morgaine (1991) stated:

One conclusion from this emerging field (of cognitive science) is that knowledge (especially expert knowledge) is often specific to a particular activity or area of expertise, and that for most people effective learning requires a context that matters to them. In particular, most learning (including learning in the workplace) takes place in ways quite different from the form it takes in schools. Most learning takes place in groups and requires cooperation, while most school-based learning is an individual activity; (most learning) relies on using both simple and complex tools, whereas school-based learning emphasizes thinking that is relatively independent of tools. Most importantly, schools emphasize relatively abstract forms of learning disconnected from the "real worlds" of work, family, and community—as schools themselves are disconnected from these worlds—rather than connecting learning to events, people, and objects that have some meaning to them such as the tasks required on the job, the chores necessary around the home, or the routine activities of community members and citizens. . . . But, of course, vocational education has always tried to provide a context for learning which is intrinsically important—to teach the use of tools and to use tools as aids to further learning and to promote learning in groups and group projects rather than individual learning; therefore, it seems to exemplify the emerging principles of cognitive science. (pp. 9–10)

In an integrated program of instruction, let us be clear; the objective is more, not less, academic knowledge. The objective is to be reached by embodying the pedagogical strengths of vocational practice into the presentation of theoretical concepts. Through use of those pedagogical strengths, academic knowledge is made more accessible to a majority of the student population, perhaps for the first time. In an ideal program, may I suggest, virtually all students would meet the requirements of the college prep curriculum while at the same time gaining skills for entering a career line. That combination offers many more options to students who attain it than most students in this country have today. Of course, the ideal requires a longer than average school day and school year than we have and certain other conditions that must be met.

3. Cooperative Learning in Secondary Schools

As I understand the practice, cooperative learning means that students spend not an insignificant proportion of school time working in groups, often working on group projects. Here is an example I have witnessed. At Thomas Jefferson High School for Science and Technology in Alexandria, Virginia, I saw a group of some six students working in a darkroom on a set of problems in laser technology. The instructor was not in evidence, though obviously at some point he had to help the students set up the experiment. The students were clearly engaged and closely involved in their work. As they watched the laser beams go through their gyrations, they quietly posed a steady stream of questions to each other. At a point, they seemed to reach tentative agreement on how to move the experiment to a higher stage of analysis. I was told that some of the student projects at Thomas Jefferson are related to actual research and development (R & D) work in the labs of the high-tech firms of northern Virginia.

Cooperative learning does not imply an absence of competition. Students, after all, need to know how their work compares with the work of their peers. Part of a student's program at Thomas Jefferson is individualized. Additionally, student teams compete against student teams either within their own school or with teams from other schools. I was informed that a team from Thomas Jefferson had won a national contest in supercomputing. The prize was a supercomputer to take home to the school. The school won a similar contest a second year and received dedicated use of a supercomputer for a year. For 12 months, then, one high school, two supercomputers.

Not being a psychologist, I can say nothing about why students may like to spend some of their time in school working with each other, rather than working individually under the direct scrutiny of a teacher, though it does seem to be a natural kind of preference. However, one of the main advantages of cooperative learning is to turn students from passive to active learners, meaning that students are helped to take charge of their own learning processes. In passive learning, the student takes notes from the instructor's lecture, receives text assignments from the teacher, and, in general, takes the attitude that learning is fully directed by the teacher and can not occur in the teacher's absence. I see this result, moving from passive to active learning, as having implications for the work force. If, as is now frequently said, this country needs a work force that is capable of lifetime learning on the job, a passive attitude toward learning is not helpful, to say the least.

In active learning, students should gain confidence that they can learn as members of a group, with or without the presence of a teacher. They should also gain confidence in their capacity to learn using their own individual resources. These skills, I suggest, are important for lifelong learning in the work place, but there is more. High performance firms expect experienced workers to pass along knowledge about technological processes; that is, firms expect workers to teach each other. In cooperative learning groups, students function as both learners and teachers of each other. Hence, they come to see teaching as an easy and natural act.

In writing about active learning, and about how the instructor "fades" as the learning group approaches maturity, Schoenfeld (1988) stated:

> I have a sense of what . . . problems will serve as fertile sources of ideas and explorations. . . . It is essential for me to find fertile grounds for mathematical exploration . . . . It is equally essential for me gradually to remove myself from the process, moving to the side and prompting the group to resolve issues by itself. It remains engaged as a member of the community making

sure that mathematical ideas are respected (Are we really sure? Is there a counter example?). I refrain, however, from pronouncing what is right and what is wrong: I pose the issues and leave it (for as long as possible) for the class to resolve them. . . . The students work in small groups for perhaps half the class. Then, we convene as a whole to discuss these problems. . . . One day toward the end of the term I had an unavoidable conflict during the first part of the class. I asked a colleague to hand out my problem set; the students could work by themselves for a while and I would join them when I could. Unfortunately, I was detained, and only managed to get free after the class was over. I ran to the room where the class met, arriving 15 minutes after the class should have ended. All the students were still there, still in small groups, arguing over the problem. (pp. 12–13)

4. Teacher Collegiality and Collaboration

As Lortie (1975) told us, teachers tend to work in an extremely isolated fashion. As a result, students are pretty much left on their own, at least in secondary schools, to make connections among, or to see the relationships between, different subjects. Although work outside education has become increasingly multidisciplinary, educators still sort themselves out by narrow subject labels. Yet, serious efforts to achieve integration of academic and vocational education must be based on collaboration among teachers. In schools that appear to have advanced further along the path of integration, NCRVE researchers find an important precondition of success: Namely, almost all teachers in a school have a single time during the week to meet and work together as a whole school group. Advanced forms of integration afford clear examples of collegial performance: team teaching by academic and vocational faculty, joint design of programs, collaborative efforts in writing problem sets and other instructional materials, common efforts in devising new schemes of student assessment, and so on.

The idea of teachers' working together is certainly not new. In the late 1950s, the Graduate School of Education at Harvard and the Ford Foundation got together to promote a new practice: team teaching in elementary schools. The notion was that teachers should concentrate their teaching on subjects in which they had some special background or interest, such that all third-graders might receive their instruction in, say, math, from a teacher who had a strong feeling for mathematical ideas. Teacher collegiality for present purposes also assumes a natural division of labor among teacher specialties, but it goes further: In secondary schools practicing the new vocationalism, teachers would plan for and develop components of the curriculum, outreach activities, and assessment proce-dures working as a unified team. Not just teaching subjects but the design of the instructional activities of the school would become a team effort.

Interestingly enough, teacher collegiality has come under study as an important aspect of teachers' professional behavior quite independently of the integration movement in vocational education. One of the leading scholars to examine the nature of teacher collegiality is a co-worker of mine at Berkeley, Judith Warren Little. Little (1987) maintained that teacher collegiality can have, depending on its nature, either strong positive effects on the operation of schools and the achievement of students, or negative effects. Her research also indicates that teacher collegiality is a rather fragile phenomenon in the life of an educational institution.

Nevertheless, when it works right, schools become better off. Little (1987) listed the following "benefits to the school" that accrue from positive collegiality:

> Increasingly, schools must bolster public faith and enlist public support by showing that they are capable of meeting complex demands with an ever more diverse student body. Yet the twin demands that schools show steady improvement and that teachers "be professional" cannot plausibly be satisfied by the individual efforts of even the most capable, energetic, and dedicated teachers.
>
> One feature of steadily improving schools is that they are organized to influence teaching. . . . Teaching in such schools is a public enterprise. The broad values that guide daily decisions, expectations for student learning, ideas about how students learn and what we as a society wish them to learn, the planning and conduct of instruction, recurrent dilemmas in fostering student motivation and judging student progress, the principles for organizing life in classrooms — all receive the collective attention, scrutiny, insight, and refinement of peers acting as colleagues.
>
> Schools stand to benefit in three ways from promoting closer collegial ties among teachers. Schools benefit first by simply orchestrating the daily work of teaching across classrooms. Teachers, students, and parents all gain confidence in their knowledge of what is taught throughout the program and why. Teachers are better prepared to support one another's strategies and accommodate weaknesses.
>
> Second, schools that promote teacher-to-teacher work tend to be organized to examine and test new ideas, methods, and materials. They are adaptable and self-reliant in the face of new demands; they have the necessary organization to attempt school and classroom innovations that would exhaust the energy, skill, or resources of an individual teacher.
>
> Finally, schools that foster collegiality are plausibly organized to ease the strain of staff turnover, both by providing systematic assistance to the beginning teachers and by explicitly socializing all newcomers to staff values, traditions, and resources. (pp. 501–502)

5. Teaching All Aspects of the Industry

Paul Weckstein, director of the Law and Education Center, Cambridge and Washington, DC, is, I would say, the inventor and chief proponent of the process of "teaching all aspects of the industry." Though I have had conversations with Paul on the concept and recognize my debt to him, what I present here is strictly my own interpretation of what I see as an important new practice in U.S. education.

One of the most successful programs in occupational preparation in this country was agricultural education. Its notable feature was its broad scope. Students were not taught simply how to grow fodder for cattle. Rather, the program covered such topics as determinants of the price of land; measures to retain and enhance the arability of land; predicting crop yields and crop prices; study of profitable combinations of land characteristics, seed varieties, water, fertilizer, and pesticides; harvesting and storage of crops; marketing; inventory control; accounting; and negotiation of short- and long-term debt. An advantage of the broad scope is to satisfy students' natural curiosity about a line of work they might enter and to strengthen their commitment to excellence in farming. A second, and very important advantage, was that the students acquired a grounding in farm entrepreneurship, possibly superior, in some ways, to what the student might receive from a father or brother or sister. The same kind of entrepreneurship argument could be made for training in the construction trades. Instead of learning just about skills of carpentry, say, students might as well gain a lot of information about setting up their own contracting firm.

What about large-scale industry, for example, the communications industry? Here, I believe a different kind of benefit accrues to students when they study all aspects of their industry. Consider a program of training for an electronics technician. Suppose this program, beyond existing technology per se, included such topics as the following: forms of communication through history, the economic size of the communications industry and changes therein, functioning of R & D departments, emerging communications technology, patent law, international transmission of communications technology, important management techniques in the industry, environmental and social issues in communications, rights of privacy, and governmental regulations. The benefit in this case should be that workers, together with their fellow technicians, have some basis for establishing goals for improving the quality of their work life, including reducing the wall that separates management and worker. Ideally, work would become less Tayloristic and more imbued with worker decision making. It is a matter of giving a human face to work.

A third reason to urge instruction in all aspects of the industry in occupational education programs is that it can give meaning and dignity to work. In Germany, apprenticeship programs for persons who work in bookstores include such things as ordering, inventory control, accounting, marketing (basically, the entrepreneurship and cross-training subjects), but they also embrace the "significance of the printed word in the history of

Western civilization" and "production of books and journals for national and international markets." In bookstores in our country, one finds a number of wannabe writers among the workers. I asked a second-year apprentice in a German bookstore if she wrote. She responded, "No, there are more than enough people doing that already. I'm not a writer but my job is very important to writers and most other people, too."

6. Establishing an Identity for Secondary Schools

Hill, Foster, and Gendler (1991) presented evidence to the point that when secondary schools develop a focus, or a theme—in other words, define the "character" of the institution—students tend to perform at a higher standard. Given my own interest in exploring relationships between school and work, as work is discussed earlier, I am attracted to themes drawn from relationships with an industry. Examples are the High School of Fashion Industries and Murry Bergtraum High School for Business Careers in New York and the Chicago High School for Agricultural Sciences. These are stand-alone high schools with an industrial focus. In California we have a set of some 30 academies, schools within a school, that are related to such fields as health professions and electronics technology.

I speak of an "industrial connection" in general terms. I do not mean just connections with manufacturing plants. Relationships with hospitals, legal services, transport, publishing, opera and symphony, museums, major construction firms—all such activities could be industrial connections in the present context. Why might an industrial connection conceivably be important? Such a connection serves to strengthen, I would suggest, the attributes of a "good high school" that I have already mentioned. *Integration of academic and vocational studies* occurs more naturally, and with greater coherence, when the context of application of theory is centered around a single industry or a small group of industries. Projects for *cooperative learning* teams become easier to find, and different teams can more readily be working on complementary projects at the same time. Ideally, faculty and students alike are drawn into working/studying in the given school because of an interest in the industry or a discipline, such as visual or performing arts. This shared interest helps stimulate *collegiality among faculty and students* and between faculty and students. An industrial focus provides a good setting for studying *all aspects of the industry.*

An industrial focus also improves opportunities for creating cooperatively designed work experiences for secondary students—cooperatively designed, that is, by schools and employers. Nationally, a majority of high school students work while they are still students. Stern (1984) and his colleagues at NCRVE demonstrated rather convincingly, I believe, that when students work in places where learning on the job is keyed to learning in the classroom, students receive benefits. As compared with students who have typical, "pick-up" jobs, obtained through family or friends, students in designed work are more likely to think well of themselves, to see work as an interesting challenge, to be aware of career ladders, and to understand that advancement at work is based on skills and knowledge.

Insofar as an industrial connection is an important part of the new vocationalism, major metropolitan areas have a comparative advantage in establishing secondary schools with the full range of attributes of the new vocationalism, simply because cities, inside their respective community areas, have more manufacturing, commercial, artistic, and public service activities with which schools could associate. The same applies for establishing industrial connections for middle schools, as in the Jefferson–COMSAT example. A well-functioning public transport system is an asset in building these connections between school and work for students.

A BIT OF EVIDENCE: MAYBE IT WORKS

Random admission for 50% of the students entering New York City's career magnet schools has given Crain, Heebner, and Si (1992) a rare opportunity to make a tentative test of the effectiveness of the new vocationalism. Comparing academic results of students who won the lottery for admission to a career magnet school with those who lost (and attended a comprehensive high school) approximates a random assignment study, given the high proportion of New York's eighth-graders who enter the lottery for school admissions. So far the Crain results refer only to the first year of high school (ninth grade), though we hope to follow the students through high school graduation and beyond.

The career magnets are unusual schools in that they help students acquire skills for work at the same time that they prepare students to enter 4-year colleges (Mitchell, Russell, & Benson, 1989). Some might have assumed that such schools would offer benefits only to students in the upper reaches of ability levels. Crain et al.'s results suggest that they provide a setting in which the middle two thirds of students, ranked by eighth-grade reading level, make significant gains over their peers in regular comprehensive schools. The lowest 16% of the students by reading ability, alas, do not appear to benefit uniformly; for them, the results are mixed. According to Crain et al. (1992):

> Many of the effects of the career magnet programs should be considered large. . . . We would estimate the low readers who applied to, but were not accepted by the . . . magnets, are two to four times more likely to drop out or disappear from the New York City public school system between eighth and

ninth grades than are those who did receive offers. In . . . magnets, a low reader is two to four times as likely to pass Regents math than he would be if he were in a comprehensive school. Average readers in magnet schools . . . increase their reading skills at a rate at least half again faster (perhaps twice as fast) than they would in regular schools. The average readers . . . earn one-fourth more course credits than the average student in regular schools. This considerably increases their chances of getting a high school diploma, since lack of credits is a main reason for students to drop out. . . . The negative effects on low readers are also educationally significant. The gap in reading ability between poor and average readers narrows during the ninth grade in comprehensive schools; in the career magnets it widens. At the end of ninth grade, a gap has begun to appear between the number of graduation credits earned by average readers and the number earned by low readers; this gap is greater in career magnets. (p. 29)

PROBLEMS AND POSSIBILITIES

According to Prowse (1991):

Those (students) not bound for college face a common problem. Going to college is part of the American dream. The U.S. educational system is thus designed to funnel students into academic higher education. As in other predominantly Anglo-Saxon countries, vocational and technical education is poorly funded and widely despised. The academic student can see a clear path from high school to permanent well-paid employment. . . . But those whose bent is primarily practical face nothing but obstacles. Few school districts make an effort to ease the transition from school to work. Neither the private nor the public sector has a tradition of providing rigorous vocational training. Non-academic students do not even have a goal to aim at: nationally recognized technical and vocational qualifications do not exist. . . . The U.S. is in a comparable position to Britain in the early 1980s — before vocational education and training rose to the top of the political agenda. Reformers want to raise standards but focus almost exclusively on the top 30 per cent, who are already doing reasonably well. The need to learn from European experience and devise innovative forms of eduction for the remaining 70 per cent is not widely understood. The U.S. has yet to learn that economic competitiveness is determined less by the achievements of an elite than by the skill levels of the work force as a whole. (p. 1)

Can we imagine a leap forward in the quality and rigor of vocational education, with emphasis on establishment of newly designed programs in urban areas? There are plenty of signs that say no: the bad reputation of vocational education in many quarters, the strangulation of initiative imposed by master schedules, lack of time for teachers to plan and collaborate, lack of interest in teacher training institutions, the unwillingness of college admission officers to give credit for applied science courses, the indifference of most U.S. employers toward improving standards in workplace education. I do not suggest the list is complete.

At the same time, we can see signs of change in direction of educational policy, nationally and in state governments. People are becoming interested in education outside a narrowly defined college prep track. President Bush, with some show of bipartisan support, submitted the National Youth Apprenticeship Act of 1992 to Congress. The Council of Chief State School Officers issued a major policy statement on improving the school to work transition and issued grants to five states to help implement youth apprenticeship programs (Council of Chief State School Officers, 1991). The Southern Regional Education Board, under the leadership of Gene Bottoms, is sponsoring integrated education programs in 14 southern states — and Pennsylvania. At NCRVE, we have had a remarkable response from urban teachers applying to our two summer institutes on implementation of Perkins II, but that is another story for another day.

REFERENCES

Council of Chief State School Officers. (1991). *Connecting school and employment.* Washington, DC: Author.

Crain, R. L., Heebner, A. L., & Si, Y. P. (1992). *The effectiveness of New York City's career magnet schools: An evaluation of ninth grade performance using an experimental design.* Berkeley, CA: National Center for Research in Vocational Education.

Grubb, W. N., Davis, G., Lum, J., Plihal, J., & Morgaine, C. (1991). *The cunning hand, the cultured mind: Models for integrating vocational and academic education.* Berkeley, CA: National Center for Research in Vocational Education.

Hill, P. T., Foster, G. E., & Gendler, T. (1991). *High schools with character.* Santa Monica, CA: RAND.

Lave, J. (1988). *Cognition in practice: Mind, mathematics and culture in everyday life.* Cambridge, England: Cambridge University Press.

Little, J. W. (1987). Teachers as colleagues. In V. Richardson-Kilheck (Ed.), *Educators' handbook: A research perspective* (pp. 501–502). New York: Longman.

Little, J. W., & Threat, S. M. (1992). *Work on the margins: The experience of vocational teachers in comprehensive high schools.* Berkeley, CA: National Center for Research in Vocational Education.

Lortie, D. (1975). *Schoolteacher.* Chicago: University of Chicago Press.

Mitchell, V., Russell, E. S., & Benson, C. (1989). *Exemplary urban career-oriented secondary school programs.* Berkeley, CA: National Center for Research in Vocational Education.

Pennsylvania Council on Vocational Education. (1991). *22nd annual report.* Harrisburg, PA: State Department of Education.

Prowse, M. (1991, August 16). At the bottom of the class: The dearth of vocational education training in the United States presents the country with its biggest educational challenge says Michael Prowse. *Financial Times of London,* p. 1.

Raizen, S. A. (1989). *Reforming education for work: A cognitive science perspective.* Berkeley, CA: National Center for Research in Vocational Education.

Resnick, L. B. (1984). *Everyday cognition: Its development in social context.* Cambridge, MA: Harvard University Press.

Schoenfeld, A. H. (1988). *Ideas in the air.* Palo Alto, CA: Institute for Research on Learning.

Scribner, S. (1986). Thinking in action: Some characteristics of practical thought. In R. J. Sternberg & R. K. Wagner (Eds.), *Practical intelligence: Nature and origins of competence.* Cambridge, England: Cambridge University Press.

Selvin, M., Oakes, J., Hare, S., Ramsey, K., & Schoeff, D. (1990). *Who gets what and why: Curriculum decisionmaking at three comprehensive high schools.* Berkeley, CA: National Center for Research in Vocational Education.

Sewall, G. T. (1987). The national assessment of vocational education. In National Assessment of Vocational Education, *Design papers for the national assessment of vocational education* (pp. 2-10). Washington, DC: U.S. Department of Education.

Stern, D. (1984). School based enterprise and the quality of work experience. *Youth and Society, 15*(4), 401-427.

Whitehead, A. N. (1929). *The aims of education.* Chicago: University of Chicago Press.

15

Environmental Education for the 21st Century

Lester W. Milbrath
State University of New York at Buffalo

A CURIOUS AND UNSETTLING MYSTERY:
WHY DID WE ABANDON ENVIRONMENTAL EDUCATION?

Knowing how nature works and how humans should relate themselves to it has always been central for our ability to live successfully on planet earth. Primitive people, even when they did not have formal schools, took great pains to instill awareness and knowledge of nature into all of their young people. Only during the last two centuries, with the pursuit of science, technology, and industrialization, has environmental education (EE) slipped from the educational agenda.

As I have studied the history of the relationship between humans and nature, I have been astonished at the sweeping changes in perspective that accompanied colonialism and the early stages of the Industrial Revolution. Instead of the long-standing traditional perspective that humans should live harmoniously with nature, we shifted to a perspective of being master, even rapist, of nature. This was especially true of the "pioneers" who led the European invasion and exploitation of such undeveloped continents as North and South America, Africa, Australia, and New Zealand. The European conquerors/colonists displaced indigenous humans, slashed down forests, mined for resources, squandered natural wealth, dumped their wastes everywhere, and transformed ecosystems—even climates.

A new belief system was developed to support the ascendance of science, technology, and industrialism during and after the colonial era; it empha- sized the following:

1. It is right and proper for humans to dominate and control nature.
2. Science and technology are powerful means for domination and control; their development should be emphasized; progress need never cease.
3. Acquiring material goods is the key to a good life.
4. The world is vast; there are plenty of resources, so we need not be concerned about running out.
5. Nature will absorb our wastes.

Dunlap (1983) called this belief system the "human exemptionalist paradigm," because it assumes that humans are not bound by the laws of nature that restrain the behavior of all other creatures. This belief system characterized not only the natural sciences but carried over into the social sciences, which became thoroughly anthropocentric. They all implicitly assumed that humans could live apart from nature, which they simply ignored.

We pursued our false beliefs to ridiculous extremes; this flaw is now evident in the serious environmental problems all around us. Humans now intrude so injuriously into nature that we have begun to change the way bio-geo-chemical systems work. We are in danger of wrecking the good functioning of planet earth's life systems. We never intended to do that; we merely fulfilled a false belief system. What is the nature of the predicament we have gotten ourselves into?

MAJOR ELEMENTS OF OUR
ENVIRONMENTAL PREDICAMENT

Consider the following nine environmental problems:

1. Human population on planet earth is exploding. Just in this century, human population has doubled twice from 1.5 billion to 3 billion to 6 billion. Every current trend suggests another doubling in 50 years to 12 billion. If the population of any other creature grew like this, we would consider it an epidemic; we surely are an epidemic to all other creatures.

2. All of these new people would like to live an affluent lifestyle (although many will not be able to). Our rate of throughput (the rate we take materials from the earth, make products, consume them, and throw the wastes away) is growing many times faster than population. We humans now consume 40% of our planet's bioproduct (photosynthetic product) and at this rate of growth, we will soon consume more than 80%. We cannot do that without crowding many other creatures from their niches. Do we want to wipe them out? Will we have suitable habitat if there is no suitable

habitat for other creatures? Can our lives be good if we humans try to take over everything?

3. The extinction of species is accelerating. It is difficult to be certain of the rate because several million species have never been cataloged, but hundreds extinguish every day. That process surely diminishes humans and all of the rest of the life system. Some geneticists believe that allowing mass extinctions is the one failure our children will have most difficulty forgiving.

4. Human emissions of greenhouse gases are bringing on global warming. Gradual warming will be devastating to creatures in many habitats. Bad as that is, we have no assurance that the changes induced by the warming will be gradual. Warming to some unknown point could trigger sudden climatic changes, even oscillations, that would be catastrophic to plant and animal life as well as to our civilization and our way of life. Our whole lives, especially our economies, are built on the premise of continuity; chaos in the climate system would destroy that premise, thus collapsing the whole socioeconomic–political system.

5. Emissions of chlorine atoms, especially the release of chloroflourocarbons (CFCs), are destroying the stratospheric ozone layer that shields us from injurious ultraviolet B rays. Not only will these rays bring more skin cancer and eye cataracts to humans but they also interfere with the ability of plants to take carbon dioxide (a greenhouse gas) from the atmosphere and make plant food. This is especially injurious to the phytoplankton in the ocean that are the beginning of the oceanic food chain.

6. Human demand for forest products, and jobs, is leading to swift deforestation all over the planet. Not only does this devastate forest ecosystems and extinguish species but it also releases carbon dioxide when the trees are broken down. We should be growing trees (one of the best ways to remove carbon dioxide from the air) rather than cutting them down.

7. As poverty stricken humans scramble to stay alive in many parts of the world, they destroy their ecosystems— people will pull up the last plant or eat the seed just to stay alive one more day. Overpopulation and poor management are turning more and more of the planet's land surface to desert. The destruction of plant life also changes the climate, which accelerates desertification.

8. Pollution of air, water, and soil is getting worse all over the planet leading to illness and death of humans as well as other creatures. We literally are poisoning life systems. The growth of human numbers, and their voracious appetites, seems to overwhelm whatever gains are made by antipollution laws, stricter enforcement of them, and new technologies.

9. "Everything has to go somewhere" is a law of nature; whatever we throw away does not disappear—it always goes somewhere. Everything we use or consume sooner or later becomes waste. We easily see the waste

carted away from our households (5–7 pounds a day for each person); to that must be added industrial and construction waste as well as hazardous waste. Senator Gore (1992) totaled all the waste for the United States and divided it by our population; from that he estimated that each person, directly or indirectly, generates more than twice his weight in waste *every day* (p. 147). Nature can eventually break down some wastes but hazardous wastes are poisonous to living things; they are especially resistant to breakdown. They circulate from air to water to soil to food, around and around—endlessly. We literally live in a chemical soup and it is getting worse.

The list of consequences flowing from our false beliefs could go on, but those listed illustrate my chief point that we are drastically reducing the carrying capacity of the planet at the same time that human numbers and appetites are soaring. We have created a civilization that cannot be sustained. We have no other choice than to change. If we stubbornly refuse to change, nature will force change on us. Resisting change will make us victims of change. Many people have studied this nested set of problems and have offered various proposals for transforming our society to a more sustainable mode (Clark, 1989; Milbrath, 1989; United Nations Conference on Environment and Development Agenda 21, 1992; World Commission on Environment and Development, 1987). Without exception, those proposals call for much more and better environmental education. Now, when we need it more than ever, environmental education is not on the agenda of our educational system. The U.S. educational system (and that of most other countries) has responded to this crisis by ignoring it. (The educational systems in The Netherlands, Norway, and Brazil are exceptions.)

THE RESISTANCE OF SCHOOL SYSTEMS TO ENVIRONMENTAL EDUCATION

It would not be fair to say that educational leaders actively oppose environmental education; they either fail to even think about it or they oppose adding new subjects to their overburdened curricula. In recent years, many proposals have been made for educational reform. There have been calls for more vocationally oriented education, for more attention to science and technology, and for tougher standards to make us more competitive in worldwide economic competition. None of these reforms have made any allusion to environmental education even though the environmental crisis is many times more urgent and potentially more devastating than the crises the other reforms are intended to relieve.

The New York State Education Department claims that it has a program in environmental education; it is a sham. I and two colleagues conducted a study in 1990 of levels of environmental knowledge, awareness, and concern among 11th-graders in New York State schools (Hausbeck, Milbrath, & Enright, 1993). We found abysmal levels of environmental knowledge. If a regents exam existed for environmental knowledge, most students would have failed; in some schools every student would have failed. These same students had fairly high levels of environmental awareness and concern that they got mainly from the media, not in their schools.

(In fairness, there were a few schools that did a decent job with EE; this was usually because a specific teacher, or administrator, or school board member felt EE is vital and took the extra effort to do something about it. More than 90% of the schools, however, made no effort whatsoever.)

The New York State Board of Regents (1991) listed educational goals for the state. Goal 7 states that "each student will acquire knowledge of the ecological consequences of choices in the use of environment and natural resources." The New York State Education Department and New York State schools have made no concerted effort to implement that goal. They tried to have their cake and eat it too by adopting a policy of infusing environmental examples and principles into currently standard curricula. Such efforts have been modest and have produced almost no substantive learning of environmental principles. When time pressures require choices, and they always do, environmental content is sacrificed for the standard content of the subject. Close observers of EE nationwide have concluded that infusion is inadequate to the task (Disinger, 1990, p. 33).

Teachers are given no signals that they are expected to include environmental learning in their teaching. The New York State Regents exam designers were told to include environmental questions in their standard exams. They failed to do so, presumably because the designers believed other topics were more important. A bill was introduced into the New York State legislature that would have required every student graduating from a teacher training program to have a basic course in environmental principles. The New York State Education Department opposed the bill and it never got out of committee. The New York State legislature did pass a bill in 1990 setting up a task force to inventory EE resources in the state; after a feeble start, and the passage of 3 years, the report still has not been issued. Congress passed an environmental education bill, they did not ask Health, Education, and Welfare (HEW) to implement the program; they gave it to the Environmental Protection Agency (EPA) where it would be more sympathetically implemented—but then failed to support the program with money. (EPA diverted minuscule resources from other parts of their budget to set up a token program.)

Parents and the public fail to pressure the schools to implement EE. The New York State PTA convention in 1989 considered a resolution urging EE;

it was defeated. A workshop on EE was scheduled for the New York State PTA 1991 convention; approximately 20 persons (out of more than 1,000 delegates) showed up; it was preaching to the converted—those who most needed to hear were not listening. We mailed a brief report on our 1990 study of environmental knowledge, awareness and concern to every PTA in New York State; it elicited not even one response. Even environmental organizations give no more than polite lip service to EE.

THE MINDSET BARRIER

The phenomenon I have just been describing is a mindset that disables our society's ability to deal effectively with our environmental predicament. The ignorance and indifference of our people is rooted in our outmoded beliefs about the relationship between humans and nature that still imprison our minds today. There are other aspects of the mindset that should be clarified:

1. *Environment is a special interest.* An EE program would be pandering to a special interest—schools are too busy to do that. I tried to show earlier that this mindset is false and dangerous. I am convinced that EE is just as basic to the learning needed in the 21st century as reading, writing, arithmetic, and history. In college, it should be just as basic as English 101. Just as we would not consider persons to be educated who had never studied history, they cannot be educated if they have never studied the environment. We can always find room in school curricula for the basics of being educated.

2. *EE is mainly outdoor education.* Intimate contact with nature excites students and engenders a love of nature that is important for learning. Love of nature is a good start for EE programs but typical outdoor education does not deliver a knowledge of ecological principles nor an understanding as to how social-economic-political actions can reduce injuries to life systems; good classroom instruction can do that.

3. *EE is the province of the science curriculum.* Knowledge as to how natural systems work is taught partially in earth science and partially in biology. Important as that is, it does not explain to students how economic, social, and political actions affect the good functioning of life systems. Nor does it clarify for students how they might work for a better environment. We got into our environmental predicament by building the society we have; we will extricate ourselves from the predicament only by changing our society. Good EE is interdisciplinary (perspectives from different disciplines in the same classroom) rather than the province of science—or even multidisciplinary.

Many New York State schools compound their narrow-mindedness by setting up an ecology course in the science curriculum. They routinely steer weaker students who can not hack chemistry and physics (but who still must take a science course to get a high school diploma) into this course. This practice tells students that EE is not important. It also systematically steers tomorrow's leaders away from a solid grounding in environmental principles, and an environmental way of thinking, even though that knowledge will be crucial for their effective leadership in the 21st century.

We cannot successfully make it to the end of the 21st century without changing this anti-EE mindset. How can this be done? I have tried every way I know and I must confess that I am defeated, at least for now. The mindset will change; but if nature must force the change, her lessons are very painful: disease, injury, privation, and death. I urge you to help change the mindset before nature forces her harsh lesson upon us.

HOW SHOULD ENVIRONMENTAL STUDIES IDEALLY BE STRUCTURED?

The following recommendations may serve as a guideline:

1. It should be interdisciplinary, drawing teachers and relevant knowledge from the natural and social sciences as well as humanities.

2. It should require learning basic concepts and principles so that students will not make errors in analysis. Students should learn to think integratively, systemically, holistically, and in a futures mode. Environmental systems cannot be understood by mechanistic cause and effect thinking.

3. It should encourage students to discuss their deep concerns about real problems. Many will want to move to personal actions to alleviate environmental problems.

4. Consideration of alternative solutions to problems requires weighing values; do not try to escape this necessity. Students should learn how to clarify their own values and to perceive the values pursued by various actors in environmental controversies. Teachers should not seek to impose their own values but they can encourage students to think more clearly about their values and to make confident and sound individual decisions.

5. It should address both local and global environmental problems. Students will eagerly study problems they encounter in their daily lives. Urban students will wish to discuss such problems as overcrowding, pollution, rodents, garbage, and urban decay. Students should be helped to link local problems to global problems.

6. Ideally, it should involve hands-on contact with nature: field trips, hiking, camping, park, roadside, and stream cleanups. These experiences develop a love of nature and enrich and deepen environmental knowledge and awareness.

SPECIFIC RECOMMENDATIONS TO EDUCATIONAL POLICY MAKERS

In establishing EE as a major component of the school curriculum, educators should:

1. Restore the idea that EE is a basic component of "being educated."
   a. Accord EE the same status as reading, history, and mathematics.
   b. Basic EE is for all students. Beware of the temptation to channel the best students away from EE.
2. Infuse environmental principles and examples into all curricula, K–12.
3. Find ways to offer experiences with nature to students. Helping students to bond with nature will be a blessing for life. Seek the collaboration of nature and environmental groups (who will be glad to help).
4. Require a basic course in EE during high school that is requisite for receiving a high school diploma.
5. Develop a statewide exam in EE (as is now done for other subjects).
6. Encourage/require all school systems to offer an advanced course in EE as an elective in the 11th or 12th grade.
7. Launch and support a program of teacher training in EE.
   a. Require a minimum preparation in environmental studies of all persons seeking a teaching certificate (as we now do for history).
   b. Establish and support in-service training in EE for present teachers.
   c. Encourage/require colleges to offer specialization in EE for prospective teachers.
8. Develop model curricula for the basic and the advanced courses in EE.

CONCLUSION

It is abundantly clear to me, and hopefully now to you, that establishing effective environmental education is a crucial aspect of the effort to avert global environmental catastrophe. It also is an essential component of literacy for the 21st century. The media can communicate environmental awareness and concern but they are not very effective in teaching basic principles and ecological ways of thinking. Our schools could do that better, but they must be disabused of their mindset about EE before they can undertake the task.

Humans are the only living creatures who can remember the past and foresee the future; it is this gift that makes us moral creatures. We can be held responsible for what we do or do not do with respect to the future, especially by our children and grandchildren. I have given you a brief view of the future as honestly as I know how. Now that you have seen the future, whether or not you try to initiate EE becomes a moral decision; even deciding not to decide is a moral decision. I urge you to join in attempting to break through the EE mindset barrier. If not you, then who?

REFERENCES

Clark, M. E. (1989). *Ariadne's thread: The search for new modes of thinking.* New York: St. Martin's Press.

Disinger, J. F. (1990). Needs and mechanisms for environmental learning in Schools. *Educational Horizons, 69*(1), 29–36.

Dunlap, R. E. (1983). Ecologist vs. exemptionalist: The Ehrlich–Simon debate. *Social Science Quarterly, 64,* 200–203.

Gore, A. (1992). *Earth in the balance: Ecology and the human spirit.* New York: Houghton Mifflin.

Hausbeck, K. W., Milbrath, L., & Enright, S. (1993). An inquiry into environmental knowledge, awareness, and concern among eleventh grade students: The New York State example. *Journal of Environmental Education, 24*(1), 27–34.

Milbrath, L. (1989). *Envisioning a sustainable society: Learning our way out.* Albany, NY: SUNY Press.

1991 Revised Reports Goals. (1991, November). The University of the State of New York, State Education Dept., Albany, NY.

United Nations Conference on Environment and Development (Earth Summit, Rio). (1992). *Agenda 21.*

World Commission on Environment and Development. (1987). *Our common future.* London: Oxford University Press.

16

Literacy in the Future

Howard F. Didsbury, Jr.
Kean College of New Jersey

In a world characterized by rapid and complex change and influenced by the effects of scientific and technological innovations, a sustained concern about the future is imperative. The distinguished futurist John Pratt (personal communication, November 1992) stated:

> To survive, we must suddenly find out how to solve our problems in advance. . . . It will take problem-solving by anticipation, global systems analysis, and collective decision-making with stabilizing feedbacks. Anticipatory decision-making comes to be of central importance for management and survival.

This is the rationale for what has frequently been designated *the study of the future* understood as a consideration of the likely economic, social, political, and ecological impacts of science and technology. To deal with anticipatory decision making requires a more systems based and literate view of the universe than most of us have attained.

NEGATIVE ATTRIBUTES AND PROBLEM SOLVING

The study of the future is often burdened with three unhelpful attitudes. One perspective is what may be described as "gee-whiz" technological optimism. In this view an exaggerated faith is placed in the inevitable scientific and technological breakthroughs, which serves as the deus ex machina to save us from catastrophe at the last minute. This view gives rise to a facile optimism that can easily result in complacency and impotence. As the distinguished French existentialist, Albert Camus, noted, comfortable optimism seems like a bad joke in today's world. Complacency discourages concern and action.

A second view is *gloom and doom pessimism*: a view that regards the challenges of tomorrow as so numerous, complex, and intractable and human nature so short-sighted, selfish, and/or ignorant that the possibility of timely, prudent action is poor or nonexistent. The gloom and doom perspective results in apathy, inaction, and ultimately, complacency.

The nostalgia trap is a third hapless attitude in planning for the future. In this case, we have an appeal to recapture the "good old days." Frequently, the conception of former times is the result of a romantic distortion of the past, of the passage of time, and of a fuzzy knowledge of history while reminiscing about myths of the golden age. To attempt to recapture the past in the future encourages pursuit of the unattainable, and often, the undesirable.

TEMPERED OPTIMISM

In contrast, *tempered optimism* supports the view that many of our problems are of human origin and subject to human intervention. The past is beyond our control except as myth; the future is the realm of possibility for human action. However, history can serve as an antidote to pessimism. Spurring us to creative thought and action, history is a record of the realization of impossible dreams. Many of the ideas, inventions, and forms that we take for granted as normal forms of life—current world views of social, political, and economic constructs—were once viewed as impossible, impractical, or utopian. John McHale (1971) stated: "The future of the future is the present." The tempered optimist operates on the premise that we have many futures—possible, preferable, and probable.

THE ROLE OF TECHNOLOGICAL FORECASTING

Human knowledge and determination can function to solve social, economic, political, and environmental problems. Knowing this, technological forecasting anticipates scientific and technological developments that can be applied to the problems of development. Forecasting serves a valuable social function in providing self-negating forecasts; forecasting states that "such and such" will take place "unless x and y are done." The forecast may be sufficiently disturbing or provocative to serve as a catalyst for appropriate action to prevent the predicted outcome.

The problem of meaningful employment in a high-tech society in which an amalgam of computers, automation, artificial intelligence, and robotics may drastically reduce the knowledge and skill required to perform many jobs is an area of growing concern. These high-tech jobs mandate only a certain amount of tending the machines by workers. The likely outcome is a reduction in numbers of workers, evident today in many basic industries and in agriculture. Further, reduction in middle range positions is under way and may increase with the widespread utilization of intelligent machines.

When technological unemployment is discussed, the familiar refrain that growth in services will compensate for displacements by absorbing the unemployed is often heard. However, the multitude of service jobs available now and in the future may be jobs that do not require much education or technical sophistication. The information society may be an exciting place for those of exceptional ability and creativity—an elite by any criterion. For a great number of workers, however, this society may offer jobs beneath their educational level and ability. If the information society concentrates on everincreasing efficiency and higher productivity, the substitution of machines operated by robots and/or guided by artificial intelligence will replace humans. Ultimately, a genuine job necessitating high intelligence and a sense of individual responsibility will be rare.

Moreover, the continual emphasis on the growth of production, both nationally and internationally, leads to a society and a world engaged in intense competition to dispose of what it has produced. Massive overproduction and overcapacity suggest that there are limits to productivity and to competition. The overproduction of arms is a case in point. We sell obsolete weapons to less developed nations who engage in civil wars that often must be stopped by the international community. Thus, we see that intense competition on a worldwide basis can lead to economic chaos, political tension, and social collapse.

THE NEW WORLD OF LITERACY

What of literacy in this new world? Literacy is defined as communicative competence in the many changing systems of a modern society. The definition implies knowledge of scientific and social change or lack of it in a world society. It implies a knowledge of the customs and beliefs of cultures, modern or otherwise, in this global conception of literacy. These cultures reflect many languages, customs, and beliefs: different attitudes toward gender, toward work, toward property, and toward communication itself. Literacy can no longer be interpreted as merely speaking, listening, reading, writing, and thinking in a given language. Literate forms must, at root, be considered reflective of a way of life. In the United States today, we can no longer consider that we are concerned with a single culture or country and its language. Calfee (this volume) writes, "The literate use of language is to problem-solve and communicate—it includes the capacity for action, understanding, and insight."

In addition to cultural literacy, we will be developing specialized technological literacies—computer programs and video programs that inform individuals as apprentices in learning new concepts, new jobs, and new roles. Far from becoming less literate at a verbal level, we will need reading, writing, thinking, speaking, and viewing abilities to accommodate highly sophisticated jobs. Service jobs will have to be regarded as some form of production, and not merely services. To manage job requirements in a high-tech era, one will need to be trained on an annual or semiannual basis. Those persons who get the most interesting positions will be those who can assimilate new ideas and tasks most quickly. Interpersonal communication competencies will be requisite in this fast-paced information age. The need for developing visual literacy for many new forms of learning will be integrated with the verbal means that predominate currently.

Embracing change will become a way of life. The old defensive behaviors of exaggerated faith in the brilliance of others and/or the newly developing technologies, the depression of gloom and doom helplessness, or longing for the good old days will not suffice. An attitude of being open to the wealth of information presented us in all its forms becomes a way of thinking. The excitement of having the world at our fingertips, of being rich in information and ideas quickly and with little effort, will force us to change the way we process information. Recently a colleague working from his desk on a personal computer found that he could access all of the printed data in the Smithsonian using a total area network (LAN) system. Soon, the visually pictured tour of artifacts housed there will be available also, not just the archives.

One problem will be that of information selection: How can we decide what we want to learn today? How fast can we learn it? And what are we going to do with these ideas once we possess them? Decision making will consist of checking the *Internet* or *Compuserve Newsletter* on your screen to choose a selection for the day.

If we are becoming a technological society with all of the possibilities that infinite information sources can bring, then surely we can provide options that make most of us literate, informed, and interesting. Verbal language with its graphic presentations will not be diminished; rather, its literate, linear forms will be enhanced with new forms of visual literacy and, probably, new myths to sustain the life of the soul.

SUMMARY

The need for a reconceptualization of literacy as the world grows in interrelatedness, complexity, and accelerated change is mandated. The challenges as well as the opportunities before humanity are growing. New forms of literacy, combined with fascination with the future and a willingness to change may provide a richness of opportunities, unanticipated by previous generations.

REFERENCES

McHale, J. (1971). *The future of the future.* New York: Ballantine Books.

Author Index

Subject Index

DATE DUE

SEP 15 2000		
JAN -2 2003		

Demco